Self Publishing Made Easy: Cookbooks

The Food Bloggers Guide to Writing, Publishing and Marketing a Cookbook

By Jason Logsdon

Copyright © 2016 by Primolicious LLC

All rights reserved. Printed in the United States of America. No part of this book may be used or reproduced in any manner whatsoever without written permission except in the case of brief quotations embodied in critical articles and reviews.

For more information please contact Primolicious LLC at 12 Pimlico Road, Wolcott CT 06716.

ISBN-13: 978-1-945185-00-7
ISBN-10: 1-945185-00-7

Other Books By Jason Logsdon

Modernist Cooking Made Easy: Infusions

Modernist Cooking Made Easy: Sous Vide

Modernist Cooking Made Easy: Getting Started

Modernist Cooking Made Easy: Party Foods

Modernist Cooking Made Easy: The Whipping Siphon

Beginning Sous Vide

Sous Vide: Help for the Busy Cook

Sous Vide Grilling

TABLE OF CONTENTS

PREFACE: IS SELF PUBLISHING RIGHT FOR YOU?	1
Why Should You Write a Cookbook?	2
HOW TO USE THIS BOOK	5
Jason Says	6

BEFORE YOU GET STARTED

FIRST STEPS	2
Overview of the Publishing Process	3
Goals of Publishing a Cookbook	4
Types of Cookbooks	7
Consider a Sample Book	8
Self Publishing Versus Traditional Publishing	10

RESEARCHING AND WRITING YOUR COOKBOOK

DETERMINING YOUR COOKBOOK SUBJECT	16
What Makes a Good Cookbook Subject	17
Brainstorming Cookbook Subjects	18
Determine the Competition In a Cookbook Subject	22
Complementary vs Competitive Products	27
Finding Complementary and Competitive Products on Amazon	31
Competitive Breakdown of an Amazon Sales Category	35
Finally Choosing Your Cookbook Subject	36
RESEARCHING YOUR COOKBOOK SUBJECT	39
Choosing Your Avatars	40
Researching the Cookbook Subject	41
Researching Material for Your Cookbook	45
Outlining and Note Taking Tools	47
WRITING YOUR COOKBOOK AND RECIPES	53
Keys to a Well Written Book	54
Components to a Recipe	55
Recipe Layouts	60
Recipe Attribution	67
Book Writing Tools	69
How to Back Up Your Cookbook Files	73
PHOTOGRAPHING AND TESTING RECIPES	75
How to Test Cookbook Recipes	76
Recipe Testing Worksheet Templates	77
Food Photography Tips	82

PROOFREADING AND EDITING YOUR COOKBOOK	**87**
Types of Cookbook Editing	88
Tips for Self Editing Your Cookbook	88
Finding Outside Editing Help	90
Proofreading and Editing Resources	93

DESIGNING AND PUBLISHING YOUR COOKBOOK

PUBLISHING FORMATS AND PLATFORMS	**98**
Types of Cookbook Publishing Formats	99
Choosing a Self Publishing Printer	101
Types of Printing Platforms	103
Comparison of Print on Demand Cookbook Printers	105
eBook Publishers and Distributors	110
Should You Use an eBook Distributor?	111

DESIGNING YOUR COOKBOOK	**115**
Cookbook Design and Formatting Guidelines	116
Choosing A Great Cookbook Title	122
How to Design a Cookbook Cover	123
What Fonts to Use in Your Cookbook	126
Cookbook Front Matter	128
Cookbook Back Matter	135
In-Book Marketing	142
Finding Outside Design Help	143

EBOOK SPECIFIC DESIGN	**147**
How to Design an eBook	148
How to Create an ePub File	149
Previewing and Testing eBooks	151

PRE-PUBLISHING STEPS	**153**
How to Price Your Cookbook	154
How to Write a Selling Book Description	157
Determining Your Amazon Categories	161
Choosing Publishing Keywords	164

PUBLISHING YOUR COOKBOOK	**169**
How to Publish on Amazon With CreateSpace	170
How to Publish On the Kindle	184
Linking Your Print and Kindle Versions	196
How to Publish on the Nook	197
How to Publish on iTunes	205
How to Publish Your Book Through Smashwords	211
How to Create and Sell a PDF on Your Blog	213

SELLING AND MARKETING YOUR COOKBOOK

PROMOTING YOUR COOKBOOK — 216
How to Launch Your Cookbook Successfully — 217
Getting Amazon Reviews — 219
Newsletter Promotions — 226
Free Content and Previews on Your Blog — 228
How to Get Blogs to Write About Your Cookbook — 231

WHOLESALING YOUR COOKBOOK — 233
Methods of Cookbook Wholesaling — 234
Where to Wholesale Your Cookbook — 234
Developing a Wholesaling Line Sheet — 237
How to Get A Cookbook in Bookstores — 239

APPENDIX

DEEPER LOOKS — 242
All About ISBN Numbers — 243
How Do Cookbook Royalties Work? — 246
What is the Amazon Sales Rank? — 249
What is DRM? — 253
KDP Select - What Is It and Is It Worth It? — 254
Case Study: Sales Channel Breakdown — 259
Cookbook Writing and Marketing Templates — 261
Financing Your Self Published Cookbook — 262

SELF PUBLISHING RESOURCES — 263
Writing and Publishing Resources — 263
Food Information, Connections and Descriptions — 265
Technical and Scientific Resources — 266

DID YOU ENJOY THIS BOOK? — 269

ABOUT THE AUTHOR — 271

Preface: Is Self Publishing Right for You?

Who Can Write a Cookbook?

Anybody.

Or more accurately, anybody who is willing to put in the time and energy.

Writing a cookbook is not easy, it is a lot of hard work. But if you are committed to learning about the process and willing to work hard to make it happen, you can definitely write and publish a great cookbook of your own.

Right now, self publishing is easy. You don't need money. You don't need a place to store thousands of books. And you definitely don't need to get permission from anyone else. All you need is an idea for a book and the work ethic to actually create it.

This book is focused on food bloggers who are looking to create a cookbook. Luckily, as a food blogger, you are uniquely positioned to write a cookbook. You understand recipe development and writing, food photography and how to connect with readers. These are all critical skills to writing a cookbook and food bloggers have a leg up on other potential authors. You also have a built in marketing base with your readers and your network of other food bloggers.

At the end of this book you will believe that YOU can write a book, you'll feel comfortable with the self publishing process and you will understand how self publishing fits into your blogging strategy.

WHY SHOULD YOU WRITE A COOKBOOK?

There are many reasons to publish a cookbook and here are my top five.

5) INCREASE AUTHORITY

Number 5 is the increase in authority you acquire. Most people view someone that has written a book on a subject as more of an authority than someone who hasn't. Part of this is that to write a book on a subject, you need to BECOME an authority.

This authority manifests itself in many ways. Your readers will view you as more of an expert than they do now. New readers will automatically give you more trust up front. Other bloggers will look up to you and view you as a larger presence than you were before you published. Companies, retailers, and other potential partners or clients will also view a published author as having more credibility than a "regular" blogger.

4) INCREASE BRAND RECOGNITION

The number 4 reason to self publish is that having a published cookbook out there increases your brand recognition. This is especially true within your niche. It's a great feeling to send an email to a company and hear back from their in-house chef who says they have your book on their shelf and love your work.

3) INCREASE NETWORK

This increase in authority and brand recognition also leads to an increase in the size of your network, the number 3 reason to self publish. It's easier to reach out to other bloggers and you will get a better response from them. Cold calls to companies that are potential partners or clients become easier.

You can also leverage your book to increase the size of your network. Contact the 5 or 10 largest blogs in your niche and find a way to work with them. Are they willing to hold a contest to give away some copies of your books to their readers? If you have a PDF, set up an affiliate network where these blogs are getting paid for helping sell your book. Provide guest posts that are recipes from your book. All of these are ways you can provide free content, swag, and revenue to bloggers in your niche with little to no cost to yourself.

2) Increase Revenue

The number 2 reason to self publish is to increase your revenue. Publishing a cookbook, whether print, ebook or PDF, allows you to add another revenue stream to your blog. Book income can be more than enough to live off of, especially when you have published multiple books.

It's also largely a passive revenue stream, meaning you continue to get paid for work you did in the past. I've been publishing books for 8 years now and during all this time, my second book was either my #1 or #2 best seller, despite it being several years old and no longer the focus of my marketing. In fact, it brought in more money in 2014 than it had in any other year.

1) Increase Opportunities

And what is the end result of increasing your authority, brand recognition, network, and revenue? Number 1, increasing your opportunities for future success. Don't get me wrong, revenue is great, but through the process of publishing you will find opportunities you wouldn't have otherwise, even if you don't sell thousands of books.

Does that large client want to work with you because you're a published author? Did the major blog finally get back to you about guest posting because they remember seeing your name come up in Amazon search results? Can you speak at a conference because you have more name recognition that someone else? Do you get the job writing columns for a magazine because you have the most credibility of the people that applied?

Some of the best opportunities that arise from publishing a book are things that you might not even have been aware of before you began writing it.

How to Use This Book

Welcome to Self Publishing Made Easy: Cookbooks! We are so excited you've decided to take the first step towards publishing a cookbook of your own.

This book is laid out in a step by step manner that makes it easy for you to go through the entire book writing and self publishing process. We've also tried to break up the information into discrete enough chunks that you can quickly skip around and pick up the information you are currently interested in.

Go ahead and begin your self publishing journey by learning what you need to know before you start in the "First Steps" chapter, or jump directly to a section that looks interesting to you!

We recommend taking some time and at least reading through the "Overview of the Publishing Process" and the different section intros for the publishing process steps. This will give you a good idea of what to expect during the publishing process. It will also alert you to things that should be started early on in the process. This includes things like understanding the different book formats and types of printers, as well as many tasks to promote your cookbook such as newsletter list building and networking that should be worked on as you go along for full effect.

We provide links in this book to many products, programs, and other websites. Many of the URLs listed in this book have been shortened to make it easier for you to type in. So don't be concerned by the strange, seemingly random format!

Most importantly, never forget that YOU can write and publish a cookbook.

Now go get writing!

Jason Says

Hi! I'm Jason Logsdon, from Amazing Food Made Easy and Self Publishing Made Easy. I'm so excited to be sharing this information on self publishing with you. Self publishing changed the entire focus of my blogging strategy and I can't wait to show you how it can do the same for yours.

Over the last 8 years I've self published 9 cookbooks which have sold over 60,000 copies in paperback and electronic formats. One of them, Modernist Cooking Made Easy: Sous Vide, even made the Amazon top 20 cookbook list and hit the #1 spot on Amazon for both Slow Cooking and Gourmet Cooking.

During this time, my website has grown from a from a small blog with a few hundred visitors a month to an establish site with several hundred thousand visitors. My income has also grown from a few hundred dollars a month to six figures a year and I owe it all to self publishing.

This book was written to be as general as possible so many different cookbook authors can learn from it. However, I wanted to share a lot of my personal tips and self publishing experiences I've had over the years I've been publishing. So look for the "Jason Says" boxes sprinkled throughout the book. These will contain my thoughts on publishing and my experiences going through this process for 9 different books.

Hopefully these insights will help add a personal touch to the sometimes impersonal process of self publishing. And if you have any questions, please don't hesitate to reach out to me on our Facebook Group at www.spmeasy.com/Facebook.

I can't wait to see the incredible work you are going to do!

Before You Get Started

FIRST STEPS

It can be tempting to jump right into writing a cookbook. We all have so many ideas and recipes floating around in our heads and we just want to get them down in a book. However, to make the process go smoothly, it's best to first step back, understand the publishing process, and consider some questions.

In this chapter we provide an overview of the self publishing process, as well as places to find more information in the book. We also discuss what makes a successful cookbook, what the different types of cookbooks are, and how sample books can be used. Finally, we discuss the differences between traditional and self publishing.

Overview of the Publishing Process

The path to publishing a cookbook is long and has many steps but when it's broken down into pieces the process is easy to understand and follow. Here is the general process for self publishing a cookbook, with directions to find more details about each step of the process.

The first step is to determine what your cookbook will be about and what content it will contain. The second step is to research, write, and edit the book. The third step is to design and publish the book. The fourth step is to promote and distribute the cookbook.

1) Determine What the Book is About

The biggest decision early on is to determine what your cookbook is going to be about. To accomplish this, you need to figure out the goals of your cookbook. This is critical and affects all your publishing decisions.

You also need to familiarize yourself with the types of cookbooks you can write including Recipe-Based, Historical or Story-Based, Informational, and Collaborative.

Once you have those basics covered you can begin to look at various cookbook subjects and try to determine which ones would most likely be successful for you.

This process of exploring how to determine the subject of your cookbook is one of the most important steps in successful book publication.

2) Research, Write and Edit the Cookbook

Gathering enough information for your book involves researching your cookbook, including what type of information it will contain and what that information actually is.

Once you have a real good idea of the content the book will include you can start writing the recipes and other material.

Once the content and recipes are written, you need to photograph and test your recipes, then proofread and edit the cookbook.

3) Design and Publish the Book

After recipes testing and editing is done, you need to determine what format it will be in, including print, digital, or even both. This also entails picking a printing or distribution platform.

Based on the format and/or printer picked, the design of your cookbook will be implemented, including the title, table of contents, typography, and general formatting.

After the design is completed you are finally ready to publish your cookbook on the platforms of your choice!

4) Promote and Distribute the Book

Once your cookbook is available for sale you can promote it through various channels, gather reviews, and create good press and coverage.

You can also expand your distribution though many different options including wholesaling, partnerships, and affiliate programs.

Goals of Publishing a Cookbook

When people think of a successful book they tend to think of a best selling, famous novel like the Harry Potter series or the Da Vinci Code. However, there are many ways of defining success for a book, not just in terms of profit made or number sold.

We refer to cookbooks as being one of three types, either a Monetizing cookbook, Marketing cookbook or Viral cookbook, depending on what it is trying to accomplish. These aren't exclusive goals, and we tend to think of them on a spectrum. However, you need to focus on a main book goal since there are several mutually exclusive decisions you have to make. Due to these trade-offs inherent in the different goals, how you define success for your cookbook will impact many of your decisions during the book publishing process.

Monetizing Cookbook

Monetizing cookbooks are all about making money and maximizing the profit they earn. Decisions are made with a mind towards how the bottom line will be affected. If a feature of the book will not increase the bottom line, then it's probably not worth implementing. For example, it might be better to use a slightly lower quality printer if it is less expensive or faster to work with. Maybe a black and white book will suffice instead of cutting your royalty in half by using color.

Pricing should be set as high as possible to maximize the royalties, even at the loss of of some customers. For example, it's better to sell 10 books a month at $50 each than 20 books at $20.

> **Jason Says**
> One thing I'd like to strongly state is that publishing a Monetizing cookbook does not mean producing a low quality, shoddy book that readers will not enjoy. I think one key to maximizing the profit of a book is to over-deliver to your customers, leaving them happy and wanting more books from you in the future.

VIRAL COOKBOOKS

Viral cookbooks have one purpose, to spread an idea into the world. They are designed to sell, or give away, copies and to effectively communicate the ideas inside them. Whether you have a great cooking or health idea, or just a passion you feel needs a champion, a Viral cookbook is all about sharing it.

Similar to a Monetizing cookbook, decisions to reduce the quality, or leave out extraneous features that would increase the cost of the book must be considered. The less you charge for the book the more copies it will sell, at least within reason, go too low and people may think it is low quality. With a Viral cookbook it's much better to sell 30 books at $10 each than 10 books at $50 - even though you're leaving money on the table, you are getting your ideas to more people.

Viral cookbooks can also be easily made into ebooks and sold for $1 or even given away on many devices, further spreading your ideas.

MARKETING COOKBOOK

Marketing cookbooks are all about one thing - promotion. Whether the promotion is for you, your blog, or an organization you represent, a Marketing cookbook is designed to wow the readers and showcase your skills.

There are many reasons to create a Marketing cookbook. Some people create a cookbook to attract a traditional publisher. Many recipe developers or food photographers can use a Marketing cookbook as a portfolio to send to clients. Bloggers often work with large brands to promote their products and having a great looking cookbook can do wonders to seal the deal with potential companies.

For Marketing cookbooks, the price of the book isn't nearly as important as ensuring that it is designed to wow the group you are marketing to. Some Marketing cookbooks may never be sold, only sent to prospective clients as marketing material.

COMBINING GOALS

As mentioned above, the cookbook goals are more of a spectrum than an absolute definition. You may want to mainly spread your ideas with a Viral cookbook but still want to make money off of it. Or you may want to maximize the profit of a Monetizing book while ensuring you have something worthy to market your skills with as well.

The three definitions function best as a way to frame your decision making, and remind you of why you're creating the book in the first place.

> **Jason Says**
> I find it can be helpful to assign percentages to the goals. For instance, most of my books are 70% Monetizing, 25% Viral, and 5% Marketing. I make most of my decisions around the profit and cost of the book, but I do sacrifice some short-term profit in order to be more viral. Of course, that's mainly because I believe having a wider exposure will lead to more long term sales.

Types of Cookbooks

Everyone is familiar with the classic, recipe-based cookbook but there are several other options that might suit your writing style better. Here's an overview of the main types of cookbooks you might want to consider.

Recipe-Based Cookbooks

The most common kind of cookbook, Recipe-Based cookbooks are all about the recipes.

The *The Essential New York Times Cookbook* (http://amzn.to/1T7ZKuE) is a great example of a Recipe-Cased cookbook. In the 1,000 page book there are only about 50 pages of introduction or descriptive text. Even the recipe intros are only 1 to 2 paragraphs long. Their goal is not to educate you, wow you with photographs (there are almost none), or tell you a story. Their goal is to provide you with the best recipe (in their mind) for just about anything you want to cook.

Informational Cookbooks

Informational cookbooks have a much larger focus on teaching and explaining concepts instead of just presenting recipes.

Michael Ruhlman's new books are an example of Informational cookbooks. His book *How to Roast* (http://amzn.to/1O3b1pC) is 160 pages long and contains only 20 recipes. His main hope is that after reading his book you will so fully understand roasting that you won't need any more recipes, you'll be able to do it on your own.

> **Jason Says**
> Most of my books fall in between the Recipe-Based and Informational types of cookbooks. They usually have 50 to 100 recipes but my goal is that after using my book you will understand the technique it is teaching and be able to create your own fantastic recipes. My recipes are geared towards highlighting the techniques and explaining them, not just providing recipes to be followed blindly.

COLLABORATIVE COOKBOOKS

Collaborative cookbooks usually fall into the Recipe-Based or Informational types of cookbooks but they include recipes from a wide variety of sources.

These books can be a great way to split out the recipe creation and testing to other people. It is also easier to get publicity for them because often the people contributing recipes will take pride in the book and write about it. One caveat, all the recipes in Collaborative books should be given with direct permission from the author you are taking them from.

> **Jason Says**
> I was asked to contribute to At Home with Sous Vide (http://amzn.to/1O3bbxh) along with several chefs and authors. I also often include a handful of recipes in my books provided from other authors I respect and reached out to for contributions.

BIOGRAPHICAL, HISTORICAL, AND STORY-BASED COOKBOOKS

Biographical, Historical, and Story-based cookbooks are a combination of a traditional novel or non-fiction book with a cookbook. They have many more stories than a traditional cookbook, and the recipes and cooking information might be secondary to the stories themselves and may be interspersed throughout the book.

Some great examples of these books are: *When French Women Cook* (http://amzn.to/1T8180g), *High on the Hog* (http://amzn.to/1O3bMPf) and *The Art of Living According to Joe Beef* (http://amzn.to/1O3bLLt).

CONSIDER A SAMPLE BOOK

We all want to jump right into the deep end and publish an awesome cookbook, but doing a smaller, less visible book is great practice. It will help you learn the publishing process, discover what works for you and your writing style, and iron out many of the wrinkles you will run into.

For example, if you have been blogging for over a year do you still have the same blog design, recipe layout, writing style, and color scheme as when you started? Almost no one does. Because our style, design, and layout evolves as we get more familiar with producing content and the tools available to us. The exact same thing occurs with publishing cookbooks.

That's why we recommend doing a smaller, sample book first. Do a "best of" collection of recipes from your blog. Put together your favorite 25 family recipes and write a book around them. Showcase your top 30 food photographs and write about the circumstances that went into creating them. The book only has to be 50 to 100 pages, nothing major.

Take that simple idea and go through the whole publishing process. Write the book, test the recipes, photograph whatever is needed. Then design the book and publish it on Amazon. Create an ebook and publish it for the Kindle, Nook, and Smashwords. Sell a PDF version on your site. In other words, really treat it like a full cookbook, but your goal isn't to be #1 on Amazon, it's to get practice for your next cookbook.

You will learn so much during this process that your next cookbook will be an order of magnitude better than it would've been otherwise.

> **Jason Says**
> My second book was much, much better than my first book. I really don't think my books were professional quality until after my fourth one. Even my latest two books are markedly better than my previous ones. Trying to learn how to write, format, design, and publish a cookbook, all at the same time, will result in a lot of stress and you most likely won't be happy with your first result anyway.

There can be some concerns about publishing a sample book if you are sure you want to be published traditionally. Some publishers can view an unsuccessful sample book as a black mark on your record. If you are confident you will want to be published traditionally, it may be best to put the sample book out under a pseudonym. This is easy to do through all of the self publishers, since they have a place for you to enter in your name during the publishing processes. You can still market it on your blog and through your contacts as a book you highly recommend, or even helped published, without having to take credit as the author.

SELF PUBLISHING VERSUS TRADITIONAL PUBLISHING

Self publishing is a very different processes than publishing through a traditional publisher. Both methods have their advantages and disadvantages and only you can determine the method that will work best for you.

COOKBOOK ROYALTIES

Royalties are simply the amount of money the author gets paid every time a book is sold and they are one of the main concerns for many authors. There are a few differences between royalties for self published and traditionally published books.

For traditionally published books, royalties are negotiated ahead of time and are usually 1% to 10%, depending on how established an author is. For most authors the 5% to 8% range will apply. This is usually based off the profit of each book sold, not the list price.

Royalties for self published books tend to be much higher than for traditionally published books. They are almost always 100% of the profit of each book, which is often in 20% to 40% of the list price. You also have control over how large your royalties are when self publishing by changing the list price, allowing you to maximize profit or sales, depending on the goals of your book.

For more information on royalties you can read the Appendix section "How Do Cookbook Royalties Work?".

COOKBOOK ADVANCES

Advances are the royalties an author gets paid up front. This is used to help offset the costs of creating a book. It's important to remember that it is an advance on royalties, not a bonus. So if you get a $10,000 advance and end up selling books worth $12,000 in royalties, you will get an additional check for only $2,000. Some publishing contracts will also specify that if the amount of your advance isn't met that the author has to return the excess money.

Advances don't exist in self publishing unless you externally finance your book. Most traditional advances run from $1,000 to $10,000 for a normal author who is just starting out.

CONTROL OF CONTENT AND DESIGN

One of the biggest advantages to self publishing is that you have complete control over all aspects of your book. When working with a traditional publisher they will often specify the cover, title, page layout, photography, and have input about general or specific subject matter. When you self publish you can use whatever you like so it matches your vision, potentially saving yourself lots of frustration.

Remember though, this can be a negative as well. Cookbook publishers have extensive experience determining what works for a cover, what page designs are ideal, and what content sells. When self publishing you will be relying on yourself and not their years of experience. You can supplement a lot of this knowledge with outside expertise but it will cost you money upfront and you are ultimately still responsible for every decision made.

Another negative of self publishing is that most self publishing platforms, especially print on demand printers, have more limited options for your book. You will have to go with a more standard book size, cover, and design.

WRITE THE BOOK, NOT PROPOSALS

One of the biggest challenges to becoming traditionally published is getting a publisher to accept you or your book. The vast majority of the time this requires you to obtain a literary agent who will work with you to create a lengthy proposal summarizing your book. The agent will then "shop" your proposal in an attempt to convince publishers that your subject is worth publishing.

This process can easily take months and has a high probability of coming up empty. Keep in mind that publishers are looking for authors who already have an audience. One positive aspect of this process is that if you do find a publisher it is a reasonable validation that the idea for your book is probably a sellable one.

With self publishing you can spend that time writing the actual book and publishing it. It is very empowering to be able to pick yourself (from Seth Godin: http://is.gd/kos8QD) and not wait for other people to give you permission.

DISTRIBUTION

One of the biggest negatives with self publishing is that you have to open the majority of distribution channels yourself. Some are easy to get into, such as most online book sellers, but some are almost impossible to get into, like large mega-chain book stores. Many smaller bookstores will be happy to carry your book, especially if they are local to you and like the topic, but you still have to actively find these stores, convince them to carry your book, and maintain that relationship.

Even though this lack of distribution is one of the main disadvantages of self publishing books, it is also offset in many ways by the much higher royalties you earn by self publishing.

CONTINUED DISTRIBUTION

Many traditionally published books print a specific number of books and then go out of print unless there is a large enough demand for them. This can greatly curtail sales years down the road. With a self published book it remains available until you decide not to carry it anymore.

> **Jason Says**
> Five years after I published my first book it was still selling a handful of copies every month. I eventually "retired" it because the quality wasn't up to my more recent books but it brought in an extra grand or two through the trickling in of sales long after I was done promoting it. Those sales wouldn't have happened with most traditionally published books.

SPEED OF PUBLISHING

Once the book is written, the process to get it available in stores is very different for self publishing and traditional publishing. A traditional publisher will usually take 4 to 8 months to finalize the book, print it, and set up the marketing. A self published book will usually be available on Amazon in a few weeks. This fast turn around can be a big bonus. You can also update your content if needed with a self published book, something that is usually impossible for a traditionally published one.

> **Jason Says**
> The more books you publish the faster the process will go. After publishing 9 books I know the process really well and from the time I finish writing my book and designing the cover it takes me 4-5 days to get it available on Amazon. Then only another week to convert the book to an ePub and get in the Kindle, iTunes, and Nook stores.

MARKETING

One of the biggest jobs of a traditional publishing company is the marketing and distribution of books. While I've discussed the distribution question above, the marketing is usually not as disparate between self published and traditionally published books. Granted, if you are a big-name author you will get a lot of marketing and promotional support from the company, but most small- to medium-sized authors are expected to do much of their own marketing.

PRESTIGE

There is something about publishing a book that many people find impressive and it gives a certain cachet to the author. This same prestige doesn't always translate to self published authors. Even though the quality of self published cookbooks and novels has increased drastically some people still feel like it's not a "professional" thing to do.

This lack of prestige can also translate to some distribution channels or professional reviewers who will limit themselves to traditionally published books. I've found there are enough people willing to give self published books a shot that it covers for those that don't.

> **Jason Says**
> Some people get very excited when they hear I'm a writer and have published multiple books. However, when finding out I'm self published I've had more than one person reply with "oh, well that's too bad". I tend to not care about the validation of those types of people so I try not to let it affect me, but it is something to be aware of.

Book Reviews

Similar to the prestige issues, it can be hard to get a review in a big magazine or newspaper through self publishing. Many reviewers limit themselves to books that have only been traditionally published.

Researching and Writing Your Cookbook

DETERMINING YOUR COOKBOOK SUBJECT

Choosing a subject for your cookbook can be a stressful endeavor. You are deciding what you will be working on for at least the next several months and the subject you pick will have a large impact on your sales and general success.

In this chapter we will explain what makes a good cookbook subject. Then how to brainstorm cookbook subjects that appeal to you.

Once you have some options, it's best to look into how competitive each subject is, including looking into complementary and competitive products on Amazon as well as breaking down Amazon Sales Categories.

Exploring the competition will help you eliminate the duds, then you will have to rely on your knowledge of the food space to make the call for what subject you think would work best when you finally choose your subject.

We will do our best to help you find a great cookbook subject, but unfortunately, picking a subject is more of an art than a science. We will give you the tools you need to evaluate the cookbook subjects and eliminate the poor candidates, allowing you to have more successful books than unsuccessful ones, but any given book is always a roll of the dice.

> **Jason Says**
> My best selling cookbook sells between 500 and 2,000 copies a month while my worst selling one generally sells between 20 and 30 copies. I wish I could say that each book I put out sells more than the last but it's just not true. Though in general, the more books I put out, the better they all perform.

What Makes a Good Cookbook Subject

Choosing the right subject for your cookbook is probably the most important decision you will make. The best cookbook in the world will not sell a single copy if it is on a subject no one cares about.

Regardless of the goals of your cookbook, there are several factors that make a good subject.

Focused Around Your Blog

If you have a successful blog, choosing a subject that relates to your blog is a great place to start. You are assured of an initial group of readers just based on a percent of your current fans purchasing a copy. You may also be able to reuse or rewrite large amounts of content you have already created for your website, greatly cutting down on the time needed to create the book.

Leaning on your users for helping determine the subject matter is another great idea. You can reach out to your readers early on in the process and ask them what their favorite recipes of yours are, what they wish you would cover, and what they'd like to see more of from you. The answers to those questions can give you a real good idea of the direction you could go in for a successful cookbook. On a side note, they are also good questions to ask when trying to figure out how to grow your blog in general.

Interesting to You

You almost always want to pick a subject that you find interesting. If you are going to write 40,000 words on a subject it better be something you enjoy writing about!

As your motivation comes and goes, enjoying your subject is a critical part to finishing your book and doing a good job with it. In addition, through recipe testing you are going to be eating a lot of the food you're writing about. So if you don't like fish, don't write about fish even if you found the perfect cookbook subject in that niche.

Popular But Not Crowded

In general, you want a subject that is popular, but not so popular it is saturated with books already. A subject with no interest will never attract any readers, but a subject being addressed by a lot of cookbooks already means your book will have a harder time standing out.

A great way to find subjects that fit into this mold is to find emerging trends that are just getting started. You can get in on the forefront of the trend and capitalize on the emerging popularity.

GO SMALLER TO AVOID COMPETITION

If a subject is too popular, you may be able to find a smaller niche within that subject that isn't as competitive. For instance, instead of "Italian food" you could write about "Tuscan food". Or instead of "paleo food" you could focus on "paleo desserts" or "paleo party foods" to narrow your subject and avoid competition.

Conversely, if you initially wanted to write about "Tuscan paleo desserts" you might discover that there isn't a large enough market for that subject. You can then broaden your subject until the competition level becomes too high.

> **Jason Says**
> Some of my best selling cookbooks are on smaller, more focused niches. There might be less people interested in the book, but a much larger percent of them buy it because my book is the authority on the subject instead of just another cookbook competing for readers.

BRAINSTORMING COOKBOOK SUBJECTS

Coming up with a list of potential book subjects is a critical part of the process. Sometimes you know exactly what you want to write about, but it's generally better to have a list of 100 subjects that you narrow down to a handful of options, than to only think of one or two ideas.

You want to try and pick a subject that will be successful, but be careful picking based on success alone. If you don't know as much about the subject, or care much about it, the book writing process will be a lot harder. In general, it's better to stick to subjects in your niche, that you are passionate about, or that you are passionate learning about.

There are many ways to come up with potential cookbook subjects, but here are the methods many people prefer.

> **Jason Says**
>
> I always keep a list of potential cookbook subjects around. It's a great way to have a built up reservoir of ideas when it's time to decide on a new book. It also allows me to experiment with some of the subjects on my blog. This lets me see what connects with my readers, which ones I enjoy working on the most, and what subject I may want to turn into a full book.
>
> I generally write down all the cookbook ideas I have and only eliminate them after some time has passed. This keeps my brain more open to coming up with more good ideas, even if a lot of them don't turn out to be great along the way.

WHAT MEMBERS OF YOUR COMMUNITY ARE ASKING FOR

A great place to look for cookbook subjects is by finding areas that your readers and others in your blogging area consistently have questions about. Often times you will see the same requests in blog posts or comments. If these tie into a single subject it's a great place to look for cookbook subjects.

Message boards and user forums are also good places to find areas that many people are struggling to find information.

POLL YOUR READERS

As a food blogger, you have an invaluable resource you can tap - your readers. If your subject overlaps your blog at all, it's a great idea to reach out to your readers and ask them what they'd like to see in a book about your subject.

There are many ways to reach out to them, and you probably know what method works best to drive engagement for your specific readers, but a few examples are:

- Write a basic blog post and ask users to comment about what they'd like
- Post a Facebook poll your users can vote and comment on
- Send a series of tweets asking your users their thoughts
- Post on your forums, asking for feedback
- Use a 3rd party polling company to generate a poll
- Create a survey for your users to fill out
- Send your questions in a newsletter to your readers

For more information about surveying your audience we recommend *Ask*, by Ryan Levesque (http://amzn.to/1O3edBn). He talks about asking "What is currently your greatest challenge?" as a way to get great feedback from your readers.

RELY ON YOUR EXPERTISE

If you are a successful blogger, you probably have a great feel for what is currently popular in your area of cooking and where it is trending. These popular areas can be mined for cookbook subjects.

Remember though, the cookbook will usually take between 4 and 12 months to produce. This means you have to be careful you don't pick something that is a quick fad that will be over before your book is out. This usually makes subjects that are just becoming popular better options than ones that have been popular for awhile.

TURN TO TRENDSPOTTERS

There are many places you can find information about what is trending now and in the future. Many food and cooking magazines have sections that look at trending subjects. Reading the larger blogs can also be a great way to find subjects they feel are becoming popular.

LOOK AT THE RESTAURANTS

Many of the food trends that emerge get their start in new or upscale restaurants. Once the food trend becomes popular many books on the subject start to come out. If you can be at the forefront of the books you can capitalize on the emerging popularity.

When you go out to eat at a nice restaurant, start paying more attention to what is unique on the menu, and what you are starting to see on menus across restaurants. Going online and looking at restaurant menus is another great way to get ideas without having to actually go to many of the places.

CHECK OUT THE EQUIPMENT

There are lots of new types of equipment coming out every year and there are often people looking for how to use them or get more out of them. Writing a smaller, dedicated book about a piece of equipment focused around your niche can be very successful. This is especially true if you can find ways that a popular piece of equipment can be used that the more general cookbooks don't focus on.

TWEAK POPULAR SUBJECTS FOR YOUR NICHE

There are many subjects that are saturated with cookbooks describing the subject in general. It's possible to take the general subject and focus only on an underrepresented portion that touches on or relates to your niche.

For example, fresh juices are currently very popular and there are tons of books on juices. But if you write about ice cream a lot, you could write a book focused on making ice cream or sherbet from fresh juices. You can tap into the popularity of juicing (and ice cream making) but in a way that you are still differentiating yourself from the other generalized books.

Once you have decided on a few cookbook subjects, you will want to try and narrow down which ones are good ideas and which ones should be passed on. The following sections will give you several methods for accomplishing that.

Determine the Competition In a Cookbook Subject

Once you have come up with your list of cookbook subjects, you will want to figure out the level of competition that exists in your subject. You are looking for a subject that has some competition but isn't so popular that your cookbook will just get lost in all the other books. There are many ways to get a feel for the popularity of a subject.

General Amazon Search

A great first step to determining the popularity of a subject is to do a simple Amazon search. From these searches you can get a good idea of the amount of relevant competition and the quality of the books. This search should be a book-only search, which you can set using the drop down box. You will want to do this search for different iterations of the words in your subject.

To illustrate how to use the search to determine competition, we will use two sample searches, one for Gluten Free Baking and the other for Grilling Desserts. Since new books are always being added to Amazon, we've captured the search results in two images below.

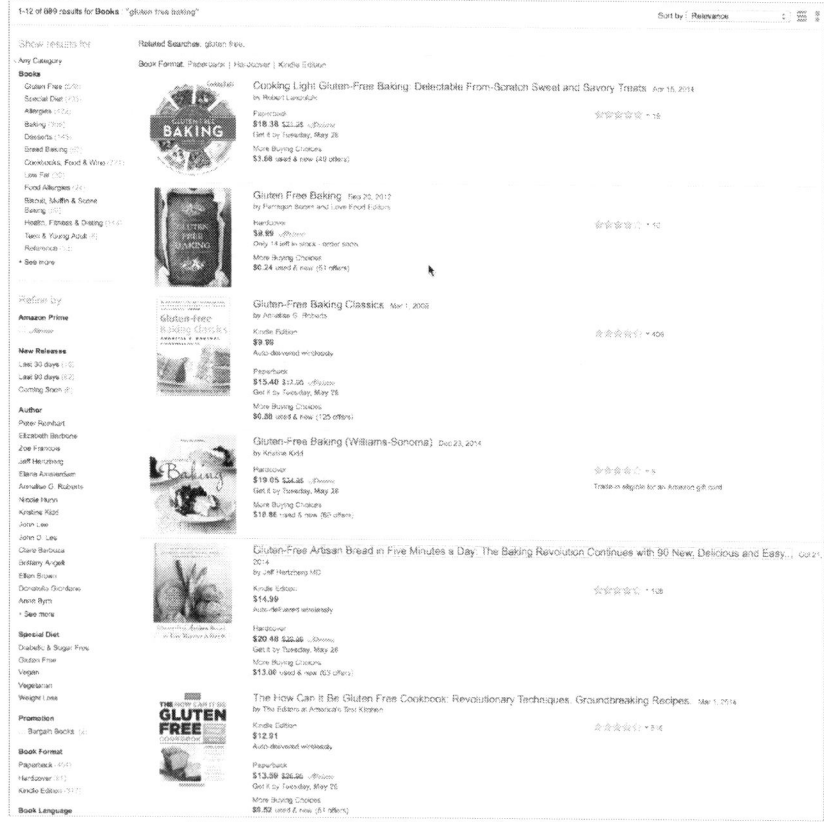

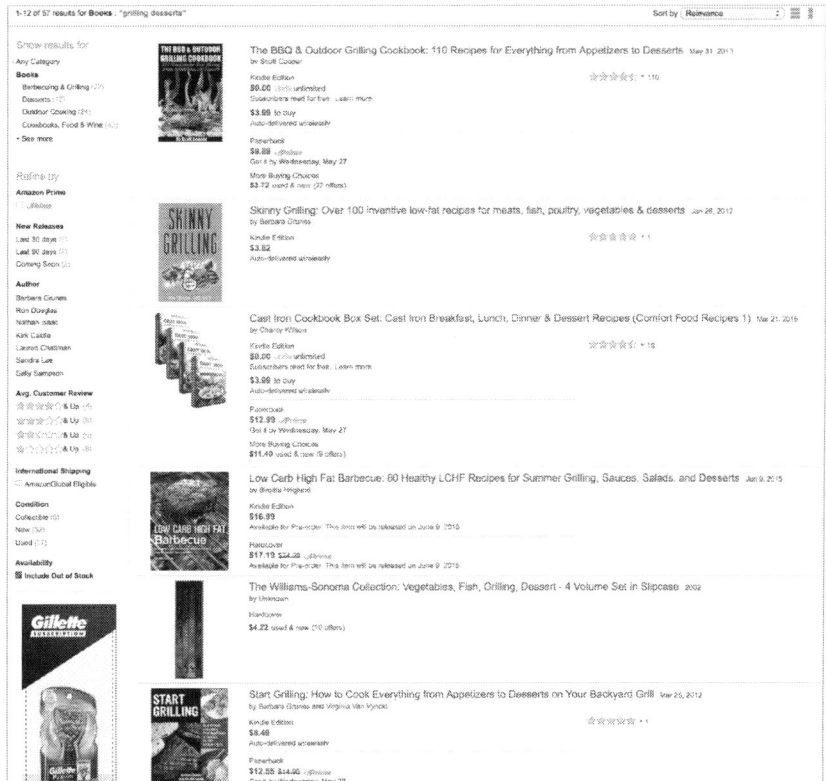

Relevancy of Search Results

The first thing to look for in the search results is how many of the results are actually relevant to the subject. For "gluten free baking" the first 10 results are all relevant and specifically about "gluten free baking". This indicates strong competition in that subject because all of the results are relevant, meaning your cookbook would be just one more book competing with all of these existing ones.

Compare this to the results for "grilling desserts". Here, the books returned only lightly mention desserts in the titles and none are 100% focused on desserts. This means a cookbook focused on grilling desserts would definitely stand out.

Quality of Books in Search Results

There are many ways to judge the quality of a book, but a simple method is to check out the aggregate rating of the reviews. Amazon provides the aggregate directly in the search results, which makes it easy to see how good the books are at a glance. It's important to look at both the number of stars, 1 to 5, and the number of reviews submitted.

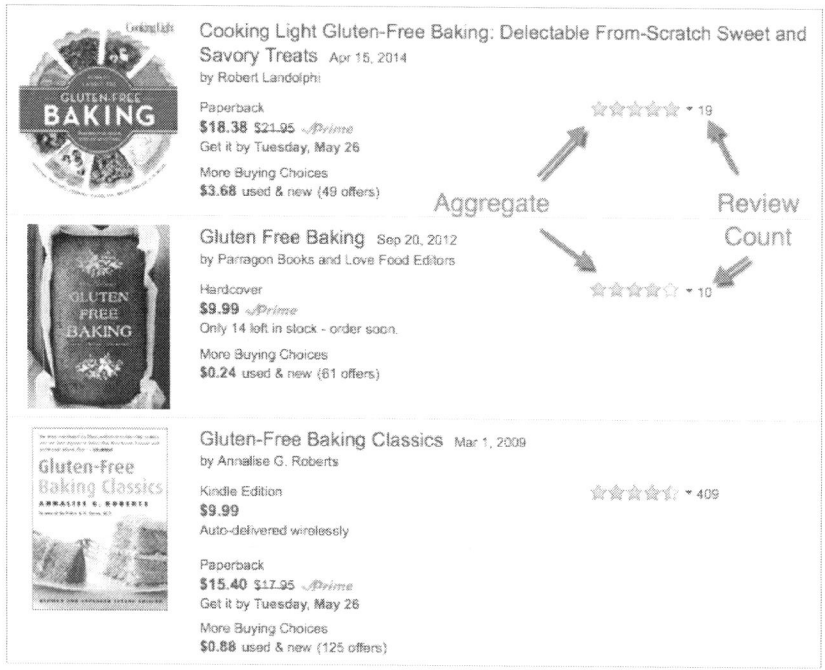

The cookbooks returned from the "gluten free baking" search are generally highly rated. The first few are all over 4 stars with 19, 10, and 409 reviews. The more reviews there are, the stronger the indication it is a high quality book. Generally, 10 reviews is the minimum to get a good feel for it. Anything over 20 or 30 reviews is a lot and should strongly indicate the quality of the book.

By way of comparison, only two of the "grilling desserts" books have more than 1 review. One with 110 reviews and the other with 19. Those two books are strong competition and most likely high quality but the others probably don't sell well and would be easy to displace with a strong cookbook of your own.

AMAZON SALES RANKS

If the subject still has potential after the General Amazon Search research, you can dig in deeper to the results you generated. Using the Amazon Sales Rank for these books allows you to estimate both the copies of the book sold and how hard it would be to break into the subject.

Using the Amazon Sales Ranks is a more nuanced factor than some of the other factors. If all the competition has a very poor Amazon Sales Rank then it is a good indication that people actually aren't interested in this subject. Conversely, if all the books have good sales ranks you might have a hard time breaking into the category because these books would all show up above your book in the results.

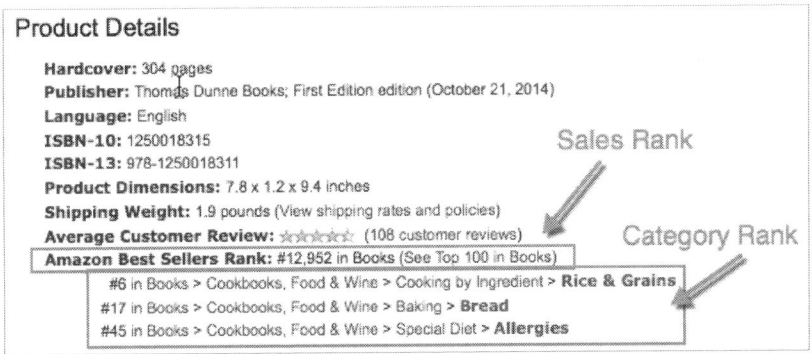

To view the Amazon Sales Rank of a book, click through to the book's product page. Scroll down the page until you find the "Product Details" section. It will list the "Amazon Best Sellers Rank" below the "Average Customer Reviews". If the book has enough sales to rank in a specific book category they will also show up here.

> **Jason Says**
> I generally look for a subject that has one or two books with a good Amazon Sales Rank and several books that aren't selling well. This indicates there's a demand for good books that isn't being fulfilled by the current selection.

You can read the "What is the Amazon Sale Rank?" section in the Appendix for more information about how the sales rank is calculated and what it does.

COMPLEMENTARY VS COMPETITIVE PRODUCTS

Another way to determine the popularity and competitiveness of a subject is through finding complementary and competitive products in the subject.

Complementary products are products that people would purchase in addition to your cookbook; competitive products are products that people would purchase instead of your cookbook. There is also a gray area here since many books might overlap with your cookbook but people may purchase both of them. For example, a book on BBQ might cover grilling as well, but many people might still buy an in-depth grilling cookbook.

COMPLEMENTARY PRODUCTS

Complementary products are products that are used with the recipes in your cookbook or other books that add to or fill out the knowledge you provide. So if you are selling a book about grilling, then some complementary products would be grills, spatulas, and charcoal. Also, cookbooks about marinades, BBQ sauces, dry rubs, and smoking might be complementary products.

Complementary products are important for several reasons. The amount of complementary products available helps to illustrate how popular a subject is. If there are a large number of products, there's usually a lot of customers willing to spend money on that subject. This is a great indicator that there is a demand for cookbooks in that category.

Another important factor for complementary products is the Amazon "Frequently Bought Together" and "Customers Who Bought This Item Also Bought" product listings. Having your cookbook show up in those locations is a great way to garner free marketing to the customers who might be explicitly looking for your cookbook. The more complementary products there are, the more chances you have to get in front of potential customers.

COMPETITIVE PRODUCTS

Competitive products are those products that provide the same, or similar, information and recipes as your cookbook. They are all products that people would buy instead of your cookbook. Though one thing to keep in mind is that a customer might still buy your book even if they buy a competing book. Many people will purchase several books on a subject they feel passionately about.

Competitive products are a two edged sword. The more competitive products there are, the higher the chance the subject matter is popular. However, the more competitive products there are, the harder it is to get noticed in that subject. If there are no competitive products it is easy to stand out but it might also indicate there is limited interest in that subject.

For example, searching on Amazon for "grilling" results in thousands of grilling books. Definitely a popular subject, but would your book ever stand out?

Conversely, searching on Amazon for "Goats in Trees" only returns a few relevant results. You'd easily get to the top of the search results...but would anyone be looking for your book?

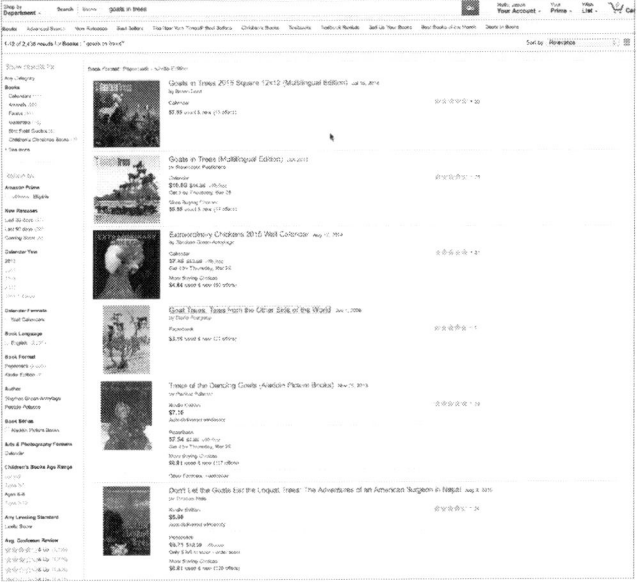

It is easy to identify and eliminate subjects at the end of the spectrum but there is a wide gray area in the middle. There are many ways to determine how the competition stacks up in a certain subject.

COMPLEMENTARY AND COMPETITIVE PRODUCT RATIO

One of the important criteria for entering a market is the ratio of complementary products to competitive products. If you can find a market with a high number of complementary products (shows customers are interested in that subject) with a low number of competitive products (easier to stand out in) then it is a good indicator that people are interested in a book on that subject and that the book will easily stand out.

FINDING COMPLEMENTARY AND COMPETITIVE PRODUCTS ON AMAZON

There are several methods for finding complementary and competitive products on Amazon. The main methods are general keyword searches, "book" keyword searches, "Customers Who Bought This Item Also Bought" listings, and Amazon Best Sellers lists.

It's a good process to take your list of cookbook subjects and go through the following methods, getting a feel for the complementary products in each subject, and the other cookbooks you'd be competing against.

If you need help on finding and evaluating keywords, you can see the "Choosing Publishing Keywords" section of the "Pre-Publishing Steps" chapter and apply many of the same principles here.

GENERAL KEYWORD SEARCHES

General keyword searches are a great way to find complementary products, and to see if there are any highly ranked competitive books. To do a general keyword search, go to Amazon and set the search area to "All" or "All Departments" and type in your keyword.

The search results will be a combination of books and other products having to do with your keyword. It's a great way to find the top complementary products for your keyword and also discover how high the competitive books rank.

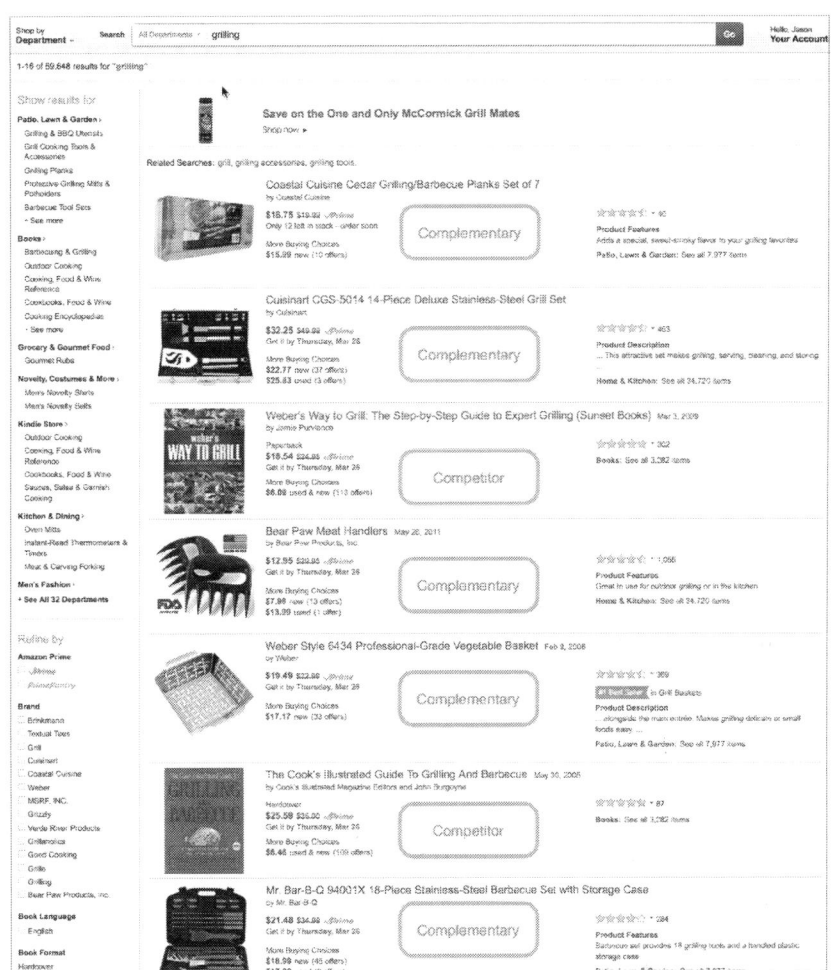

Researching and Writing: Determining Your Subject 32

BOOK-SPECIFIC KEYWORD SEARCHES

The next search type is a book-only search for any associated keywords. Just set the search area to "Books" and type in a keyword.

This will show you the general competition for your subject keywords and many of the books you will be competing against.

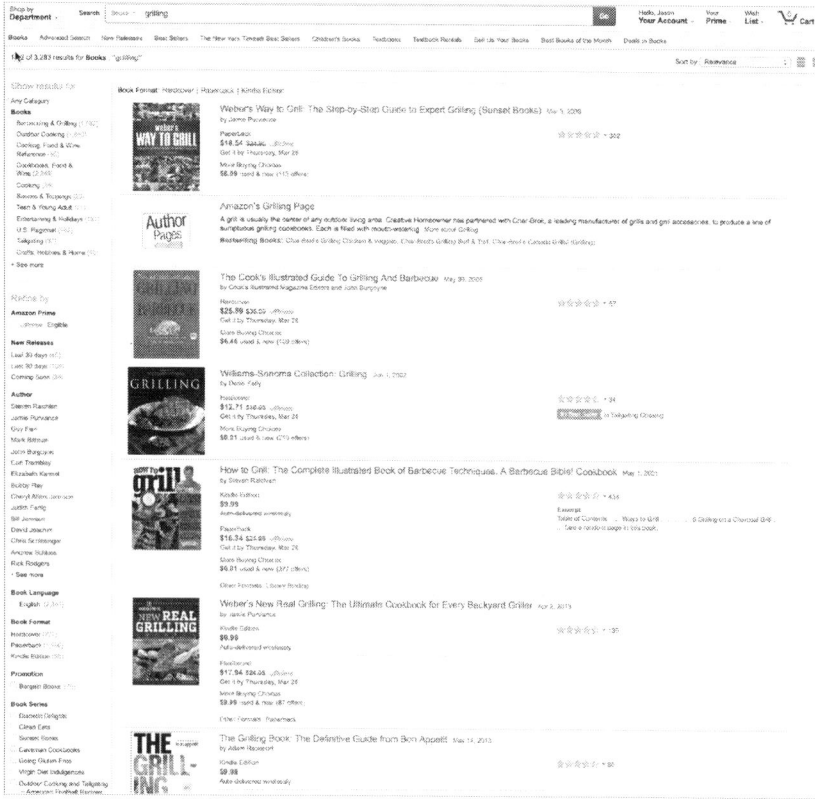

It's important to realize that even if your book isn't on the same subject, these books are still your indirect competition because you are fighting with them to show up higher in the search listings. For example, you might be writing a book on "Brewing beer" and only 2 of the top 10 results for "beer" are about brewing, but you still want to show up ahead of the other books that are on "beer tasting" and similar subjects.

AMAZON "CUSTOMERS WHO BOUGHT THIS ITEM ALSO BOUGHT" LISTINGS

For the top competing and complementary items you find, it's helpful to look at the "Customers Who Bought This Item Also Bought" listings.

These listings show other books that are potential competitors to you as well as many complementary products. It also helps you judge if most people interested in the subject purchase more than one book of that type.

AMAZON BEST SELLERS LISTS

Amazon maintains a list of best sellers in many different subjects. These subjects are a great place to find successful cookbooks that are competitors to your cookbook. You can access the best sellers from the sales rank listing on any best seller's product page or by going directly to a subject like Books (http://amzn.to/1o2qSiN) or Cookbooks (http://amzn.to/1o6J6Am).

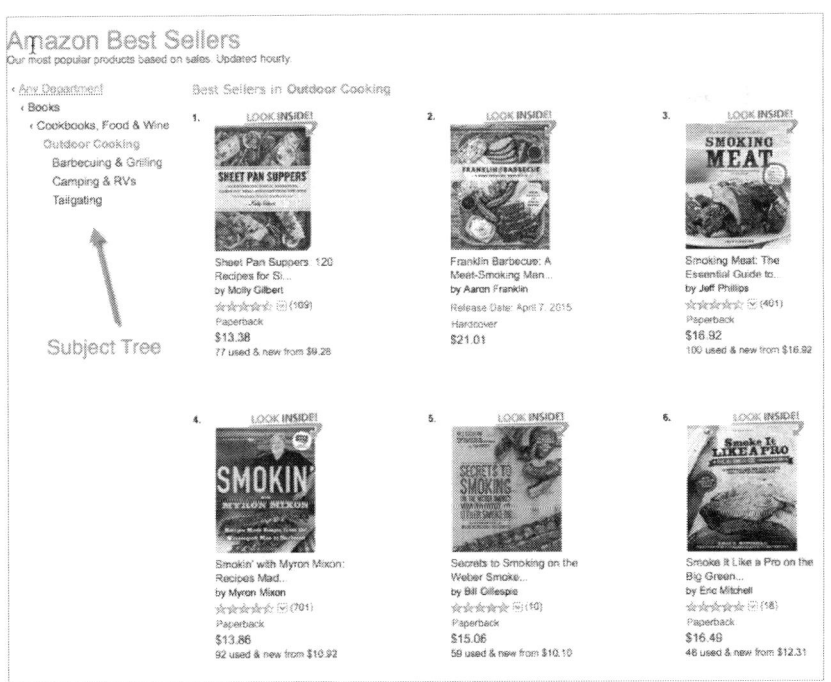

Once on the Amazon Best Sellers list, you can work your way up or down the subject tree, looking for subjects that interest you.

Another good way to find subjects that might apply to you is by looking at the Amazon Sales Rank area of the "Product Info" for some of the competitive books you found. There are many subjects spread throughout Amazon that aren't listed directly under the "Cookbooks" section and they can be easily found using this technique.

Product Details

Series: Sunset Books
Paperback: 320 pages
Publisher: Oxmoor House; 1 edition (March 3, 2009)
Language: English
ISBN-10: 0376020598
ISBN-13: 978-0376020598
Product Dimensions: 9 x 0.8 x 11.4 inches
Shipping Weight: 2.8 pounds (View shipping rates and policies)
Average Customer Review: ★★★★★ (302 customer reviews)
Amazon Best Sellers Rank: #4,924 in Books (See Top 100 in Books)
　　#8 in Books > Cookbooks, Food & Wine > Outdoor Cooking > Barbecuing & Grilling
　　#9 in Books > Reference > Encyclopedias & Subject Guides > Cooking
　　#10 in Books > Cookbooks, Food & Wine > Cooking Education & Reference > Reference

Would you like to update product info, give feedback on images, or tell us about a lower price?

Once you have found several categories that best fit your subject, you can do a competitive breakdown of each category.

COMPETITIVE BREAKDOWN OF AN AMAZON SALES CATEGORY

Determining how competitive an Amazon Sales Category is can help you figure out if you want to attack that market or not. There are a few ways to gauge the strength of a category but the most effective is to check the Amazon Sales Rank of the books in that category.

You can get a good baseline of how many books you would have to sell to rank in that category by checking the sales rank for the books in the top 10 as well as #25, #50, #75, and #100. Different categories can require vastly different sales ranks to break into the top of the charts.

For instance, currently in the Pacific Rim category (http://amzn.to/1SjmYz7), the top book has a sales rank of 24,000, the

35 Self Publishing Made Easy: Cookbooks

number ten book has a sales rank of 150,000, and the number 100 book has a sales rank of 890,000. Compare this to the Quick and Easy category (http://amzn.to/1o6JJdd), where the top book has a sales rank of 480, the number ten book has a rank of 2,100, and the number 100 book has a rank of 17,000.

This means that with the same sales, your Pacific Rim cookbook could be ranked #1 and your Quick and Easy cookbook might not even be in the top 100. Of course, if you do manage to get ranked in Quick and Easy it will drive a lot more readers to your book than if you were ranked in a smaller category.

FINALLY CHOOSING YOUR COOKBOOK SUBJECT

While going through the steps in this section you have learned what makes a good subject, brainstormed potential subjects, determined the competition, found complementary and competitive products, and broke down the Amazon Categories. This should have eliminated several potential subjects and narrowed your list down to a handful of candidates.

Now the final decision is here and you want to look at your remaining subjects and find the one that is the best mix of the following criteria:

- An interesting topic to you
- In a popular area, but not too popular
- Has several complimentary products, but few competitive products
- Is broad enough to have potential readers, but narrow enough that you can stand out
- Tied into your current blog
- Is getting more popular, not less popular

As we mentioned earlier, it's more art than science to picking a subject, and there's no way to guarantee success with any subject. But putting all those criteria together will allow you to select a cookbook subject that will more often than not be a success for you, especially when applied over multiple books.

> **Jason Says**
>
> The amount of research you do will depend on your personality and how intimately you know your market. I tend to do less research than many authors, mainly because most of my books are on the fringes of the market (not much competition out there to get information about) and I'm very aware of what the modernist community is actively asking for more information about. Researching a market can be very valuable before you go into it, but in a majority of the situations it won't be perfect for identifying a successful or unsuccessful book and you will have to rely on your gut.

Once you've picked your cookbook subject, it's time to start researching and writing it!

Researching Your Cookbook Subject

There are two main components to look at when researching your cookbook. The first is to research the subject your cookbook is about and the second is to research the actual information that will be in the book. During the researching process there are also many outlining and note taking tools you can take advantage of. We will also teach you how to use "avatars" to more easily narrow down your book content.

Choosing Your Avatars

The first step to determining what content your cookbook should cover is to figure out who you are actually writing it for. This "typical reader", "audience" or "avatar" is who you envision will actually read your book. It is good to be specific with these avatars, the closer to real people they are the easier it is to figure out what information they need from you.

For example, if you are writing a book on baking bread, there are several potential avatars you might choose from:

- First time bakers looking to learn the ins and outs of basic bread making
- Professional bakers hoping to perfect their craft
- People familiar with bread baking who are looking for ways to expand their cooking repertoire
- Health-conscious mothers looking to provide healthy, home-cooked food for their families
- Gluten-intolerant fathers exploring gluten-free baking
- Busy professionals trying to fit bread baking into their busy schedules

As you can see, there are a wide variety of people that might be interested in learning more about baking. Part of crafting a successful cookbook is choosing who to focus on and then tailoring the content specifically for them.

A book for "Professional bakers hoping to perfect their craft" would be filled with higher-end recipes, technical descriptions of the minutia of bread baking, considerations for baking in bulk, how to manage a team of bakers, esoteric or ethnic breads, making the most of an expensive bread oven, and similar high end, professionally-focused content.

A book for "First time bakers looking to learn the ins and outs of basic bread making" would have a very high-level look at how bread baking works, basic recipes for simple and popular breads, how to fit bread baking into a normal weekday schedule, how to properly measure ingredients for bread, what properly kneaded bread looks like, and more accessible, home cooking-based content.

Despite both being about bread baking, these two books would cover completely different aspects of the process and be filled with content applicable to only those readers. There's no need to talk about how to properly measure flour if the book is for people who are already cooking bread for a living, and there's no need to discuss the ins and outs of expensive bread ovens for people cooking only at home.

Most books will have 2 or 3 avatars they are written for and your book will be a blend of the content they desire.

Once you have decided on who your avatars will be, you can use their perceived needs to start to research the actual content your book will contain.

RESEARCHING THE COOKBOOK SUBJECT

Once you have picked your avatars you can start to really narrow down what content they will want. This usually takes the form of a rough outline of topics. It's normally best to start with a high-level look and then drill down into specifics as you go along.

There are many ways to keep track of this information and we offer some recommendations for outlining tools that you can use in the last section of this chapter. At its most basic, a simple text-based outline will work fine at this point, for example:

BAKING BOOK EXAMPLE OUTLINE
Bread Baking Basics
 How To Measure
  Dry Ingredients
  Wet Ingredients
 How To Knead
Recipes
 Boule
 Baguette
 Sandwich Bread
 Rye Bread

You shouldn't worry much about sections, chapters, or too many other specifics at this point, you mainly want a detailed list of the information you intend to cover. The organization of it into the form of a book can come once you know what most of your content topics will be.

There are many places to get ideas for the content you should be covering and you always need to keep the desires of your avatars in mind as you search through it.

CONTENT FROM YOUR EXPERIENCE

In most cases, you will be writing a book about a cooking subject that you already have experience in. With your knowledge you can begin to sketch out the content you think people will need. Use your experience from writing recipes and articles on your blog, as well as learning the information yourself.

- What questions did you run into when learning this information initially?
- Read back over your comment threads for blog posts similar to the subject your book is on. What questions did people have?
- Have readers or friends emailed you questions about your book's subject? What were they?

All of these avenues from your personal experience will help you start outlining your content.

CHECK OUT THE COMPETITION

Take your list of complementary and competitive products and read through all the reviews and "Customer Questions & Answers" entries. What questions are often asked? What do people like about the competing books? What do they say is missing? If some of the complementary products are popular, should you cover them in your book?

Also look at the table of contents and "Look Inside" feature of the competing cookbooks. What do they cover? What seems to be missing?

Remember though, not all of the competitive and complementary products for your book's subject will be right for the avatars you picked. Be sure to filter the content based on what your avatar actually needs and do not feel obligated to include it all.

Ask Your Readers

Just as in determining a subject, talking to your readers is a great way to get information.

We discussed talking to your readers in the "Brainstorming Cookbook Subjects" section of the "Determining Book Subject" chapter.

Talk With Your Network

One of the most valuable methods of learning what people want in your cookbook subject is to sit down and talk with them. This can be done through email, IM, texting, tweeting, or other online methods, but it's most valuable over the phone or face-to-face.

Do you have a friend that is interested in your cookbook subject? Invite them out for a beer or some coffee. Ask them what they find interesting about that subject and what they'd like to learn about it. If they already are involved in your subject, ask them what challenges they face and what difficulties they run into. Ask them what they now know that they wish they knew when they started.

Conversations like this can lead to some great insights about must-have content for your book.

Force People To Do It

Another great way to determine content is to find someone that fits your avatar and get them to actually cook what your book is about. So find a friend that is interested in baking bread and get together and make some bread together. Talk them through the steps and encourage them to ask questions. What is easy for them? What questions do they have? What do they struggle with? What would they like more information about?

These interactions will help uncover a lot of nuanced content you weren't aware you needed.

> **Jason Says**
>
> When you are writing a book you often become so immersed in the subject that you forget many people don't know even the most general details. In my book on whipping siphons I tried to give a full explanation about how the siphon works, what the pressure does, and how it could be used effectively.
>
> Then during my testing the most asked question was "Which way do I hold this?"
>
> Despite my best attempts to provide a comprehensive look at the mechanics of the whipping siphon, I had forgotten to mention how to hold it upright. It only took one person at my testing party shooting the foam on the wall to make me realize I should probably mention it in my book.

FOLLOW THE CRIES FOR HELP

One of the great things about the internet is that you can get an answer for any question you have. There are lots of places to find questions people have including message boards, Reddit's cooking subreddits, Seasoned Advice, Yahoo Answers and blog comments. Try to search these sites for questions about your cookbook subject. If people regularly have these questions, there's a good chance you should be covering them in your book.

On many of these subject specific sites you can also ask them what they'd like to see in a book on your subject. Most community members are more than happy to share their thoughts about what would go into a good cookbook.

We dive into more detail about these online communities in the next section, "Researching Material for Your Cookbook".

RESEARCHING MATERIAL FOR YOUR COOKBOOK

Once you have figured out what content you want to include in your cookbook you will have to make sure you can write knowledgeably about all of it. Unless it is a subject you are truly an expert in already, you will have to do research to fill in the gaps in your knowledge. Luckily, there are very few cooking questions that don't have answers if you search hard enough for them. Here are a few of our go-to places to do research for our cookbooks.

As a general note, if you find information in only one other cookbook or website and you include a variation in your book, it's considered good form to credit the place and author you obtained the information from. Cooking and recipe creation is often a collaborative process and there's no shame in recognizing the contributions of others.

OTHER COOKBOOKS

One of the best places to do research about your cookbook is through other cookbooks. These can be cookbooks that either you like and respect, or are on the subject you are writing about. Purchase the most highly regarded cookbook or two in your niche and see how they approach the subject; it can be a great way to examine your niche from another point of view.

For more technical help you can turn to books more focused around the science and techniques of cooking. We put together a list of great books to learn about food and cooking in the Self Publishing Resources chapter.

BLOGS AND WEBSITES

There's not many cooking subjects that someone somewhere isn't blogging about. Reading about various approaches to solving a cooking problem can help you narrow down the approach you will want to write about in your book. The comments on many articles can also provide great feedback from a wide variety of cooks at various skill levels.

These articles are usually pretty easy to find if you do enough Google searches. Be sure not to just copy anything you read, you can use other people's work for guidance and direction, but if you don't make it your own you should give credit where credit is due.

If someone makes a great point, or describes a process in a way you love, you can also reach out and ask if you can quote them in your book. Most bloggers and writers will be more than happy to let you use some of their content in exchange for a mention of their blog.

WIKIPEDIA
Wikipedia is a wonderful resource for learning about cooking techniques, ingredients, and different cuisines. It won't provide recipes for you but you can go really in-depth on many different topics. This information can either be used to help shape the direction of your book or it can be used to flesh out the more informational areas.

ONLINE COMMUNITIES
There are many online communities you can tap to try and get answers to your questions.

Message Boards and Forums
Message boards are a great resource both for finding old discussions about your topic or to ask questions to start new discussions. They normally include a wide range of people answering, which helps expand your view of a topic. Each niche has it's own message boards but we highly recommend eGullet (http://forums.egullet.org/) as a general resource.

Reddit
Reddit is a wonderful community full of helpful, insightful people...and several jerks. If you use Reddit, you need to quickly learn to listen to the helpful people while tuning out and not engaging with the others.

With that caveat in place, Reddit is a great place to ask questions and get feedback about various cooking issues. There are many specific niches called SubReddits (http://www.reddit.com/subreddits/) you can search through for different types of cooking. There are also generic subreddits for asking culinary questions (http://www.reddit.com/r/AskCulinary/), cooking (http://www.reddit.com/r/Cooking/), food (http://www.reddit.com/r/

food/), and recipes (http://www.reddit.com/r/recipes/). The best way to ask questions is to do a "text post" that people can comment on.

Seasoned Advice

Seasoned Advice (http://cooking.stackexchange.com/) is a place dedicated to asking and answering culinary questions. The feedback and comments tend to be of a higher quality than those in some other communities.

Twitter and Facebook

Reaching out for help on Twitter and Facebook is another great way to get advice. The people in your network are usually very happy to help you answer any questions you might have.

COOKS AND CHEFS YOU KNOW

If you know great cooks or chefs in your niche they can be invaluable resources. They can often provide direct answers, and if not, they can almost always point you in the right direction to find an answer. Many chefs of local restaurants are also happy to make time for people interested in their craft, especially if you can quote or acknowledge them in your book or on your website.

OUTLINING AND NOTE TAKING TOOLS

When researching your cookbook you will come across lots of information you need to process. These outlining and note taking tools will help you keep it all organized.

We will look at specific online tool options for the two different outlining and note taking approaches. The first group is an outlining tool or "outliner". These programs work directly with text, a master topic has sub-topics, each with its own sub-sub-topics. The second group is a mind mapping tool or "mind mapper" which uses a visual diagram containing a concept in the center with branches and sub-branches extending off in numerous directions instead of just words.

On his website, Sid Savara briefly compares 3 common note taking strategies: Outline System, Cornell Note Taking Method and Flow-Based Note Taking (http://bit.ly/1mAJZja). If one seems to resonate with your natural way of doing things, you can look into the technique further. These basic strategies can be implemented with the online programs we recommend.

If you are interested in learning more about the background of mind mapping techniques The Mind Map Book: How to Use Radiant Thinking to Maximize Your Brain's Untapped Potential by Tony Buzan (http://amzn.to/1SOH3hq) is a comprehensive look at the subject. This is the basic theory behind today's online mind mapping tools.

Regardless which of the outlining and note taking tools you select, always opt for the program that aligns best with your personality and work style!

OUTLINING TOOLS
Evernote
Evernote (http://evernote.com/) is a robust web-based note taking and note collecting app perfect for researching books. It offers flexibility and utility for multiple types of personal projects. Evernote makes it effortless to take notes and store info online for access anywhere, on any device. This program handles not only free form notes like a champ, but it lets you upload images and use both tags and separate notebooks to organize your data.

Jotted down some quick notes by hand while you were out? Just scan your handwritten notes into Evernote, and it will use image recognition technology to allow you to search for them within the app.

With the widely encompassing free plan you can send Evernote 60MB of data traffic per month as you make and take notes, but there's no limit on how much you can store. That includes uploading photos, videos, emails, webpages, and documents. A $49-a-year premium version adds even more features, such as the ability to work offline, search inside stored files, and increases the new uploads to 10 GB per month.

Evernote has good online "getting started" tutorials on its website. If you would like a visual tour of the free Evernote version and the web clipper, Keith Everett's informative 10 minute YouTube presentation may be just the thing (https://www.youtube.com/watch?v=qhHeAOzw2R4). David A Cox has a more detailed 45 minute tutorial that covers the premium Evernote tool (https://www.youtube.com/watch?v=7RzXo_eD4Vk). Due to the popularity of Evernote, you can find tutorials on just about any aspect of this outliner program on the internet!

WorkFlowy
WorkFlowy (https://workflowy.com/) is a very simple web-based outlining/workflow management tool that falls somewhere between a basic to-do list and a mature word processor. Its interface uses animations in an unpretentious, non-distracting way that makes everything feel more engaging. You can use Workflowy on your smartphone or tablet. And to help you use its power, documentation is offered as a series of short, no-nonsense videos demonstrating every aspect of the product. Their free plan only allows one list which is limited to 500 monthly documents, but that is probably enough to get started. Pro users who pay $49 per year get unlimited lists and a few extra goodies.

Simplenote
This very simple outlining tool is aptly named Simplenote (http://simplenote.com/). It's a great program for taking an endless amount of short notes and easily retrieving them later. Written changes are saved immediately, syncing is fast and the version history is accessible. Simplenote allows you to share and collaborate on notes with others by tagging your note with an email address. It's a good program for quickly getting ideas down but not robust enough for more structured writing.

Checkvist
Checkvist (https://checkvist.com/) is a responsive web tool for creating online outlines, hierarchical task lists, and collecting and structuring all kinds of information. It is a fast, mature, polished outliner with innovative keyboard shortcuts. Most outliners use Ctrl-key combinations, Checkvist uses Vim-like keystroke sequences. Markdown, code highlighting, import and export (OPML, text) make Checkvist an ideal hub for working on complex computer projects. Checkvist's free version offers more than enough functionality for most users. If you need full HTTPS support, file attachment, repeating tasks, and task assignment

options for collaborating with others, the paid version costs $3 per month.

OmniOutliner
OmniOutliner (https://www.omnigroup.com/omnioutliner) is a Mac-only outlining program. It is a flexible start-to-finish writing tool for creating, collecting, and organizing information. It is made to take great notes and turn them into a cohesive structured outline. OmniOutliner has many of the same features you get in the other outlining applications. OmniOutliner only has a 14 day free trial, and then you have to sign up for the standard plan at $49.99; seems a little pricey in light of the other less expensive options. Upgrading to the $99.99 Pro edition adds advanced features such as column visibility, reference links, Word export, and advanced style controls.

MIND MAPPING TOOLS
SpiderScribe
SpiderScribe (http://www.spiderscribe.net/plans.php) is a sharp looking Flash-based online mind mapping and brainstorming tool. Unlike a typical mind mapper app, this one gives you the ability to embed a variety of links, notes, files, and other content into your mind map. In addition, it lets you brainstorm collaboratively with others by simultaneously editing shared multimedia mind maps.

SpiderScribe is free for individuals who don't need more than three private maps and 300 MB files and images space; public maps are unlimited. This plan is for a single user but does include full sharing capabilities. For professionals, SpiderScribe offers a $5/month plan with unlimited private and public maps and 2 GB files and images space. They also offer business and education plans.

Trello
Trello (https://trello.com/) is simple on the surface, but the flexible Kanban / notecard based mind mapping program can help you visually group and organize your thoughts and subjects. As a management tool it allows you to see everything about your project just by glancing at the board, and it updates in real-time. Trello is free to use but you can purchase apps for your mobile devices, the web and Windows to add extra capabilities.

FreeMind

FreeMind (http://freemind.sourceforge.net/) is a free open source mind mapping tool that is programmed in Java and thus cross-platform compatible. It has a hierarchical structure but the information is presented in a visual format instead of a simple list. FreeMind is keyboard friendly--it's possible to create your entire outline without your hands leaving the keyboard. This software offers retractable and expandable branches and hyper-linking between different branches to make it easier to organize and connect ideas.

MindMeister

MindMeister (https://www.mindmeister.com/) is a web-based visually oriented mind mapping program. It is a robust tool with powerful collaboration features and a slick historical view of previous mind map versions. By using cloud storage, it distributes real-time changes to all users on all devices. MindMeister's controls work a little differently than most, so creating that first mind map may take a little work but after that it's an easy-to-use tool. MindMeister doesn't let you link each thought with more than one parent, nor does it not let you specify the relationship or type of link. For some users, this can be a frustrating aspect. MindMeister offers a free basic plan that includes 3 mind maps for a single user with full-sharing ability. Additional features with the $4.99/month personal subscription include the ability to add images and photos and export maps.

Writing Your Cookbook and Recipes

Once you've researched your cookbook it's finally time to start writing it! There are two main components to a typical cookbook, the introductory and descriptive sections and the recipes themselves. Both components take different skills to write and both are very important.

We will start off by covering the keys to a well written book and move into discussing the components of a recipe and how recipe attribution works. We also suggest many book writing tools and offer tips on how to backup your files.

> **Jason Says**
> Writing an entire cookbook can be a really daunting task. What helps me to get through it is to focus on small daily goals.
>
> For instance, I'll set a goal to wake up every day and write either a page of content or a recipe until the book is ready for testing and proofing. I do this before I do anything else in my day. This ensures that I'm slowly making progress on my book and not letting the work back up. Some days I'll be inspired and get much more writing done, but starting the day off with a small win is a great way to build up momentum.

KEYS TO A WELL WRITTEN BOOK

Having strong writing is one of the most important factors in creating a successful cookbook. A poorly written book, or one filled with errors, will regularly garner negative reviews, leading to fewer and fewer sales. There are some broad areas you can focus on to ensure your writing is up to the task.

WRITING STYLE

Having a strong and distinctive writing style is a key component to a successfully written cookbook. Unless your book is strictly a book of recipes, the style you use in your introduction sections and your recipe headnotes will help set the tone of your book. This is where your personality can shine through.

We provide several suggestions of books that can help you improve your writing in the "Self Publishing Resources" chapter.

EASY TO FOLLOW RECIPES

The most important job a cookbook has is to help people actually cook food. Recipes that are easy to follow and consistently turn out great food is the key to any well-written cookbook. Accurately showing the list of ingredients, having clearly stated directions, and good notes for successful execution are all critical to good recipes.

As a food blogger you probably already have a recipe style you prefer to use but if you want more information we look at components of a recipe in more detail in the next section.

KEEP YOUR AVATARS IN MIND

Make sure when writing your introductions and recipes you keep your avatars in mind. Different types of people need different information and directions. Always writing for your audience will prevent you from providing too much, or too little, information.

WELL ORGANIZED

Having a well organized and easy to scan cookbook is also very important. Many people will be using your cookbook while they have a pot on the stove, food in the oven, or are rushed for time.

Making sure the information they need is right at their finger tips is critical to ensuring they will think highly of your book.

WELL EDITED

Ensuring that your cookbook is well edited is also a major factor in creating a professional book. This is covered in much more detail in the "Proofreading and Editing Your Cookbook" chapter and is one of the biggest failings of many self published books.

COMPONENTS TO A RECIPE

Writing a recipe for a cookbook is very similar to writing it for a blog so you may be familiar with the process but here is an overview of the different components that can go into a recipe. A recipe really only needs either ingredients or directions (the preparation method) to be considered complete. At a minimum most recipes have a title, ingredients list, and preparation method.

If you need a more robust look at recipe writing we highly recommend The Recipe Writer's Handbook (http://amzn.to/1VefBqQ). It's a comprehensive guide to writing recipes including the different components, proper styles, and other important considerations.

RECIPE TITLE

The title of the recipe is the name used to refer to the recipe throughout the text of the book, including the table of contents and the index. The name should usually be simple and declarative, quickly conveying what the recipe is for. Some of my latest recipe titles are:

- Spicy Pickled Watermelon Rind
- Spring Pea Soup with Carrot Pearls
- Bacon-Bourbon BBQ Jam
- Honey Goat Cheese Flatbreads with Port-Infused Figs
- Chocolate Mint Rum
- White Russian Pudding
- Mom's Sweet Potato Casserole Bites

You know at a glance what the recipe is about, and what its main components are. It can be tempting to be clever with your recipe titles, but often times this makes it harder for the readers.

RECIPE YIELD

The yield of the recipe lets the reader know how much food the recipe actually makes and is a valuable part of any recipe. This can be expressed several ways:

As servings (how many it can feed)
- 4 Servings
- 8 Servings as a side
- Makes 4 Servings, 12 as an appetizer
- Feeds 12

As an Amount
- 4 Cups Chutney
- 2 Gallons Iced Tea

Try to be consistent with the yield throughout the recipes in your book, both in wording and in relative size. Readers will get confused if all your main courses serve 12 but the sides only serve 4.

If you have a recipe or two that deviates greatly in size, it's best to call it out in the headnote as well. Something like "This great party food will serve 20 so be sure to only cook it when you're having a bunch of people over" will alert your readers that it's not a normal, weekday meal for 4.

RECIPE HEADNOTE

Headnotes are the introductory text at the front of a recipe. Many cookbooks, especially more recently written ones, make extensive use of headnotes. Headnotes are a place to sell the reader on the recipe, provide more information they may need, and paint a picture of what the final dish will be.

Here are some example headnotes.

Sample Headnote One

Some flatbreads use pesto as a base sauce but this recipe separates out the pesto components and allows them to shine on their own. The basil is turned into a thick drizzle for the flatbread while the other ingredients remain whole and add bursts of flavor.

Sample Headnote Two

My mother-in-law is a huge fan of beets but I never ate them growing up so I'm still not completely sold. I've been trying to work beets into my cooking so I can develop a better appreciation for them. Turning them into crispy chips is one way I've found that I really enjoy beets, especially when served with flavorful dips.

Sample Headnote Three

I love how the sweetness of caramel complements pork. This recipe uses a rosemary caramel to act as a sauce for some sous vided pork. You can season the caramel with many different spices and it gives you a wide variety of flavors you can add to a dish.

Headnotes can be personal, technical, matter-of-fact or a mix. Just try to be consistent in the style and voice you use in the headnotes.

INGREDIENT LIST

The ingredient list is one of the most important parts of a recipe. It lays out all the ingredients that a reader will need to recreate the recipe at home. It should contain the amount of the ingredient needed, as well as the name of the ingredient. It's best practice to include anything you use in the recipe in the ingredients list.

Normally each ingredient is on a separate line and listed in the order it is used in the recipe. If your dish has multiple components it can be helpful to separate each component under its own heading.

Ingredients
For the Thai Infused Rum
1 lime
½ stalk lemongrass, coarsely chopped
¼ cup shredded or flaked coconut
6 basil leaves
2 teaspoons grated fresh ginger
1.5 cups rum, preferably overproof

Ingredients
For the Spice Rub
1g thyme
8g paprika
5g ancho pepper powder
5g ground coriander
4g ground cumin
10g salt
3g black pepper

For the Pulled Pork
2,000-3,000g pork shoulder or pork butt, 5-6 pounds, can be multiple pieces
150g onion, 1 medium, sliced
30g garlic, 6-8 cloves, diced
Chicken stock
Water

Ingredients
For the French Onion Soup
Olive oil
1000g onions, peeled and sliced
800g water
100g red wine
2 bay leaves
3g thyme leaves
2g rosemary leaves
Salt and pepper

There is always discussion about what type of measurements you should use. Most cookbooks published in the United States use volume measurements such as "1 cup" or "2 tablespoons" for their ingredients. Many European books, and several baking or dessert books, use weight measurements such as "10 ounces" or "20 grams" instead. There's no right answer, you will have to try and understand what your target market, and your avatars, would prefer.

PREPARATION METHOD
The preparation method is another very important part of your recipes. It explains to the reader, step by step, exactly what they need to do to prepare the dish at home. The amount of detail you go into will depend on your avatars and the complexity of your recipe. It's almost always better to err on the side of too much information than too little information. You will often have to rely on recipe testing to get feedback about whether your preparation methods are clear or not.

NUTRITIONAL INFORMATION
If your book is focused around healthy eating, providing the nutritional information can be invaluable for your readers. There are many different ways to provide the nutritional information ranging from a simple statement of "this has no sugar in it" to a more complex gram breakdown of fat, sugar, and carbohydrates.

TIMING
It can be very helpful to your readers if you let them know how much time a recipe will take to make. This can take the form of

the total time or it can be broken down into the preparation time, cooking time, and total time. It's also good to use the headnotes to clearly call out if a part of the recipe will take a really long period of time, such as marinating over night.

REQUIREMENTS

If your recipe requires something that people don't always have on hand in their kitchen you should let them know about it up front. This can take the form of equipment, specialty ingredients, or other unusual requirements. Some examples of requirements could be "A standing mixer with kneading hook", "prepared sourdough starter", or "a cool, dry location such as a cellar".

RECIPE VARIATIONS

Providing variations on your recipe is a great way to help readers think of new ways to customize the recipe. This can take the form of suggestions for substitutions, alternate preparation methods, or different directions the recipe can be taken. Some recipe variations are detailed, others are just simple suggestions.

Example Recipe Variation One

For a vegetarian take on this dish, substitute the ground meat with 2 large portobello mushrooms that have been finely diced.

Example Recipe Variation Two

For an upscale modernist take you can turn the blue cheese sauce into a thick foam using a whipping siphon. Omit the olive oil and increase the heavy cream to ¾ cup. Blend everything together then pour it into a whipping siphon. Seal and charge the siphon then dispense onto the steaks. The blue cheese foam can be made a day or two ahead of time and stored in the refrigerator.

Example Recipe Variation Three

This marinade also works well with fish, just replace the chipotle peppers with lemon peel and cumin.

RECIPE NOTES

Recipe notes are a place where you can share more information with the reader. This can include places to purchase hard-to-find ingredients, storage tips, suggestions for timing, re-heating ideas, alternative ingredients, drink pairings and anything else that doesn't fit into the other components of the recipe.

The information in recipe notes can be similar to what is included in the headnotes but it is usually called out separately from the rest of the recipe.

Recipe Layouts

There are countless ways to format a recipe for a cookbook. We highly recommend looking through some of your favorite cookbooks and seeing which formats you like best.

We've included some of the more popular variations commonly used for self published cookbooks below. They are generally easy to implement in most word processors and easy to tweak around a wide variety of recipes.

LAYOUT ONE

This format has the header at the top, follow by any yield, timing, and requirement information. The headnote follows this and spans both columns of the recipe. The ingredient list and preparation method are side by side and split apart by the part of the recipe they are focused on. Recipes in this layout have a nice golden ratio-type feel to them.

ROASTED RED PEPPER SOUP

Makes: 7 to 12 servings • Needs: Agar, whipping siphon

Roasted red peppers are a classic Italian offering and this recipe uses the whipping siphon to aerate them into a light, smooth soup. The amount of agar can be adjusted to easily control the thickness of the soup.

I prefer making my own roasted peppers but high-quality store bought ones can be used if you are in a pinch. In addition to serving it as a soup, this foam can be used in many different ways to turn traditional dishes into modern masterpieces. It's great on fish, asparagus, or even steaks.

Ingredients

For the Roasted Pepper Puree
5-6 red peppers
Olive oil
Salt and pepper
3 cloves garlic, diced
4 sprigs thyme, stems removed
100g water or stock

For the Foam
400g roasted pepper puree, from above
100g water
2.5g agar, 0.5%

To Assemble
Lemon zest
Thyme leaves
Parmesan cheese strips

For the Roasted Pepper Puree
Toss the red peppers with the olive oil then salt and pepper them. Cook them on a grill, or in a hot oven, rotating as needed, until the skins begin to blacken then remove from the heat. For a more refined presentation the charred skin can be peeled off, though sometimes I leave them on since the char adds a pleasant bitterness to the foam.

Combine the roasted peppers, garlic, thyme, and water in a pot. Bring to a simmer then blend well. Strain the puree and set aside.

For the Foam
Blend the roasted red pepper puree, water, and agar together. Pour into a pot and bring to a boil. Let simmer for 3 to 5 minutes then pour into a container and let it set completely.

Once it is set, cube the gel and puree with a blender until smooth. Add some water if you need to thin it. Pour the fluid gel into your whipping siphon and charge.

To Assemble
When you are ready to serve, dispense the foam into bowls. Garnish with the lemon zest, thyme leaves, and parmesan cheese strips.

It's also easy to add a small photograph to the recipe without taking up much space.

Roasted Red Pepper Soup

Makes: 7 to 12 servings • Needs: Agar, whipping siphon

Roasted red peppers are a classic Italian offering and this recipe uses the whipping siphon to aerate them into a light, smooth soup. The amount of agar can be adjusted to easily control the thickness of the soup.

I prefer making my own roasted peppers but high-quality store bought ones can be used if you are in a pinch. In addition to serving it as a soup, this foam can be used in many different ways to turn traditional dishes into modern masterpieces. It's great on fish, asparagus, or even steaks.

Ingredients

For the Roasted Pepper Puree
5-6 red peppers
Olive oil
Salt and pepper
3 cloves garlic, diced
4 sprigs thyme, stems removed
100g water or stock

For the Foam
400g roasted pepper puree, from above
100g water
2.5g agar, 0.5%

To Assemble
Lemon zest
Thyme leaves
Parmesan cheese strips

For the Roasted Pepper Puree

Toss the red peppers with the olive oil then salt and pepper them. Cook them on a grill, or in a hot oven, rotating as needed, until the skins begin to blacken then remove from the heat. For a more refined presentation the charred skin can be peeled off, though sometimes I leave them on since the char adds a pleasant bitterness to the foam.

Combine the roasted peppers, garlic, thyme, and water in a pot. Bring to a simmer then blend well. Strain the puree and set aside.

For the Foam

Blend the roasted red pepper puree, water, and agar together. Pour into a pot and bring to a boil. Let simmer for 3 to 5 minutes then pour into a container and let it set completely.

Once it is set, cube the gel and puree with a blender until smooth. Add some water if you need to thin it. Pour the fluid gel into your whipping siphon and charge.

To Assemble

When you are ready to serve, dispense the foam into bowls. Garnish with the lemon zest, thyme leaves, and parmesan cheese strips.

To really showcase your photography you can insert a large image below the headnote and push the recipe to two pages.

LAYOUT TWO

This is a simple recipe format that has the headnote and ingredient list share a column opposite the preparation instructions. It's a compact and easy format to lay out.

MANGO HABANERO FROTH

This froth adds a spicy, tropical flavor to many dishes. I really like it on soft tacos or as a topper to gazpacho. You can also freeze the foam in molds and use it as a spicy topping on desserts.

The amount of habanero you use will depend on how hot you like your food, and how spicy you want the foam to be. You can also use other juices besides mango, I really like orange or peach juice as well.

If you don't want to make your own mango juice you can find it at many nicer supermarkets or health food stores. You can always use Goya canned juice if you can't find any fresh juice.

Tools Needed
Xanthan gum
Standing or immersion blender

Ingredients
For the Mango-Habanero Infusion
450 grams fresh mango juice
¼-1 habanero, seeds removed and cut in half

For the Foam
400 grams mango-habanero infusion
2.4 grams xanthan gum, 0.6%

For the Mango-Habanero Infusion
Pour the mango juice in a pot and add the habanero pepper. Bring to a boil then simmer for 5 to 10 minutes. Remove the habanero pepper and any seeds.

For the Foam
Blend the mango-habanero infusion and xanthan gum together. Pour into a whipping siphon and charge. You can heat the whipping siphon or leave it at room temperature until you are ready to dispense the foam.

Small images can easily be inserted at the top or bottom of the columns.

Mango Habanero Froth

This froth adds a spicy, tropical flavor to many dishes. I really like it on soft tacos or as a topper to gazpacho. You can also freeze the foam in molds and use it as a spicy topping on desserts.

The amount of habanero you use will depend on how hot you like your food, and how spicy you want the foam to be. You can also use other juices besides mango, I really like orange or peach juice as well.

If you don't want to make your own mango juice you can find it at many nicer supermarkets or health food stores. You can always use Goya canned juice if you can't find any fresh juice.

Tools Needed
Xanthan gum
Standing or immersion blender

Ingredients
For the Mango-Habanero Infusion
450 grams fresh mango juice
¼-1 habanero, seeds removed and cut in half

For the Foam
400 grams mango-habanero infusion
2.4 grams xanthan gum, 0.6%

For the Mango-Habanero Infusion
Pour the mango juice in a pot and add the habanero pepper. Bring to a boil then simmer for 5 to 10 minutes. Remove the habanero pepper and any seeds.

For the Foam
Blend the mango-habanero infusion and xanthan gum together. Pour into a whipping siphon and charge. You can heat the whipping siphon or leave it at room temperature until you are ready to dispense the foam.

Larger images can be inserted at the bottom of the recipe and span the entire width.

Mango Habanero Froth

This froth adds a spicy, tropical flavor to many dishes. I really like it on soft tacos or as a topper to gazpacho. You can also freeze the foam in molds and use it as a spicy topping on desserts.

The amount of habanero you use will depend on how hot you like your food, and how spicy you want the foam to be. You can also use other juices besides mango, I really like orange or peach juice as well.

Tools Needed
Xanthan gum
Standing or immersion blender

Ingredients
For the Mango-Habanero Infusion
450 grams fresh mango juice
¼-1 habanero, seeds removed and cut in half

For the Foam
400 grams mango-habanero infusion
2.4 grams xanthan gum, 0.6%

For the Mango-Habanero Infusion
Pour the mango juice in a pot and add the habanero pepper. Bring to a boil then simmer for 5 to 10 minutes. Remove the habanero pepper and any seeds.

For the Foam
Blend the mango-habanero infusion and xanthan gum together. Pour into a whipping siphon and charge. You can heat the whipping siphon or leave it at room temperature until you are ready to dispense the foam.

LAYOUT THREE

Similar to Layout Two, this layout just moves the headnote into the same column as the preparation method and shrinks the width of the ingredients column. Images can be added in a similar manner to Layout Two.

Mango Habanero Froth

This froth adds a spicy, tropical flavor to many dishes. I really like it on soft tacos or as a topper to gazpacho. You can also freeze the foam in molds and use it as a spicy topping on desserts.

The amount of habanero you use will depend on how hot you like your food, and how spicy you want the foam to be. You can also use other juices besides mango, I really like orange or peach juice as well.

If you don't want to make your own mango juice you can find it at many nicer supermarkets or health food stores. You can always use Goya canned juice if you can't find any fresh juice.

Tools Needed
Xanthan gum
Standing or immersion blender

Ingredients

For the Mango-Habanero Infusion
450 grams fresh mango juice
¼-1 habanero, seeds removed and cut in half

For the Foam
400 grams mango-habanero infusion
2.4 grams xanthan gum, 0.6%

For the Mango-Habanero Infusion
Pour the mango juice in a pot and add the habanero pepper. Bring to a boil then simmer for 5 to 10 minutes. Remove the habanero pepper and any seeds.

For the Foam
Blend the mango-habanero infusion and xanthan gum together. Pour into a whipping siphon and charge. You can heat the whipping siphon or leave it at room temperature until you are ready to dispense the foam.

LAYOUT FOUR

This layout runs the content together in a single column. It can split into multiple columns for the ingredients, if desired. Images can be inserted after the headnote, or at the end of the preparation method.

MANGO HABANERO FROTH

This froth adds a spicy, tropical flavor to many dishes. I really like it on soft tacos or as a topper to gazpacho. You can also freeze the foam in molds and use it as a spicy topping on desserts.

The amount of habanero you use will depend on how hot you like your food, and how spicy you want the foam to be. You can also use other juices besides mango, I really like orange or peach juice as well.

If you don't want to make your own mango juice you can find it at many nicer supermarkets or health food stores. You can always use Goya canned juice if you can't find any fresh juice.

Tools Needed

Xanthan gum   Standing or immersion blender

Ingredients

For the Mango-Habanero Infusion   *For the Foam*
450 grams fresh mango juice   400 grams mango-habanero infusion
¼-1 habanero, seeds removed and cut in half   2.4 grams xanthan gum, 0.6%

For the Mango-Habanero Infusion

Pour the mango juice in a pot and add the habanero pepper. Bring to a boil then simmer for 5 to 10 minutes. Remove the habanero pepper and any seeds.

For the Foam

Blend the mango-habanero infusion and xanthan gum together. Pour into a whipping siphon and charge. You can heat the whipping siphon or leave it at room temperature until you are ready to dispense the foam.

RECIPE ATTRIBUTION

There is significant ethical debate among food writers about recipe attribution. There are very clear ends of the spectrum but a whole lot of gray in the middle. It's pretty obvious that you shouldn't just copy somebody's recipe verbatim and take credit for it, and it's also clear that you don't have to credit anyone if it's a recipe you came up with on your own. But what do you do if a recipe inspired you and you ended up changing several of the ingredients and the cooking method, does the original recipe writer deserve credit? What if a recipe you wrote was based on 3 or 4 different recipes, do all the writers deserve credit?

To start answering these questions, I want to first share the legal responsibilities you have. First, of course, a disclaimer! *We are cookbook writers, not lawyers, and any advice we give is just our opinion, before relying on any advice you should speak to an actual lawyer.*

With that out of the way, the law basically says that a recipe writer doesn't own the list of ingredients or the method of cooking food, they only own the words describing it. So technically, I could get my favorite Bobby Flay cookbook, copy the ingredients from each recipe, rewrite the instructions, and legally publish it under my name. Here is the actual wording from the copyright office.

> Copyright law does not protect recipes that are mere listings of ingredients. Nor does it protect other mere listings of ingredients such as those found in formulas, compounds, or prescriptions. Copyright protection may, however, extend to substantial literary expression - a description, explanation, or illustration, for example - that accompanies a recipe or formula or to a combination of recipes, as in a cookbook.

Because the bar is set so low to follow the law, it really becomes an ethical decision to determine "what is right." This means that everyone needs to make their own decisions about what they feel comfortable doing. And just like everything else where individuals have to determine what they think is right, there is a ton of disagreement.

Don't forget that crediting other recipe writers is a great way to expand your network, most writers are excited to hear that you were touched by a recipe they wrote.

> **Jason Says**
>
> I personally try to treat other recipe writers as I would like to be treated myself, or like I would treat a friend if it was their recipe. If a recipe directly inspires me I will give credit to the original writer or restaurant, even if I've changed the seasoning, cooking method, or other large parts of the recipe.
>
> If I'm researching a specific dish, I'll usually pull up several online recipes for that dish to get my bearings. Unless one of those really jumps out in a unique way, I don't credit all the other recipes because they were just used in aggregate.

Many food bloggers deal with this type of ethical question when writing on their blogs and many of the same considerations should go into effect. I highly recommend you choose a method you are comfortable with and stick to it, both on your blog and in your books.

For some good information and views from both sides, I recommend reading the comments from Adjusting a Recipe Doesn't Make It Yours (http://diannej.com/2010/adjusting-a-recipe-doesnt-make-it-yours) and the article and comments for Recipe Attribution from the Food Blog Alliance (http://foodblogalliance.com/2009/04/01/recipe-attribution). Dianne Jacob also has a great book on writing cookbooks called Will Write for Food that discusses these and other ethical issues (http://amzn.to/1XtczjN).

Book Writing Tools

There are many tools you can use for successful book writing. Some of these tools are general word processors and some are book publishing-specific tools. Choosing the correct tool to write your book in is a personal decision but we've provided several options below.

One thing to remember is that during the process of writing your book you should be focused on actually writing. You don't need to be focused on the book design, formatting, layout, or look and feel. Because of this, many authors look for a writing tool that is simple, quick and easy to use, and focuses around the actual writing process, not the book making process. Once the book is written, they will move it into a more robust word processor where they can add images and design the book. We cover design and formatting in much more detail in the "Designing Your Cookbook" chapter.

> **Jason Says**
> I use Pages '09 for all my books because I am the most familiar with it, though I will be switching to Microsoft Word for my coming books because Pages '09 is no longer being supported. If you are working on your first book I recommend using something you are already used to writing in. I personally have enough trouble focusing on the writing process that I hate to be interrupted by trying to figure out how a new program works at the same time.

It is also hard to know what your word processor is missing when you are working on your first book so many features of the more robust programs may be lost on you. You can always move your text into Word or another program later, once it is already written.

WORD PROCESSORS
Microsoft Word
Microsoft Word is probably the most commonly used word processor for book writing. This is because many people already know how to use it, it has many helpful tools for PDF and ePub creation, and it is relatively easy to navigate. Many publishers also provide Word templates to speed up the initial creation of the book. Even people that don't write their book in Microsoft Word will often use it to design and publish the book once the text is written elsewhere.

Apple Pages
Most Mac users are familiar with Pages, Apple's answer to Microsoft Word. Pages has been used often to create books over the years but unfortunately Apple removed many of the features in their latest version that are helpful when designing and publishing

a book. It is hard to recommend Pages anymore for anything but writing the book unless you are already intimately familiar with it.

Google Docs

You can also use the word processor from Google Docs if you want your documents stored online for easy access (https://apps.google.com/docs-showcase). It's a pretty basic word processor but it does a lot of what you need, especially for the initial writing process and through the first few drafts.

Using Google Docs also makes it easier to share your cookbook with testers and editors since it's online and you can give them access to make comments directly in the document. You can also automate many repetitive tasks using the Google Docs scripting. For a much more detailed look at writing books in Google Docs you can see this article by Jamie Rubin (http://www.jamierubin.net/2014/08/08/how-i-use-google-docs-for-writing).

Scrivener

Generally considered one of the best book writing programs, Scrivener is a 100% book writing-based program (http://www.literatureandlatte.com/scrivener.php). Because of this, it is also an organizational tool that combines note taking, outlining, and writing all in one place. Once the book is designed you can also publish Kindle, ePub, and print formats directly from Scrivener.

If you are interested in Scrivener there is a great video program that will walk you through everything you need to know about Scrivener (http://learnscrivenerfast.com).

iaWriter

ia Writer (https://ia.net/writer/mac/) stores documents in plain text for ease of portability. There are also iPhone and iPad apps so you can easily write anywhere.

OpenOffice

If you want a more robust word processor like Word without paying for it, OpenOffice provides free word processing tools (http://www.openoffice.org).

Other Word Processors
Other tools people use are Ulysses (http://www.ulyssesapp.com), Fast Pencil (http://www.fastpencil.com/company/book_writing_software), and Plume Creator (http://www.plume-creator.eu/site/index.php/en/).

DISTRACTION FREE WRITING
Regardless of what tool you use to write your book, sometimes you just need to block out everything else and focus on the writing. To help with that, there are several distraction free writing tools.

Scrivener and iA Writer Pro already have this feature built in. Some other writing programs also have good distraction free modes, such as WriteRoom (https://itunes.apple.com/us/app/writeroom/id417967324), Zen Writer (http://www.beenokle.com/zenwriter.html), and Write Monkey (http://writemonkey.com).

PRODUCTIVITY AND TIME TRACKING
Dragon Naturally Speaking
If you are a slow typist or just need a break for your hands, Dragon Naturally Speaking (http://www.nuance.com/dragon/index.htm) is the world's best-selling speech recognition software, it lets you dictate documents, search the web, email and more on your computer.

> **Gary Says**
> Being an extremely slow typist was the main impediment that kept me from doing much writing. In the process of transferring words from my brain to the page, I often lost my train of thought. Once I became proficient using Dragon Naturally it freed me to efficiently stream content from my mind to the page. It made writing enjoyable. So don't give up writing because you can't type - tools like Dragon can have you putting your thoughts on paper quickly and accurately in no time.

Rescue Time
Rescue Time (https://www.rescuetime.com) keeps track of what applications and programs you are using so you can get a

breakdown of how you are spending your time. It's a good way to find and eliminate inefficiencies in your work flow and time management.

How to Back Up Your Cookbook Files

If you are like most people, then you probably don't back up your computer nearly as much as you should. When it comes to your cookbook, it's time to actually start doing proper backups. It would be a devastating feeling to have months of work lost because you couldn't spare the few minutes a week it requires to back up your files.

In general, we recommend that you do a full system backup of all your important files. Bloggers and authors accumulate photographs, unpublished blog posts, business and accounting files, contact lists, email archives and other important files. Ensuring that these files will not be lost is critically important. There are many ways to backup your computer, and they are outside the scope of this course, but PC World has a good guide for PCs (http://bit.ly/1KRMbOE) and for the Mac you can use Time Machine (http://thesweetsetup.com/apps/easiest-way-to-backup-mac/) or other solutions.

In addition to full system backups, there are several tools and methods we recommend using to help manage your files. We use both full system backups and these individual tools to fully manage both our backups and our work flow.

Dropbox

Dropbox (https://db.tt/EHEyRxAF) is a cloud-based backup service that you install on your computer. It then replicates your files online. You can choose the specific files it backs up or do the majority of your computer. You can also access old versions of documents, in case you need text you had deleted from your cookbook, and it can restore deleted documents. We use Dropbox to backup the majority of our computers.

For more information on setting up Dropbox you can view this guide for the Mac (http://www.instructables.com/id/How-to-use-

Dropbox-on-your-Mac/?ALLSTEPS) and this guide for PCs (http://www.instructables.com/id/How-to-Use-Dropbox-on-Windows/?ALLSTEPS). Another helpful guide on automatically backing up your "My Documents" on your PC (http://dropboxtips.com/2012/12/how-to-make-dropbox-your-my-documents-folder/) or "Documents" folder on your Mac (http://wilsonpage.co.uk/make-your-documents-folder-your-dropbox/).

CREATING MULTIPLE FILES

Another way we manage our book writing work flow is by creating backup documents before major rewrites or changes. If we are working in the file "Baking-Book.doc" we may end up with multiple files such as:

- Baking-Book.doc
- Baking-Book-Pre-Rewrite.doc
- Baking-Book-Pre-Formatting.doc
- Baking-Book-Pre-New-Recipe-Layout.doc

We always work in the base "Baking-Book.doc" file, then before we undertake a major rewrite or large changes we will just save a copy with the file name appended with "Pre-" and the name of the change. This allows us to freely change the file, knowing that if we need something as it was before, we can easily find it in the old file and copy and paste it to the new one.

BACK YOUR FILES UP OFF SITE

Make sure you always keep a copy of your files off site. This can be through something as simple as Dropbox or even just emailing the file to yourself or a Gmail account. If you back up your files on a USB drive or external hard drive, make sure you take a copy somewhere away from your house in case of fire, flooding, or other disaster.

Photographing and Testing Recipes

Once you have written your cookbook you will need to test your recipes and photograph many of them. We've found it's a lot more efficient to photograph the recipes during the testing process, which prevents you from having to make the same dish multiple times.

HOW TO TEST COOKBOOK RECIPES

Having solid recipes in your book is critical to making readers happy and gaining good reviews. Recipe testing is a crucial part of this process.

WHO SHOULD TEST THE RECIPES

There are many ways to handle recipe testing, starting with testing your own recipes, and moving through recruiting friends, family and readers, up through using professional recipe testers. Most recipes are tested at least once by the writer of the recipe and then by at least one other person to double check they work as desired.

Testing Recipes Yourself

It's always a good idea to test your own recipes at least once before asking other people to test them. It's easy to have a typo in the ingredients or leave out a step that you don't notice before you test it. These typos and other simple mistakes can cause frustration with your testers if they are not caught up front.

Having Others Test Your Recipes

When you are having other people test your recipes it is best to have people that are in your target audience (your avatars) testing your recipes. This way the knowledge and skills of your testers will coincide with the knowledge and skills of your readers.

Friends and Family

If they are in your target audience, friends and family are a great source of recipe testers. They are usually happy to help out and give good feedback. You can also do recipe testing together with some friends, it makes a long and sometimes tedious process much more fun.

You can often ask them to test specific recipes, or let them see the draft of your book and pick out recipes that would be of interest to them.

Your Readers

If your cookbook is related to your blog, you can reach out to some of the more visible members of your community to help test recipes. You can usually offer them a free copy of the completed book as a thank you. This also doubles as a great form of promotion and can provide valuable feedback both for the recipes and the book as a whole. There is also a good chance they will be willing to give you an early review on Amazon.

Professional Testers

If you want to get real serious about recipe testing you can turn to professional testers. They will be willing to test any recipe you want and give detailed feedback for a price.

WHAT TO LOOK FOR WHEN TESTING

Regardless of who is doing the testing, there are several guidelines to keep in mind to get the most out of your testing. Be sure you are looking to check:

- All the ingredients are accounted for in the ingredient list
- The flavor and seasonings are balanced
- The directions are clear and easy to follow
- Any odd ingredients or equipment needed is called out ahead of time
- The recipe makes as many servings as it said it would
- The timing works out correctly
- The food looks and tastes great

WRITE DOWN EVERYTHING

When testing a recipe you will find things you want to change. Make sure you write down every single change you want to make. It's easy to believe that you will remember the changes, but unless you write them down you will forget some of them. It's very frustrating to go through the testing of a recipe and not remember the tweaks you had wanted to make.

Some people recommend saving all of your testing notes, even after you have updated your recipe. This allows you to go back through your changes and see why you changed the recipe and what it was before you got started.

RECIPE TESTING WORKSHEET TEMPLATES

There are many different approaches you can take to recipe testing. We provide a few templates for you, as well as links to others. Experiment with the different options and see what works best for your work flow. Feel free to take any of our templates and modify them to fit your needs. You can also access these templates in several formats including PDF, Word, and Pages from our website at http://bit.ly/1G4zqbF.

SELF TESTING TEMPLATE

Our self testing template is designed for an author to use when testing their own recipes. It's a great way to track what you need to change and keep notes on what worked and what didn't work.

Recipe Self Testing Sheet

Date _____

Book Title _____

Title of Recipe _____

Preparation Time _____

Total Time _____

Yield / Servings Made _____

What worked well?

What didn't work?

What changes are needed?

Any additional comments?

DETAILED TESTING TEMPLATE

Our detailed testing template is designed either for an author to use when testing their own recipes or when working with outside recipe testers. It's a much longer, two-part sheet designed to get the necessary information out of your testers.

Detailed Recipe Testing Sheet

Your Name _____ Date _____

Your Contact Information (email or phone) _____

Book Title _____

Title of Recipe _____

Recipe Preparation Time _____ Actual Preparation Time _____

Recipe Total Time _____ Actual Total Time _____

Recipe Yield / Servings Made _____ Actual Quantity _____

Ingredients Used   Amount

_____   -   _____
_____   -   _____
_____   -   _____
_____   -   _____
_____   -   _____
_____   -   _____
_____   -   _____
_____   -   _____
_____   -   _____
_____   -   _____

How does the food taste?   Poor   1   2   3   4   Great

Are there any changes you would make to the flavor, seasonings, or spices?

How does the food look?   Poor   1   2   3   4   Tasty

What could improve the appearance?

Powered By **Self Publishing** (MADE EASY)
www.SelfPublishACookbook.com

How clear were the directions?   Confusing   1   2   3   4   Clear

What could be explained more clearly? Would more vivid descriptions of the food's appearance at a particular stage help clarify the process?

Where the ingredients easy to find?   Yes   No

If not, which ones were difficult to find? Where did you locate them at? Online? Local specialty store?

Was there any equipment needed that you didn't already have?   Yes   No

If so, which one? If you didn't get one, how did you "work around" it?

Were there any substitutions made or ingredients omitted?   Yes   No

If so, which ones?

Was it a success?   Yes   No

What was your favorite part of the dish?

What was your least favorite?

Is there anything else you'd like to share about the recipe?

Powered By Self Publishing
www.SelfPublishACookbook.com

DOWDY CORNERS COOKBOOK CLUB

The Dowdy Corners Cookbook Club provides a nice recipe testing worksheet that they use for their club members (http://dowdycornerscookbookclub.com/club-folder/recipe-testing/).

FOOD PHOTOGRAPHY TIPS

Taking photographs for a book is very similar to taking them for a blog. As a food blogger, you probably already have a good idea of how to take great photographs. If you need a refresher, here are some important tips for food photography, as well as links to more information.

USE THE HIGHEST RESOLUTION POSSIBLE

Photos for a blog are normally used at 72 dpi which gives you a lot of leeway with resizing, cropping, and zooming using almost any type of camera. Photos used in print books are printed at 300 dpi, severely limiting the amount of cropping and resizing you can do, especially when taken with a lower resolution camera.

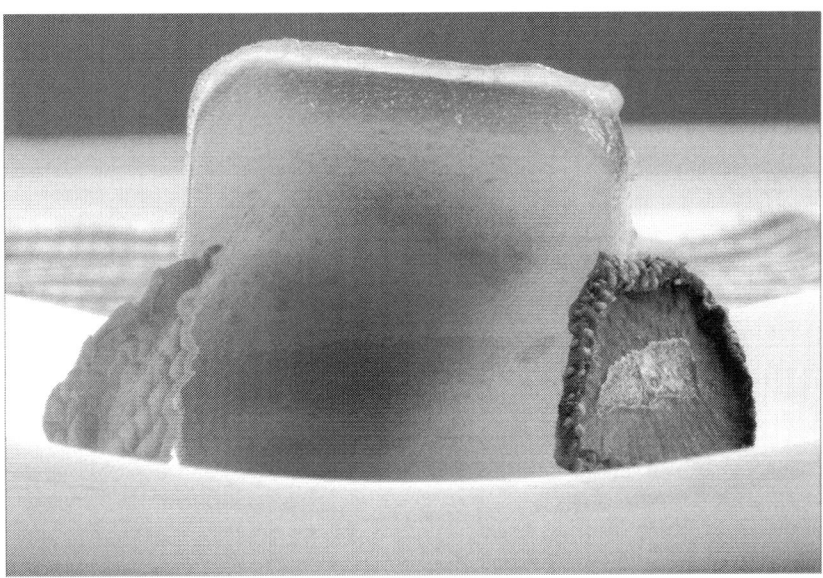

There is still some leeway with resizing and cropping but it is much more important to accurately frame your photograph from the start. It is also helpful to use the highest resolution camera you have access to.

USE GOOD LIGHTING

Good lighting is crucial to producing great photos. Natural light is a wonderful way to go if you have access to it. A box light, or stand lights are also very helpful. Never use the flash on your camera, it will result in washed out photographs.

> **Jason Says**
> Once I got serious about taking good photographs (and I was starting to do videos as well) I wanted some high-quality lights. I ended up getting the Fancierstudio Softbox Lighting Kit which comes with 3 stand lights (http://amzn.to/1oE6s0j). These lights don't get hot and are very versatile. They've met all my photography and most of my video needs, which is pretty impressive since they cost less than $150.

Using bounce boards is also a great habit to develop. These reflectors are set up at the opposite side of the food and bounce the light back, filling in shadows and rounding out the photos. A piece of foam board you can get for a few bucks at any craft store can be used as an inexpensive bounce board.

TAKE MANY SHOTS AT MULTIPLE ANGLES

Don't limit yourself to only a few angles because there are often many compelling shots you might miss out on.

It's best to start with the normal angles of an above shot, a straight front shot, and a ¾ or 45° shot. That way you know you have at least a few usable photos. From there you can start to take more unusual pictures that might not work out such as different cropped views, using harsher or softer lighting, and more or less zoom. You can also experiment with the depth of field and compositions with more unusual exposures.

Taking several shots will not only give you a wide variety of shots to choose from, it will also give you great practice and teach you what works and doesn't work with your specific type of food.

STABILIZE YOUR CAMERA

When using proper lighting you will need to have the shutter open for a longer amount of time. This makes it very hard to hold the camera steady. Using a tripod or another stabilizing device is a huge help in producing crisp photographs.

> **Jason Says**
>
> For most of my normal shots I use the Ravelli APLT2 50" Tripod (http://amzn.to/1Vh5JfQ) and it works great. Plus, for under $20 it's a great deal for a solid piece of equipment. When I'm taking photos with my phone, I use the SnapMount SM3 Tripod Mount (http://amzn.to/1XthhOC), which allows my phone to go on a normal tripod.
>
> Recently, I wanted more stability for my overhead shots so I splurged and got a combination of the Manfrotto MT055XPRO3 Pro Tripod (http://amzn.to/1oE7k53) and the Side Arm (http://amzn.to/1oE7ucB), these help me produce super-crisp shots from above.

TOUCH UP YOUR PHOTOS

Don't be scared to touch up, re-balance, and crop your photos on your computer. While some professionals might look down on this practice, most photographers can produce much, much better photos when they are touched up. Especially for a writer, the whole point of taking pictures of the food is to make it look good and inform your readers, not to showcase your natural photography skills.

Adobe Photoshop or Adobe Lightroom are the top two photo editing programs. These programs, especially Photoshop, used to be very expensive but they are now available as a subscription for only $10 to $20 a month, less than most web hosting packages. If you are serious about producing high quality work then their ability to transform your photographs is worth the monthly investment. You can also explore the other less-expensive photo editing programs available if you prefer.

SHOOT IN RAW FORMAT

To take full advantage of Lightroom, Photoshop, and the other editing programs it's best to shoot in RAW format. This format stores much more information than the standard JPG format and allows you to change many aspects of your image using simple sliders.

PHOTOGRAPHY RESOURCES

Detailed food photography is beyond the scope of this book but here are some books we highly recommend if you are looking for more help with your photography. Plate to Pixel: Digital Food Photography & Styling (http://amzn.to/1XthyRI), Food Photography: From Snapshots to Great Shots (http://amzn.to/1oE836m), and Focus on Food Photography for Bloggers (http://amzn.to/1oE87D3) all provide great overviews of food photography that will work for both bloggers and publishers.

For a general look at photography we recommend Understanding Exposure: How to Shoot Great Photographs with Any Camera (http://amzn.to/1XthDop).

If you need help with your food styling, Food Styling: The Art of Preparing Food for the Camera (http://amzn.to/1XthCAQ) and The Food Stylist's Handbook (http://amzn.to/1oE8mhm) both provide great information.

Proofreading and Editing Your Cookbook

One of the hardest parts of self publishing a cookbook is ensuring that the proofreading and editing is held to a high standard. A poorly edited book filled with spelling and grammatical errors will usually get many bad reviews and end up hurting your sales. You've gone through the long process of writing a great book, now it's time to make sure it reads like one.

We will first help you familiarize yourself with the types of editing that are done on completed books then provide several tips for how to effectively self edit your cookbook. We discuss finding outside people to help with editing and give you several recommended editing and proofreading resources.

Types of Cookbook Editing

There are three main types of editing that you should be concerned with once your cookbook is written: substantive editing, copy editing, and proofreading.

You can go through these editing processes yourself, use friends or your blog network, or turn to outside parties. We highly recommend you have at least one outside person, and preferably 2 to 3, look at your book before publishing it. Things that seem clear to you may not be clear to other readers and the more pairs of eyes you have on the book the less mistakes will get through.

Substantive Editing
Substantive editing, or line editing, is a rigorous process where the editor rewrites sentences, moves information around, and generally makes your book easier to read. They also view the book as a whole to ensure it conforms to any standards or general formatting you have set and keeps a consistent voice throughout.

Copy Editing
Copy editing is the next step in the editing process. A copy editor looks for errors of spelling, grammar, capitalization, punctuation and other writing mistakes. Occasionally they may correct awkwardly written sentences but most of the editing is for grammatical issues.

Proofreading
Proofreading is the final editing phase and is normally undertaken once the pages are fully laid out. It looks for major mistakes, bad formatting, and overt grammatical errors such as spelling and bad tense.

Tips for Self Editing Your Cookbook

Whether or not you end up using friends or an outside service to help you edit, you should still spend time editing your own work. The more complete the manuscript you give to friends the happier they will be and the less money you will have to spend on an outside service.

Depending on your preferences, you can either print out your book and work from the hard copy or do it directly in your word processor. Some people also recommend going through your final copy on your iPad or tablet, this gives you a different view of the content and forces your brain to re-think how some of it fits together.

FINDING SENTENCE STRUCTURE ERRORS

A great way to find errors in sentence structure is by reading the text out loud. When you do this, most awkward sentences will jump right out to you. You can then rework them until they sound correct.

It can also be a good idea to take a week or so off before editing for sentence structure. Because you are so immersed in your book you will often know what you are trying to say even if the words don't actually say that. Taking a little time off will help you forget what you meant to say and you'll see what you actually wrote.

SEARCH FOR THE WORD "THAT"

Often the word "that" and some of the words around it can be eliminated by carefully rewording the sentence. This results in cleaner and more concise writing.

MINIMIZE YOUR COPY

A good rule of thumb is to try to use the fewest words possible to convey the same amount of information. Cutting out extraneous words, extra sentences, and other pieces of text that don't help convey your message will help tighten up your writing, making it easier on the reader. Some sentences can be made more direct, getting to the point more quickly.

This does not mean you want to change the tone of your writing, or the amount of information presented. It just ensures you are doing it the most efficient way possible.

VIVID COPY

There are many words that do not convey much information and it's best to eliminate them. Some of these words are "nice", "good", and "ok". They do not add any information and can easily be replaced by more impactful and descriptive words.

PICTURE YOURSELF AS YOUR READER

When you are editing your book it is very helpful to picture yourself as your avatars. Keeping their mental states and existing knowledge in mind, as well as what they hope to learn from your book, is a great way to pick up on areas that might need more clarification.

FINDING GRAMMAR AND SPELLING ERRORS

While it sounds like a no-brainer, the first place to start is by running the spell check and grammar check in your word processor. This will catch many low-level issues you need to fix. You can also use external grammar checkers like Grammarly (http://grammarly.com).

Many people recommend reading your text backwards to find spelling and grammar errors. Our brains have the tendency to auto-complete sentences and smooth over bumps in the text, going backwards removes this process, allowing errors to show more clearly. Some people recommend reading each word backwards one at a time, others do a paragraph at once. Experiment and see what works best for you.

FINDING OUTSIDE EDITING HELP

It is very hard to successfully edit and proofread a cookbook by yourself and we highly recommend you get at least one other person, and preferably 2 or 3, to look at it before you publish it. There are two main ways to elicit outside editing or proofreading: your friends or outside editors.

Note: Before sending your cookbook to an outside source you should always edit your cookbook yourself. This will make it easier on your friends and save you money with outsourcers.

ENLISTING YOUR FRIENDS TO EDIT

The easiest way to get editing and proofreading help is by turning to your friends or network of fellow bloggers. Many of your friends will be happy to help you out by reading through parts of your cookbook and giving you feedback.

A large caveat. Your friends will go much easier on your work than a professional editor will. They usually not only lack the skills of a professional editor but they will be afraid of hurting your feelings. Friends are much better for broad "this is confusing" type feedback than for nit-picky spelling or grammar mistakes.

You are also more likely to get prompt feedback from your friends if you only ask them to proof a few chapters instead of your entire book. Your friends are just as busy as you are and even though they might be excited about your book, they will have trouble spending hours proofing it for you.

It can also help to ask for very specific feedback from your friends. This will allow them to be more direct with you than they would have been otherwise.

Once they have edited the book, this group of people can also be asked for thoughts on the book that you can use as testimonials, either on the book cover or in the book description. They can also be tapped during your pre-launch to contribute reviews on Amazon.

HIRING AN OUTSIDE EDITOR

Hiring an outside editor will guarantee that you have a professional sounding cookbook with most spelling, grammar, and punctuation mistakes corrected. A substantive or line editor can help with your sentence structure, continuity and grammar, or you can focus on a copy editor or proofreader to catch the spelling, punctuation and other grammatical mistakes.

There are many ways to find outside editors. You can look on job sites such as eLance (http://bit.ly/1Xl54eu) or Upwork (http://bit.ly/23hC669). The Editorial Freelancers Association has common editing rates listed on their website (http://www.the-efa.org/res/rates.php) as well as a member directory where you can find editors (http://bit.ly/1N1bgaX).

Absolute Write Water Cooler is a writers forum for self publishers (http://bit.ly/23oJKIE). This huge community of writers can offer conversation, discussion and enlightenment on many writing-related topics.

The Independent Book Publishers Association (https://www.ibpa-online.org/) is aimed at "helping each other achieve and succeed" and often has good recommendations.

There are also many companies that handle all aspects of the editing process.

Regardless of how you find them, there are a few considerations you should keep in mind before agreeing to work with an editor.

Price
Price is often a big concern for self publishers. You don't need to work with the most expensive editor but going the cheapest route can often mean working with someone of much lower quality. Picking an editor priced in the upper-side of the middle range often works well. You can also take a risk on a less-experienced editor if you are trying to save money since they will usually charge less as they try to build up their portfolio.

Work History
You should always check the work history of an editor you are going to employ. Have they done cookbooks before? How many books have they edited? Are they willing to provide you with names or references for previous work? It's not critical to find a cookbook editor, but someone who specializes in cookbooks can give you more insights than someone who never cooks.

Sample Edits
Most editors will provide you a free "sample edit". This means you send them a few pages or a chapter of your book and they will edit it and send it back. This allows you to see how they work and if their editing style is right for you. It is a very common practice and can save you time and many headaches by avoiding editors that have styles which clash with yours.

Work Process
It's good to learn how they handle the editing process. Will you get everything back at once or a chapter at a time? How long do they anticipate it to take? What file formats do they prefer? How will they communicate with you? Also double check what type of editor they are - you don't want to hire a substantive editor when all you wanted was a proofreader.

Your Personal Preferences

There are many nuances in grammar and cookbook writing that can go either way. Do you prefer to use "tablespoon", "tbsp.", or "T" in your recipes? Do you prefer "chile pepper" or "chili pepper"? Do you love or hate the Oxford comma? If you feel strongly, let them know ahead of time so they don't erroneously mark up your book.

Once you get back your cookbook, always make sure you do a self edit or proofread before publishing it to ensure they didn't mess anything up or make any decisions you don't agree with. You also don't have to follow all their recommendations, it's still your book and you can handle it how you like.

PROOFREADING AND EDITING RESOURCES

There are many resources you can use to help make the cookbook editing and proofing process much easier on yourself.

FOOD AND GRAMMAR REFERENCES

When writing and editing your cookbook, you will often have questions about proper grammar and the spelling of words, especially types of food. These food and grammar references are a great place to get all your questions answered.

Google

If you are looking for a specific usage question you can usually turn to Google for most of your answers. Typing queries like "their vs there" or "is 'googling' capitalized" will often present several results that discuss the ins and outs of your question, allowing you to make an educated decision. Karen Wise, a cookbook editor, also recommends googling products and looking at the labels in the images to determine the correct way to spell them.

Food Lover's Companion

The Deluxe Food Lover's Companion (http://amzn.to/25IRQAu) is the latest entry in this series of dictionary-like books and contains more than 7,000 alphabetically arranged entries on types of food, cuisine, dishes, and other culinary items. This tome is not a cookbook or a wealth of recipes; it does not address the topics of food storage and handling, temperatures, wrapping, sealing, preservation and canning, or safety essentials. However it is a practical, well researched reference book on the food trade that will demystify most of your queries.

Chicago Manual of Style
The Chicago Manual of Style (http://amzn.to/1MjFFkQ) is the definitive guide to editing and what is considered grammatically correct. The sixteenth edition offers updated information on producing electronic publications, including web-based content and ebooks. An updated appendix on production and digital technology explains the process of electronic workflow and offers the basics of XML markup. In addition, a revised glossary includes a host of terms associated with electronic as well as print publishing.

Grammar Girl
One of the most often seen Google results for grammar queries is QuickAndDirtyTips.com, the website of Grammar Girl. Mignon Fogarty addresses many different aspects of grammar and editing. Her easy to follow, casual writing style makes understanding and remembering her grammar tips simple. In addition, she has a weekly podcast that helps listeners use good grammar and write more effectively.

ONLINE GRAMMAR CHECKERS
The real value of an online grammar checker is when it is used as a tool, rather than a stand-alone editor. These programs should not be considered the final word in spelling, syntax and grammar, but rather helpful assistants when a spelling and grammar check is needed. The following are three of the better online grammar checkers currently out there.

Grammarly
Grammarly (https://www.grammarly.com/) is an online grammar checker that you pay a monthly fee to use. It is a more well-rounded and comprehensive option than most word processor grammar checkers. It's easy to use and provides useful feedback. However, its lengthy explanations provide more information than usually necessary.

WhiteSmoke
The WhiteSmoke online checker (http://www.whitesmoke.com/) doesn't catch all grammar mistakes, but it will help improve your

writing and it is easy to use. Its strengths lay in offering the most modern interfaces available and in providing robust full service customer support. WhiteSmoke proposes several fee schedules to choose from, i.e. monthly, quarterly, yearly and lifetime. This online checker cannot pinpoint plagiarism.

CorrectEnglish

In addition to boosting the quickest processing speed to find mistakes, the CorrectEnglish online checker (http://www.correctenglish.com/) has superior grammar correction accuracy over the others. CorrectEnglish's drawback stems from the user interface not being as modern and sleek; it also lacks any kind of mobile versions. However, this is a solid service to help you find, correct and learn about your grammar mistakes.

Designing and Publishing Your Cookbook

PUBLISHING FORMATS AND PLATFORMS

Once your book is written, tested, and fully edited, the next step is to decide which formats you want to publish your book in. This includes print and PDF, as well as the various ebook formats like Kindle, Nook, and iTunes. You can publish in multiple formats and you can maximize your revenue by publishing in as many as possible.

If you are interested in publishing print books, we explore the self publishing printers and print on demand printers, as well as provide in-depth reviews of CreateSpace and IngramSpark, the two largest self publishing printers.

For electronic books we cover many of the distributors and publishers you can use and discuss the differences between them.

Types of Cookbook Publishing Formats

There are many different formats you can publish a cookbook in. The most popular are

Print Cookbooks
- Hardback
- Paperback
- Pamphlet or Flyer

Electronic Cookbooks
- Kindle
- Nook
- iBook
- PDF
- Interactive Book

The book format you choose can affect the layout, length, photography, and design of your book so it's important to at least have an idea ahead of time if possible. Each book format has its own quirks, positives, negatives, and things to keep in mind.

Print Books

Print books are the most popular format for the major publishing houses and until recently were the only real way to purchase a cookbook. These are the books you find in every book store. They usually have full-color covers and their interiors are either color or black and white. Most printed cookbooks have 100 to 300 pages and range from 30 to 100 recipes, depending on the type of cookbook.

There tends to be no main difference between paperbacks and hardback cookbooks, besides the material of the cover. Pamphlets tend to run much smaller, between 40 and 100 pages.

You can get a lot more information about print books in the "Choosing a Self Publishing Printer" section.

Electronic Cookbooks

Electronic cookbooks first entered the marketplace as PDF files and were usually self published. However, over the last several years electronic cookbooks have become more and more popular, driven primarily by the Kindle and expanding into the Nook, iBook, and other electronic formats based largely on the ePub specifications. You can get a lot more information about ebook publishers and distributors in the "eBook Publishers and Distributors" section.

Electronic cookbooks tend to break down into two major categories, print-like cookbooks and electronic-only cookbooks.

Print-Like Cookbooks

Print-like books are works that follow traditional cookbook styles. They are often an electronic version of a printed cookbook and follow the typical page and recipe counts found in print cookbooks. They are usually sold side-by-side with print versions of the same book.

Electronic-Only Cookbooks

Electronic-only cookbooks can follow the traditional guidelines but they can also break from them in many ways. The two main paths these books deviate are by selling them for very little money or by creating an interactive book.

Without needing to cover print costs, electronic books can be sold for very little, or even given away. This strategy can be used to increase distribution of a book or to monetize smaller books that contain much less content. It's not unheard of to sell a 50 page cookbook in electronic format for $1, something that isn't possible for print books (unless they are in the bargain bin).

Interactive books go the other direction and deliver more content than a traditional print book does. This may include audio snippets, videos or calculators and other tools. The cookbook might be more in the format of a magazine or a cooking show. Or the cookbook might just have an amazing design and innovative ways to access the recipes and content. Interactive cookbooks usually cost the most to produce.

WHICH FORMAT TO CHOOSE?

The type of format you choose will depend a lot on the goals for your cookbook. If you are trying to maximize your income, then producing a book that works in as many formats as possible should be your goal. If you want to spread your ideas, then a variety of formats is also important, though focusing on a lower cost. If you want to market yourself, then pick a format or two that will let you create the best product to show your expertise.

> **Jason Says**
> I tend to publish my books in as many formats as I can. This opens up sales on several platforms and allows me to make use of the same content in multiple locations. Moving from one book format to another is usually a pretty easy process, especially compared to writing the book initially!

WHICH BOOK FORMAT TO WRITE AND DESIGN FOR

When writing your book, you don't have to focus on a format, but once you move into the design phase the format you choose will affect many things. It is a good idea to initially focus on the format that is most important to you and that you will spend the majority of your marketing energy on. Then you can tweak that design into the other formats.

> **Jason Says**
> For my books I tend to focus on the print versions. They are my largest sellers and money makers. I start off optimizing my books for the print format then convert the finalized book into the other formats.

SALES COMPARISONS OF BOOK FORMATS

To help show how the sales can vary between the different formats we released our 2014 sales comparison in the Appendix as "Case Study: Sales Channel Breakdown".

CHOOSING A SELF PUBLISHING PRINTER

When publishing a printed book, there are two services that are important, the printing and the distribution. Many companies can handle both services for you and there are several options for the types of printer you use. We will walk you through the different types of printing platforms available as well as the things you should keep in mind when choosing a platform.

KEY CONSIDERATIONS OF CHOOSING A PRINTING PLATFORM

Regardless of which type you are going with, there are several factors to keep in mind when choosing a printing platform.

Reputation

Probably the most important is the reputation of the printing platform with other writers. Choosing a platform that is well thought of goes a long way towards having a smooth publishing experience.

Printing and Setup Costs

There are many financial considerations as well. Different printers will charge different amounts to print and distribute the same book. Some printers also require an upfront publishing fee before they will print it. The cost to purchase additional books directly can be very important if you are planning on wholesaling or selling books directly to consumers.

Distribution

The distribution network of the printer is also very important unless you are planning on doing all the selling yourself. Getting your books on Amazon and other online retailers is a key to reaching a wide range of readers.

Ownership and Contractual Terms

Some printers have very strict contractual terms where they own some or all of the rights to your book. We highly recommend avoiding these printers.

Working with Multiple Printers

You can also mix-and-match printers, playing to each of their strengths. For example, you could publish through CreateSpace for their Amazon distribution but go through a less expensive offset printer to print your wholesale orders. Many people publish both through CreateSpace and IngramSpark to maximize their distribution. As long as you have a universal ISBN number this strategy will work fine (for more information on ISBN numbers see "All About ISBN Numbers" in the Appendix).

Types of Printing Platforms

If you are printing a cookbook there are many different platforms you can use. They break down into three main categories: digital print on demand printing, offset printing, and turnkey printing. Each type of printing category has positives and negatives that you need to be aware of.

Digital Print On Demand

Print on demand printing is probably the easiest and most common type of printing for self publishers. Print on demand takes advantage of the digital quality of books and the capability to print your book only when a copy is needed. The process is a similar, if more complicated, version of what you do at home when you print a document.

Positives of Print On Demand

The biggest benefit to print on demand printing is that cookbooks are only produced as they are needed. This eliminates the need to store cookbooks as inventory, as well as minimum order sizes. You take no risk using a print on demand company since you only pay for copies that are sold.

Many print on demand companies will work directly with Amazon or another wholesaler to receive orders from them, print your book, and ship it out without you ever being involved.

Negatives of Print On Demand

There are a few negatives with print on demand. One is a lack of control over some of the design and formatting decisions. Most print on demand companies have guidelines you have to follow because your book is printed with the same setup as many other books. This can be a major issue if you are working on a Marketing book or you want very, very specific colors, page size, paper quality, or other design considerations.

Another negative is a potential lower-quality printing compared to other types of printers. The quality varies from company to company, but most digital, print on demand quality is less than the better offset printers.

The final negative of print on demand is that there are usually no discounts for larger printings. With small- and large-batch printing you can get bulk discounts, but those discounts don't apply for print on demand. So if you are planning on ordering large quantities, it may cost more than other methods. This has been changing lately as a few printers have started offering bulk discounts.

Common Print on Demand Companies
There are several well known companies that do print on demand. We have an in-depth look at the major ones in the upcoming "Comparison of Print On Demand Cookbook Printers" section because it is the most commonly used platform for self publishers.

OFFSET PRINTING
Offset printing is the standard printing method for traditionally published cookbooks and most other professionally printed materials. It uses a process where the book is set up for printing and then a large run of them are printed out. For a more detailed look at the offset printing process in general I highly recommend the Wikipedia page about it (http://bit.ly/1RInd5A).

Positives of Offset Printing
Offset printing is the industry standard for a reason. It is relatively inexpensive for large numbers of items and the print quality is very high. You also have a whole lot of control over the look and feel of all aspects of the book.

Negatives of Offset Printing
The biggest negative to offset printing is that minimum quantities are needed. Because the press has to be set up specifically for each run, most companies require a minimum printing of 500 to 5,000 books. You or a dropship company will need to store these books and then ship them to people who purchase them. Any books that don't sell are still owned by you, and you've taken a loss on them.

Common Offset Printing Companies
There are many offset printing companies but one of the largest and most used is Ingram (http://www.ingramcontent.com/).

Turnkey Printing

Turnkey printing is the most basic type of cookbook printing. Once you've written your content, you create an account on the site and fill out forms for chapters, recipes, and other content. They will then assemble the information from the forms into a cookbook which they will then print, and sometimes distribute, for you.

Positives of Turnkey Printing

The only real benefit of a turnkey printer is that it is easy to use and no knowledge of word processing or cookbook creation is needed. If you are uncomfortable formatting documents on a computer or doing general word processing tasks, this might be the right method for you. Even then, taking a class in Microsoft Word so you can format your book for a print on demand or offset printer is probably a better investment than using a turnkey printer.

Negatives of Turnkey Printing

The biggest negative of turnkey printing is the limited control you have. They offer some subset of decisions you can choose from for design, typography, and book size but it will have to be within their guidelines.

Turnkey printers also tend to be more expensive than offset or print on demand publishers.

Common Turnkey Printing Companies

Turnkey cookbooks are a big industry and there are several large companies including Cookbook Publishers, Inc. and Morris Press (http://www.morriscookbooks.com/ and http://cookbookpublishers.com/).

Comparison of Print on Demand Cookbook Printers

Arguably the greatest boon for self publishers is the increasing availability of print on demand (POD) capabilities that are attractively priced. This allows the author to only print books once they have been sold, thus reducing the amount of upfront costs and risk associated with bringing a new book to market.

Over the last five years an increasing number of POD companies have been coming to the aid of the self publishing author. Today there are easily more than 100 of these companies vying for the hearts and minds of self publishers like yourself.

In attempting to narrow down this field to the POD company that's best suited for your book, you will need to keep in mind the type of cookbook you are planning, your cookbook goals, and the format of your book. We will give you some further assistance by listing some companies that are highly regarded, the two we recommend, and some warnings to consider as you approach your decision.

If you would like to do some additional research we would also like to recommend a website we feel has done the best job of summarizing the capabilities of a large number of these POD companies. The site is called The Independent Publishing Magazine (http://bit.ly/1MYBpaj) and is the handiwork of Mick Rooney, a publishing consultant, editor, investigative journalist, and author. Each month the magazine publishes the Publishing Service Index (https://is.gd/F1Sb7v) which is essentially a rating of the companies providing services to self publishing authors. In addition the site has an impressive collection of detailed reviews for the highest rated services.

COMPANIES WE RECOMMEND

These are two companies that we are most familiar with and are comfortable recommending as Print on Demand companies for most cookbooks. The companies have quite a few similarities, but also some important differences. As you consider the company's match for your particular cookbook, you may find that it is actually better to use them both than to select one over the other. This typically requires very little additional work or expense and allows you to leverage the unique strengths of both companies.

CreateSpace

Perhaps the greatest advantage of using CreateSpace is that it is owned by Amazon.com, which sells 64% of all printed books sold online. This relationship makes it extremely simple and quick to get your cookbook available for sale to millions of customers on Amazon with very attractive royalties.

The intent of CreateSpace is to meet the needs of the self publishing author by providing an inexpensive and user-friendly environment to create and publish a book. In addition to offering handholding along the way they also deliver reasonable customer support and a wide variety of optional services to assist the author if needed.

CreateSpace is low cost and easy to use, but it doesn't allow hard cover books and their quality can be inconsistent.

IngramSpark
Ingram Content Group is the world's largest wholesaler of print and electronic books to independent bookstores, bookstore chains, internet retailers, and specialty markets, as well as other wholesalers. They distribute to more than 38,000 retailers, libraries, schools, and distribution partners in 195 counties. IngramSpark takes full advantage of these distribution channels, getting your book into many markets and it's a good choice to maximize your distribution.

IngramSpark also has higher quality printing than CreateSpace, though their books also tend to be slightly more expensive. You also have many more printing options through IngramSpark, including hard covers, different levels of color quality, and varying paper weights.

Unlike most companies doing Print on Demand, IngramSpark does not provide a bunch of services such as proofreading, editing, typesetting, or design. Their customer service also leaves a lot to be desired since they are slow to respond and do not keep you up to date on the process as your book is being published.

Using Both Publishers
As mentioned, one way to take advantage of the distribution strengths of CreateSpace on Amazon and IngramSpark in other areas is to publish your book through both companies. When you publish your book, you can specify what distribution channels they should use, so you can only distribute from CreateSpace on Amazon and use IngramSpark for everything else.

HIGHLY REGARDED

IngramSpark and CreateSpace are the most popular printing platforms but there are many others offering similar services. Here are our recommended companies providing services to self publishers that many people use successfully.

LuLu

Lulu is an established (founded in 2002) and well respected company with a strong reputation. They have offices in the USA, Canada, UK and India. They are known for their software tools which allow authors to create a book in a very short amount of time. You can create a book essentially for free if you choose not to use any of the variety of services they have available. Their books are more expensive than CreateSpace but most believe their color offerings are of higher quality.

Outskirts Press

Outskirts Press is a relatively small publisher but is rapidly growing. They offer a wide variety of services and excellent distribution through Ingram Book Group and Baker & Taylor, Inc. They do require an upfront and nonrefundable down payment to get started.

VirtualBookWorm Publishing

VirtualBookWorm is a small publisher proud of the relationships it has with its authors. They do screen manuscripts, they have good distribution and pay competitive royalties. They also provide a wide range of services at additional cost.

Infinity Publishing

Infinity Publishing has the capability to allow bookstores to return books, which is fairly uncommon for publishers of this type outside of IngramSpark. This might result in more bookstores carrying your title in stock. Unfortunately, the company has relatively low royalties, expensive setup fees, and requires you to pay extra for distribution through Ingram Book Group and Baker & Taylor, Inc.

BookLocker

BookLocker has been around a while and has a good reputation. They have a variety of different types of programs including a DIY one for those who want to minimize expenses. They provide good royalties and a reasonable setup fee. Unfortunately, there is a significant penalty if you need to make changes to your manuscript.

Blurb

Blurb has the ability to quickly produce very high quality colored "Photo" books. Unfortunately, the high quality will cost you dearly as the printing costs are much higher than other companies. Blurb has recently partnered with Ingram to provide both worldwide distribution as well as more competitively priced color books, Blurb refers to them as "Trade Books", using Lightning Source printing capabilities. However, they are still more expensive than either IngramSpark or CreateSpace.

Mill City Press

Mill City Press is a lesser-known publisher but they do offer the full component of needed services for self publishers. Authors do get to keep 100% of the royalties after printing costs.

BUYER BEWARE

Recently a lot of companies have been rushing in to take advantage of authors during this surge in self publishing. Some of them are providing valuable services to authors but unfortunately there are quite a few that have left authors disappointed, discouraged and angry. So we recommend that you examine a potential publisher with a high degree of due diligence to be sure that you're going to get everything that you expect.

There are a couple specific areas that you will want to pay particular attention to. Perhaps the area that receives the most negative feedback is the quality of the services that are provided by some of these publishing companies. On average it appears that the services are more expensive and of lower quality than you can probably find on websites such as such as Elance and Upwork.

There also seems to be considerable consternation around the contracts and practices provided by some of these publishers that appear to be misleading at best. Far and away the company that receives the most negative feedback is Author Solutions, which is the parent company of AuthorHouse, Xlibris, iUniverse, Trafford, Palibrio, WordCray, FuseFrame, PitchFest, and Booktango. In fact they are facing two class action suits filed in May 2013 and April 2015. For numerous years authors have been complaining about poor quality products, poor quality customer service, up selling pressure and trouble with accurately reporting and paying royalties. We would strongly suggest avoiding all of these publishers.

eBook Publishers and Distributors

There are many different places you can sell ebooks and many use their own formats. Luckily there are few, if any, changes you need to make to publish with the majority of them.

You have several options when publishing an ebook. You can format and submit it to each platform yourself, or you can use an ebook distribution service like Smashwords that will convert and submit your ebook to multiple publishers.

The distribution services are usually the easiest route to go, but they do take a cut of your royalties and sometimes charge set up fees. Publishing your book yourself takes more time but you will get more money in the long run.

This section covers the ebook publishers and distributors and the next section takes a deeper look into whether publishing direct or using a distributor will be best for you. We go into more depth discussing how to submit your book to the top companies in the various sections of the "Publishing Your Cookbook" chapter.

eBook Publishers
The main online retailers of ebooks, listed in order of our sales:

- Kindle
- iTunes and iBooks
- Nook
- Kobo
- Oyster
- OverDrive
- Scribd

There are many more online retailers but this covers the ones we sold at least one book during 2015.

EBOOK DISTRIBUTORS

The major ebooks distribution services are:

- Smashwords
- Draft2Digital
- BookBaby

Often Print On Demand companies will make it easy for you to take your printed book and convert it to an ebook. For example, IngramSpark will convert your book PDF into a ePub which it will distribute to every major ebook retailer in the world: Amazon Kindle, Apple iBooks, and Kobo as well as 70 emerging ebook retailers. Similarly, CreateSpace will convert your paperback book to an ebook for $79 and distribute it through Kindle Direct Publishing.

SELLING PDFS

You can also sell PDFs directly from your blog, from your email newsletters, or through other marketing channels. This is covered in more detailed in the "How to Create and Sell a PDF on Your Blog" section of the "Publishing Your Cookbook" chapter.

SHOULD YOU USE AN EBOOK DISTRIBUTOR?

We have found that there are numerous advantages to going direct rather than through a distributor. Perhaps the most important is that you make more money with each sale since your distributor is not taking a cut of 10% to 20%. In addition, other benefits include faster payments, up-to-date sales figures, more direct control of which categories your book is listed in, and more timely changes to metadata and pricing.

Many of these benefits are critical if you plan on performing a variety of marketing activities on your ebooks. For example, if you intend to offer a discount to increase the volume of your sales, it's important to know exactly when the price will be reduced by the retailer. It would be a disaster to heavily market an attractive sale only to have the price of the book unchanged. Of course in this example you will also want to know as soon as possible how your sales were impacted by the price decrease so rapid availability of sales figures is also important.

The most significant disadvantage of going direct is having to learn how to interface with the different retailers since most have their own requirements. For example, the file format for Amazon is MOBI but for most other vendors it's an ePub file.

The most difficult retailer to interface with is Apple. Often we need to make minor changes in the ePub file to meet their very unique requirements. But arguably the biggest hurdle for interfacing with Apple is that you need to use a Mac in order to do it. This may be a showstopper for some people that don't have a Mac or access to one.

For individuals that are relatively tech savvy, learning these various interfaces is time consuming at first, but not terribly difficult. And once you do climb the learning curve of the various retailers you will be set for future books and for making changes as necessary. However, if you find that task daunting then we would suggest that you go with a distributor, they are essentially designed for individuals that want someone else to worry about all that detailed technical stuff!

Keep in mind that you don't have to go totally direct or just use a distributor. You can handle each retailer on a case-by-case basis if that works for you.

Regardless of which way you're leaning, we would strongly recommend that at a minimum you go direct for Amazon KDP. The interface to Amazon KDP is quite simple so it's easy to get your ebook submitted to the system. Also, it is highly likely that the vast majority of your ebook sales will come from Amazon and thus you want to be able to maximize your profits by going direct. You also have the advantages of placing your ebook in the categories you feel are best, easily and quickly changing your price, access to very timely sales reporting and leveraging promotional features such as KDP Select.

Jason Says

For our past books we have gone direct to Amazon, Apple iBooks, and Nook. Then used Smashwords to pick up the smaller retailers. As you would suspect our sales through Amazon totally dwarfed all the other retailers. By way of comparison, in the first third of 2016 we have sold 30 ebooks through the 12 retailers we use Smashwords for and 1,400 copies on the Kindle alone. The only Smashwords retailer with double-digit sales was Kobo. We have not finalized our decision but it's more than likely on our next book we will drop Smashwords altogether and add Kobo to our list of direct retailers.

DESIGNING YOUR COOKBOOK

Once your book is written and edited it's time to design the book and create the standard book pages. There are many components to designing a book. First, read over the "Cookbook Design and Formatting Guidelines" section for some specific tips on designing your cookbook.

We will then step you through the process of choosing a title for your book and designing your cookbook cover. Once the cover is designed, you can move inside the book and focus on choosing fonts and creating both the standard cookbook front matter and back matter. We also give you tips for adding in-book marketing.

Depending on your background and interests, some people will need more design help than others. Luckily there's a lot of outside design help available that we will help you find.

WHICH BOOK FORMAT TO WRITE AND DESIGN FOR

When writing your book, you don't have to focus on a format but once you move into the design phase the format you choose will affect many things. It is a good idea to initially focus on the format that is most important to you and that you will spend the majority of your marketing time on. Then you can tweak that design into the other formats.

> **Jason Says**
>
> For my books I tend to focus on the print versions. They are my largest sellers and money makers. I start off optimizing my books for the print format then convert the finalized book into the other formats.

COOKBOOK DESIGN AND FORMATTING GUIDELINES

There are a whole lot of things to keep in mind when designing the inner content of your cookbook. Here are some of the most important.

TEXT JUSTIFICATION

Most books use full-justification on their text. This makes the line go to the end of the page and spacing or hyphens are added to help with the various line lengths. Many books will also use automated hyphenation to help create more proper spacing. Ultimately the decision comes down to personal preference. Below are examples of left-justified text and full-justified text both with and without hyphens.

Below is standard left justified text. You can see how jagged the edges are, but the spacing between letters is consistent.

> I am a paragraph of text that is fully justified but I don't want to use hyphens. Sometimes this can get me into trouble with spacing, especially if I use several humongous words in a singular place such as: parsimonious accessories automa circumlocution winebibber, because the program has to stretch to make the words fit.

Jagged edges but even spacing between words

Using automated hyphens helps reduce the jaggedness between lines. The spacing between letters stays consistent.

> I am a paragraph of text that is fully justified but I don't want to use hyphens. Sometimes this can get me into trouble with spacing, especially if I use several humongous words in a singular place such as: parsimonious accessories automa circumlocution winebibber, because the program has to stretch to make the words fit.

Less jagged edges but still even spacing between words

Moving to full-justified text completely eliminates the jagged lines. Without using hyphens can result in noticeable spacing between letters, especially when there are multiple long words on a single line.

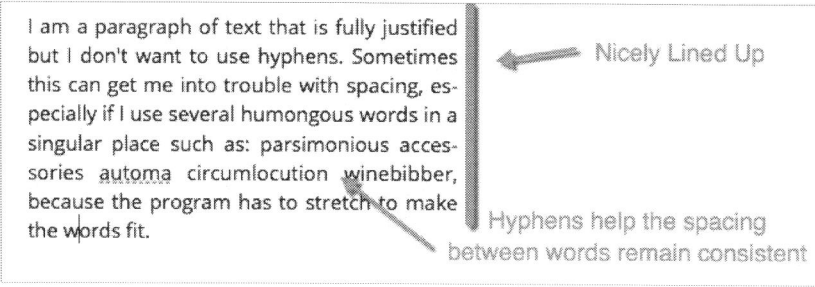

Full-justified text with hyphens minimizes the differences in letter spacing while still eliminating the jagged edges.

Spacing After Periods

Books should have only one space after a period. Many people are used to using two but the majority of fonts are set up to look best with only a single space. It's easy to do a search and replace on ". " at the end of the book writing process.

First Line Indents

Many books take advantage of a first line indent, which is simply indenting the first line of the paragraph. This is a personal preference and there isn't standard either way.

BLEED

Bleed refers to the edge of the images or backgrounds extending all the way off of the page of the book. It's a common way to add design flair and full color images to books.

> **Jason Says**
> I currently do not use bleed for my photos, only for my cookbook covers. In general, I think books with bleed look nicer but it's a more design intensive approach so I trade the gains in better design for the time savings. The impact of bleed is also reduced in black and white, which is how the majority of my books are printed.

USE STYLES

Make sure you take advantage of the styles functionality in your word processor. If you do all of your formatting using styles you can easily update all the text in your document at once, instead of doing it manually for each one. They behave very similarly to CSS styles and carry many of the same advantages.

PARAGRAPH SPACING

Spacing between paragraphs should always be a single line break. If you want larger spaces between paragraphs or headers it should be accomplished using the "Before Paragraph" and "After Paragraph" spacing. Resist the urge to simply use two line breaks to space your paragraphs. Using a single line will allow your word processor to accurately add and remove spacing at the top and bottom of pages, resulting in a much cleaner document. This also allows you to easily tweak the spacing between elements, especially if you change fonts at a later date.

PAGE MARGINS

Margins are the area between the edges of the pages and where the text or images start. The margins of your cookbook are dependent on the size of your book and your publisher but most guidelines are between 0.25" and 0.75".

If your word processor supports it, you will want to choose "Facing Pages" because the pages will be displayed facing each other, as opposed to if you just printed out the pages and stapled them together. This also allows you to do margins of different sizes.

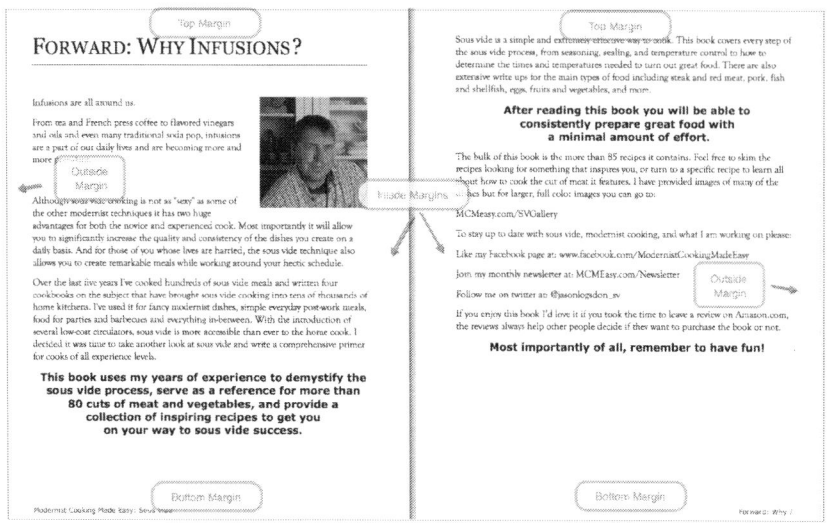

Jason Says

For my books I tend to use 0.75" for the inside margin, 0.5" for the outside margin, 0.5" for the top, and 0.4" for the bottom. The inside margin usually has some minimums depending on the number of pages - 0.375" for up to 150 pages, 0.5" for up to 300 pages - but I like the larger margin for my books so the text doesn't sink into the crevice. The top, bottom, and outside margins generally have to be larger than 0.25" and 0.5" is often recommended.

PAGE HEADERS AND FOOTERS

Some combination of page headers and page footers are often used. They are the text at the top or bottom of every page, and can be customized for both left and right pages. These are optional and when present usually consist of some combination of the name of the book, the author, the chapter you are in, the section of the book, and the page number.

> **Jason Says**
>
> I always use page footers in my books but I often skip the headers to save more room for the body text. In the footers I have the page number and book title on the left pages and the book chapter and page number on the right pages.

PAGE NUMBERING

Numbering the pages in your book is almost always a good idea. The page numbers are usually present in the header or footer for each page. Most word processors have a specific feature where you can insert the page number automatically. Most books start their page numbering at chapter one, and either use Roman numeral, or leave off page numbers, on pages earlier in the book.

USE SECTIONS

A section is a layout term used in word processing. It allows you to have a separate layout for a different part of the book. This allows you to have different headers and footers in those sections, which is key for using chapter names in them, or to control how the page numbering works.

HANGING TEXT

Hanging text, or "widows" are lines of text that are alone on another page. This is usually less than two or three lines and looks unprofessional. Once all the text for the book is done and the figures and photographs are in, one of the last things to do is remove the hanging text. This can be accomplished by re-wording phrases on the previous page or changing the kerning or line spacing for the text.

Choosing A Great Cookbook Title

The title and subtitle of a book should work together to help sell the book and pull in the reader. A good title has several characteristics regardless of where it is being published, but most of the following tips are optimized around Amazon or other online sellers.

Be Descriptive, Not Clever

A good title describes what the book is about, especially when taken in hand with the subtitle. There is often the impulse to be clever or witty in your title but in most cases it is best to resist this and use something that is easily recognizable. This is especially important when selling through Amazon, where potential buyers are scanning a list of books and you want them to instantly know if your book is right for them or not.

Keep It Short

Good titles tend to be as short as possible. Don't trade clarity for shortness, but try to use the shortest descriptive title you can. You can go into more description either on the subtitle or other text on the cover.

Keep It Simple

The language used in the title should be simple and easily understood by the majority of individuals, even those unfamiliar with your target niche. Refrain from the temptation to use long and complex words in an attempt to demonstrate expertise and authority.

Use Search Keywords In the Title

The title contributes to what searches your book will show up in, so using your top keywords in your title and subtitle makes a lot of sense. Don't give up clarity, but when in doubt go with a keyword. You will also be able to enter keywords in your description and directly in the publishing forms so don't force them in the title.

For more help on finding and evaluating keywords, you can see the "Choosing Publishing Keywords" section of the "Pre-Publishing Steps" chapter.

> **Jason Says**
>
> In my books, I'm promoting both the book and the brand so I have to sacrifice some length. I use "Modernist Cooking Made Easy" at the start of every book, after that I go with 1 to 2 words describing the book. Some examples:
>
> - Modernist Cooking Made Easy: Sous Vide
> - Modernist Cooking Made Easy: Getting Started
> - Modernist Cooking Made Easy: Party Foods
> - Modernist Cooking Made Easy: The Whipping Siphon
>
> You can see at a glance what the books are about and whether or not they are of interest to you. Our branding is also easily noticeable for people familiar with it.

EXAMPLE TITLES

For a few examples, here are the current titles of the best selling cookbooks in the "Slow Cooking" category. As you can see, they are almost all descriptive and clearly communicate what the book is about. Searching through the top selling cookbooks and looking at their titles will give you a great idea of what is currently working.

- The Paleo Slow Cooker: Healthy, Gluten-free Meals the Easy Way
- One Pot: 120+ Easy Meals from Your Skillet, Slow Cooker, Stockpot, and More
- Taste of Home Slow Cooker: 431 Hot & Hearty Classics
- The Healthy Slow Cooker Revolution
- Slow Cooking for Two: A Slow Cooker Cookbook with 101 Slow Cooker Recipes Designed for Two People

HOW TO DESIGN A COOKBOOK COVER

Designing a solid cookbook cover is one of the most important things you can do to maximize sales. Most readers will come across your book on Amazon or other websites and their first impression will be based on your front cover. A shoddy cover will turn away many potential readers and a great cover will pull them in.

Cookbook covers do not have to be complicated, many simple ones work great. If you are unsure about your graphic design skills it's much easier to develop a clean and simple cover that looks professional than a complicated one.

For great cover ideas we recommend looking at the Amazon best sellers to see what is currently working and what is in style (http://amzn.to/1SUCoYm).

Different publishers have different requirements for cover size. Most publishers provide cover templates in a variety of formats that are easy to use and update. We highly recommend you work on the largest cover size first, usually the print version, then you can easily scale down from there.

TOOLS FOR DESIGNING A COOKBOOK COVER

To design your cookbook cover you can use any graphic design tool you are familiar with. Photoshop and Sketch are great choices, as are InDesign and Illustrator. Many people also make simpler covers in MS Word. There are many free tools available as well such as InkScape or GIMP.

Depending on where you are publishing your cookbook, they also might have a built-in cover making tool you can use. CreateSpace has a popular one many people use.

You can also outsource your cover design. If you do not have the design skills and tools to create your own cover, and since the cover is so important, this is an area you may want to invest in professional assistance. We cover more of these in the "Finding Outside Design Help" section of this chapter.

SECTIONS OF A COOKBOOK COVER

There are three main sections to a cookbook cover. These are the front, the back, and the spine. Each one contributes different things to the cover design and the best covers use all three sections together to help sell the reader on the book.

Front Cookbook Cover
There is a wide variety of things you can include on a book cover but there only are few you need to have. A bold, easy to read title is very important. An eye-grabbing image or two is another key to capturing peoples' attention. A descriptive sub-title is used to provide more information. And of course your name, so people know who wrote the book at a glance.

Remember that the front cover also needs to look good at smaller thumbnail sizes since they show up in Amazon search results. Currently Amazon displays most covers at 100x100 pixels so try to make sure your photograph is clear and your title is easy to read at that size. This will be your first impression for many potential buyers, so be sure it will still draw in readers.

Your cover will normally be shown on a white background. This means if your cover is white it can blend in, especially at the edges.

If your book is related to your blog, it can be helpful to try and match some styles or include your logo on the cover. This helps spread brand awareness to new readers as well as draw in readers who are familiar with your blog.

Cookbook Spine
The spine is the area between the front cover and the back cover. It is usually best to keep this simple and just include the title of the book and your name centered vertically.

If your book is short, you may not need any text on the spine. If that is the case, just run the front and back covers together in the middle of the spine. Your printing platform should let you know if this is the case.

Back Cookbook Cover
The back cover can be used for a variety of things but you want to make sure you include a few different elements. The ISBN and barcode are the most important things to include for print books (you can read more about ISBN numbers in the Appendix). Including a description with benefits and marketing highlights is often very important as well.

If you have any blurbs or endorsements from other authors or readers this is a great place to highlight them. It can also be helpful to reiterate the title here if you want.

Some authors like to include an author bio and picture on the back cover, though we feel the space is better used for marketing the book unless you already have wide name recognition.

You can view the back covers for many books on Amazon by clicking the thumbnail below the main image on the Amazon details page.

What Fonts to Use in Your Cookbook

One of the more important parts of your cookbook design is choosing which fonts to use. Poor font selection can result in a book that is hard to read and that will frustrate your readers. Sticking to basic fonts will not make your book stand out, but you can ensure it will be as readable as possible. Print and ebooks will have different fonts because some fonts are easier to read on a computer and others are easier to read in print.

Standard Fonts for Printed Cookbooks

There are several standard fonts used for printed books. The major free ones are Georgia, Adobe Garamond Pro, Minion Pro, Palatino, Baskerville, and Goudy Old Style. These are all serif fonts, which tend to be easier to read in printed books.

The font size can vary depending on the context (such as the recipe headnote vs body text vs ingredients list) though 10 to 14 is usually used.

For headings, a larger or bolder version of the body font can be used or a more stylized font such as Bookman Old Style or Century Schoolbook.

When selecting the fonts you will use for your print cookbook, be sure to actually print some sample pages out. The fonts will look very different on your screen than they do on the printed page. It's almost impossible to accurately judge the look, feel, and size of fonts without printing them.

> **Jason Says**
> Here are the fonts I use for my most recent books.
>
> - Main Body and Regular Text: Goudy Old Style
> - Header 1: Georgia with bottom border
> - Header 2: Bookman Old Style Bold
> - Ingredient Header: Goudy Old Style Italic

STANDARD FONTS FOR EBOOKS

For Kindle and other ebooks, the generally accepted method is to set a body font that the user can then override with their device settings. The Kindle supports many basic fonts including: Arial, Baskerville, Caecilia, Courier, Georgia, Helvetica, Lucida Sans Unicode, Palatino, Times New Roman, Trebuchet, and Verdana, so it is usually best to stick to one of those as your default. You can then utilize the bold, italic, and underlined versions of this font throughout your book. A separate font can also be used for headers if desired.

> **Jason Says**
> We have published our books using Palatino, Verdana, and Georgia as our base font for different books. We then use the bold version of the font at double the size for our largest header and move the size down from there.

For fancier presentations you can also embed fonts into your Kindle books. It's usually best to only do this for headers because many readers like to pick their own body fonts. Preventing them from doing this will just upset them and lead to bad reviews.

For this reason it is also best not to lock the font size of the body text, different people like reading it at different sizes. 12pt is generally a good default font size that the reader can then override if needed.

Be sure to add in some line spacing, usually 120% to 150% works best.

For PDF books, I highly recommend using a sans serif font or one that is designed to be read on a computer screen. This will make it much easier for your readers to read it.

GENERAL COOKBOOK FONT TIPS

A good rule of thumb is to mix and match serif and sans serif fonts if your header font is different than your body font. Two different serif fonts next to each other can look a little strange. Some work well with each other but it's something to keep in mind.

It's important to remember that when most people are reading your recipes they will be in their kitchen and not in a normal reading situation. Because of this, it is best to err on the side of too large of a font instead of too small. This is especially important with print books or PDFs where you have fixed the font size.

Make sure you leave ample spacing between paragraphs. Usually a 0.8 to 2 extra lines are added.

Some people recommend always setting your text to full-justification for a more professional looking text.

You can view the fonts and styles we use in our books by downloading our sample template (http://bit.ly/1QQiEax).

COOKBOOK FRONT MATTER

At the front of most books there are several pages referred to as "Front Matter". These pages consist of the title page, copyright page, dedication, other books, table of contents, foreword, preface, and many others. The only required front matter is really a simple title page and a copyright page.

We give descriptions of the various pieces and provide basic examples in this section, but we highly recommend pulling a few of your favorite cookbooks off the shelf and looking at how they handle the front matter. You can also download a sample of the front matter from my book, Modernist Cooking Made Easy: Sous Vide for an example of the order and spacing we use (http://bit.ly/1NdsHQl).

TITLE PAGE

The title page is the first page of your cookbook with text on it. At a minimum it usually contains the title of the book. It can also have the name of the author, the subtitle, and sometimes an illustration or photograph. Some cookbooks, especially photo heavy ones, will have the title page span 2-3 pages and utilize nice pictures.

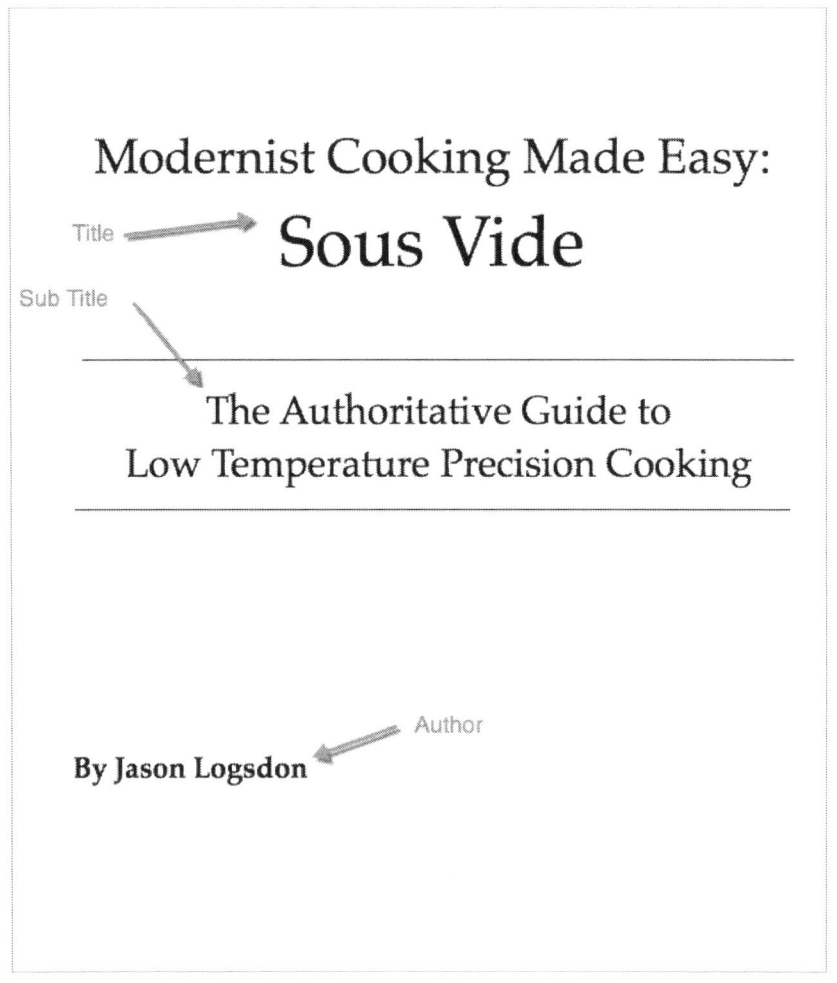

COPYRIGHT PAGE

The copyright page holds the copyright for your cookbook, your contact information, ordering information, your ISBN numbers, publication information, and any credits for design or photography.

Your copyright statement can be as short as "© 2016 Your Name. All Rights Reserved." or as long as you want it to be. We always include a standard copyright notice, our address for people to contact us, and our ISBN numbers. For a good look at various disclaimers you can check out The Book Designer (http://bit.ly/1qxTke5).

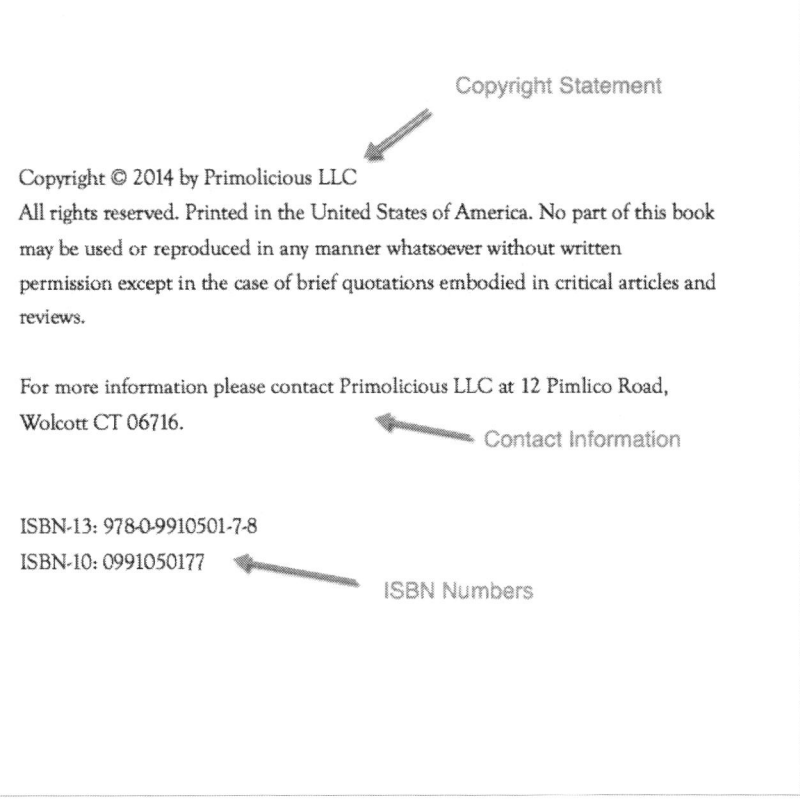

OTHER BOOKS

The Other Books page allows you to highlight the other books you have published. This section usually consists of a title followed by a list of books you have published. If you have published under several publishers the books may be broken down by publisher to give them credit. You can also include a link to your website or blog here, or any other long-form articles or guides you have written.

> **Other Books By Jason Logsdon**
>
> Modernist Cooking Made Easy: Getting Started
> Modernist Cooking Made Easy: Party Foods
> Modernist Cooking Made Easy: The Whipping Siphon
> Beginning Sous Vide
> Sous Vide: Help for the Busy Cook
> Sous Vide Grilling

DEDICATION

The dedication is completely optional but it's a great way to thank someone that has meant a lot to you, either in the publication of the book or in life in general.

> To my Mom,
> who from an early age
> gave me the confidence
> to do anything I set my mind to

EPIGRAPH OR QUOTATION

Many books lead with a quotation that applies to their cookbook or cooking philosophy. Make sure you have the right to use the quotation and are not breaking any copyright rules. Jane Friedman has a good article on when you need permission to use quotes (https://janefriedman.com/permissions/).

TESTIMONIALS

Testimonials about your cookbook, or other books you have written, are often added at the front of the book to help convince potential readers they should buy your book. Make sure you get permission from the person if you use their testimonial.

ACKNOWLEDGMENTS

Adding a section for acknowledging the people who have helped you with the book is a great way to give thanks. This could be anyone who helped edit, outline, or otherwise assist you with the creation of your book or other authors or cooks whose work you greatly leaned on.

ACKNOWLEDGMENTS

In cooking, most new dishes, flavors, and techniques are building on the work of prior generations of cooks. There are very few truly original works and we all owe a debt of gratitude to those that came before us and paved the way for us. There has been a great tradition of sharing and codifying cooking techniques from Escoffier to Ferran Adrià to Grant Achatz to Nathan Myhrvold, each of which built on the works of those that came before.

This book is no exception. I could never have written it, much less explored the latest modernist techniques, without the chefs, authors, and cooks who experimented with food, and most importantly, shared their knowledge with us in books and on the internet.

I'd especially like to mention several resources that were invaluable in creating this book. I highly recommend them for you to read if you want more in-depth knowledge.

Alinea by Grant Achatz is filled with amazing techniques and whimsical dishes. Aki Kamozawa and H. Alexander Talbot delve into the "why" in their *Ideas in Food* book, as well as their always informative website. *Texture - A hydrocolloid recipe collection*, compiled by Martin Lersch from Khymos.com, is a great compendium of recipes for many modernist ingredients. The *Hydrocolloids Primer* from Dave Arnold and the Cooking Issues website help to clarify some of the uses of and reasons for modernist ingredients . And, of course, the comprehensive *Modernist Cuisine* by Nathan Myhrvold, which covers pretty much every cooking technique you would ever need to know.

All of these resources gave me a foundation that I could use to explore the techniques and ingredients found in this book.

TABLE OF CONTENTS

The table of contents is one of the most important pages that your cookbook will have. It's used to help readers easily navigate your book. It's also often a way to market your book when potential buyers use the "Look Inside" feature on Amazon.

There are many levels of content you can include in the table of contents. The most popular is to have all sections listed, all chapters, and the major headings in those chapters. Some also show the minor headings, but it depends how fine-grained you want your table of contents to be.

We also recommend including all recipes in the table of contents. That makes it much easier for your reader to skim the recipes and find specific ones. It's also great for the "Look Inside" feature as it will show potential purchasers all the recipes your book contains.

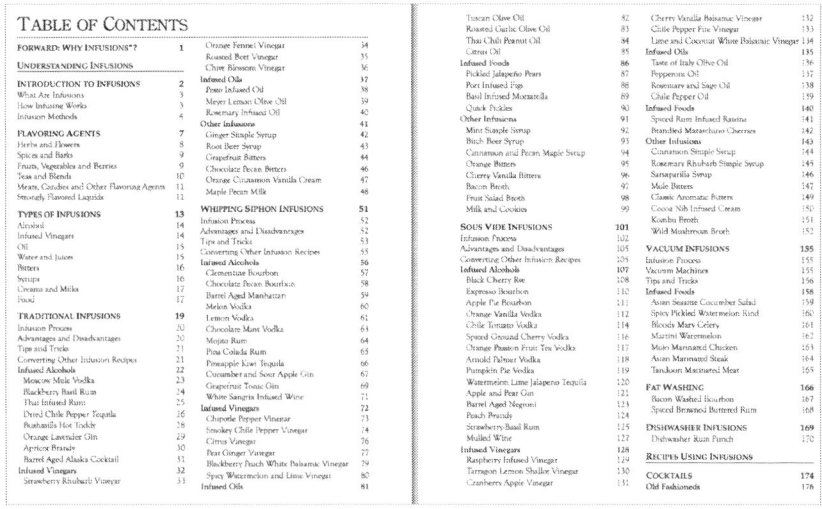

The table of contents normally goes right after the other front matter like the copyright page, dedication, and "Other Books" page at the front of the book. It is often the first page of real content, before the first section of the book starts.

FOREWORD

The foreword is an introduction to your book written by someone else. This can be done by another author or a cook or chef you are familiar with. It usually talks about why you are qualified to write the book and what they particularly liked about it.

PREFACE

The preface usually talks about why you wrote the book and what you are trying to accomplish with it. Since the preface often shows up under the Amazon "Look Inside" feature, it's a great place to market your book to potential readers by explaining what you hope to cover in it, which is usually the same as the reason they would want to buy it.

PREFACE: WHY SOUS VIDE?

I initially got my start in modernist cooking when I began exploring the sous vide process. I was fascinated with the process and hooked on learning more about the new types of cooking. Since then I've expanded into other modernist techniques and worked with everything from whipping siphons to pressure cookers and blow torches; created foams, gels and spheres; made barrel aged cocktails and brewed beer.

But the one technique I use on a daily basis is sous vide.

Although sous vide cooking is not as "sexy" as some of the other modernist techniques it has two huge advantages for both the novice and experienced cook. Most importantly it will allow you to significantly increase the quality and consistency of the dishes you create on a daily basis. And for those of you whose lives are harried, the sous vide technique also allows you to create remarkable meals while working around your hectic schedule.

Over the last five years I've cooked hundreds of sous vide meals and written four cookbooks on the subject that have brought sous vide cooking into tens of thousands of home kitchens. I've used it for fancy modernist dishes, simple everyday post-work meals, food for parties and barbecues and everything in-between. With the introduction of several low-cost circulators, sous vide is more accessible than ever to the home cook. I decided it was time to take another look at sous vide and write a comprehensive primer for cooks of all experience levels.

This book uses my years of experience to demystify the sous vide process, serve as a reference for more than 80 cuts of meat and vegetables, and provide a collection of inspiring recipes to get you on your way to sous vide success.

Sous vide is a simple and extremely effective way to cook. This book covers every step of the sous vide process, from seasoning, sealing, and temperature control to how to determine the times and temperatures needed to turn out great food. There are also extensive write ups for the main types of food including steak and red meat, pork, fish and shellfish, eggs, fruits and vegetables, and more.

After reading this book you will be able to consistently prepare great food with a minimal amount of effort.

The bulk of this book is the more than 85 recipes it contains. Feel free to skim the recipes looking for something that inspires you, or turn to a specific recipe to learn all about how to cook the cut of meat it features. I have provided images of many of the dishes but for larger, full color images you can go to:

MCMeasy.com/SVGallery

To stay up to date with sous vide, modernist cooking, and what I am working on please:

Like my Facebook page at: www.facebook.com/ModernistCookingMadeEasy

Join my monthly newsletter at: MCMEasy.com/Newsletter

Follow me on twitter at: @jasonlogsdon_sv

If you enjoy this book I'd love it if you took the time to leave a review on Amazon.com, the reviews always help other people decide if they want to purchase the book or not.

Most importantly of all, remember to have fun!

Cookbook Back Matter

There are several pieces of the book that go after the main body of the cookbook, these are called "back matter". They include content like an index, glossary, appendixes, bibliography, and resources. All of this content is optional, though an index and resources section are very common in cookbooks.

Descriptions of the various pieces of back matter are provided below with basic examples, but for more examples pull a few of your favorite cookbooks off the shelf and look at how they handle the back matter. You can also download a sample of the back matter from my book, Modernist Cooking Made Easy: Party Foods for a look at the order and spacing (http://bit.ly/1NdumW6).

INDEX

The index is a listing of key words and where they appear in the text of your book. It is a very important part of a cookbook because readers are often trying to find some recipe they vaguely remember, or because they have chicken in the fridge and want to see all your chicken recipes.

There are many ways to choose the words that go into the index, though trying to think what groupings a user would be most interested in is a good place to start. Often times the index focuses on main ingredients like types of vegetables or proteins. More specific books might focus on other distinctions, such as types of grains in a baking book, or fillings in a pie book.

> **Jason Says**
>
> Because my books are about modernist cooking or sous vide, I tend to focus my index around modernist techniques (gelling, foaming), modernist ingredients (agar, xanthan gum), and main protein types or vegetables (beef, chicken, carrots). I've found those breakdowns to be enough to give readers a good idea of where specific content is located.
>
> And if you don't think having an index in a cookbook is important, in the one book I published without one, I got more negative reviews about lacking an index than I did for printing in black and white.

Agar
Apple Cider Gel Cubes 121
Bacon-Bourbon BBQ Jam 67
Banana Ravioli 195
Banana-Mango Foam 149
Blackberry-Peach Gel Wrap 159
Buffalo Sauce Dip 66
Cayenne-Pineapple Sauce 79
Cherry Coating 211
Citrus Pudding 139
Cream Cheese Noodles 49
Curried Carrot Pearls 113
Curried Lentils 157
French Onion Pudding 40
Fruit Gels 193
Habanero-Peach Dip 55
Nectarine Pudding 186
Pea Pudding 129
Poblano Pudding 171
Raspberry Jelly 197, 209
Roasted Apple Pudding 167
Roasted Beet Pudding 123
Roasted Poblano Pearls 85
Roasted Red Pepper Soup 117
Strawberry Daiquiri Cubes 221
Tikka Masala Coating 179
Tomatillo Pudding 143

Carbonation
Cucumber and Sour Apple Gin Fizz 226
Sparkling Grape Gazpacho 109
Watermelon Soup 111

Curing
Cured Salmon 75
Homemade Lox 49
Over-Cured Salmon with Capers 93

Fluid Gel
Bacon-Bourbon BBQ Jam 67
Cayenne-Pineapple Sauce 79
Citrus Pudding 139
French Onion Pudding 40
Habanero-Peach Dip 55
Nectarine Pudding 186
Pea Pudding 129
Poblano Pudding 171
Raspberry Jelly 197, 209
Roasted Apple Pudding 167
Roasted Beet Pudding 123
Spinach-Garlic Dip 61
Tomatillo Pudding 143
White Russian Pudding 214

Foam
Banana-Mango Foam 149
Buffalo Sauce Dip 66
Butter Foam 138
Chile Oil Foam 45
Chipotle-Carrot Froth 125
Chive Air 87
Cranberry Air 183
Curry Foam 147
Easy Aioli Dip 56
Foamed Fruit Cosmos 215
Foamed Pesto 181
Foamed Singapore Sling 225
Grapefruit Foam 217
Herb Air 145
Horseradish Air 162
Lemon-Caper Air 174
Malt Vinegar Air 141
Roasted Garlic-Soy Whipped Foam 59
Roasted Red Pepper Soup 117
Tangerine-Chipotle Froth 151
Teriyaki Froth 177
Whipped Goat Cheese 77

Whipped Sriracha Dip 58
White Chocolate Clouds 191

Gel
Apple Cider Gel Cubes 121
Banana Ravioli 195
Blackberry-Peach Gel Wrap 159
Cherry Coating 211
Clam Chowder 135
Corn Custard 171
Cream Cheese Noodles 49
Curried Carrot Pearls 113
Curried Lentils 157
Fruit Gels 193
Maple-Pecan Panna Cotta 189
Roasted Poblano Pearls 85
Strawberry Daiquiri Cubes 221
Tikka Masala Coating 179

Gelatin
Cherry-Chocolate Marshmallows 211
Chocolate Covered Mint Marshmallows 207
Classic Marshmallows 203
Curry Foam 147
Foamed Fruit Cosmos 215
Foamed Singapore Sling 225
Grapefruit Foam 217
Mom's Sweet Potato Casserole Bites 205
White Chocolate Clouds 191
White Chocolate-Raspberry Marshmallow 209

Glycerin Flakes
See Mono and Diglycerides

RESOURCES

The resources section is another important part of many cookbooks. The resources point to other sources of information, equipment, and ingredients that the reader might be interested in. Some examples of what to put in the resources section:

- Do you use any ingredients that are hard to find in a small grocery store? Suggest some good online retailers.
- Do you mention a technique but don't go into more details? Point out some books or websites with more information.
- Is any specialized gear used in your recipes? Give the reader a few sources where they can purchase it.
- Are there any companion books, websites, or apps? Alert your reader to them.

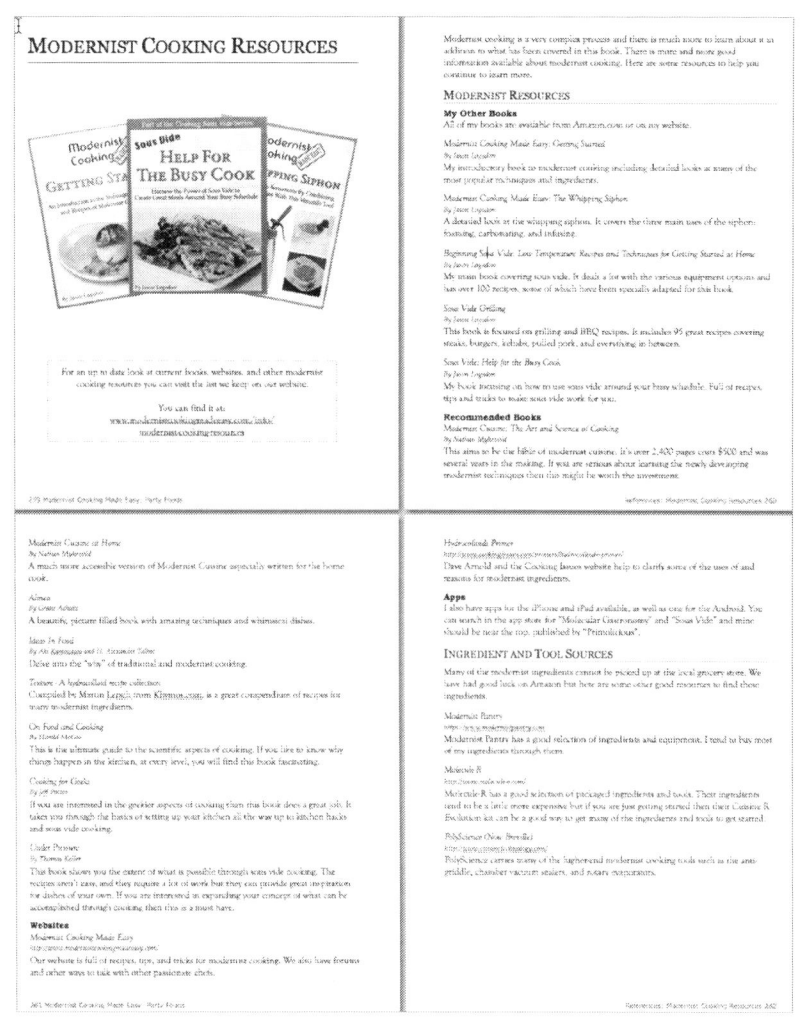

APPENDIX

The appendix will consist of any tables, charts, essays, or extended information that doesn't fit directly into the text of the book. This is a great way to provide summarized information in one easy to find location. It is also a valid place to put more technical descriptions of things you mention in passing in your actual book text.

Ingredient Techniques

Ingredient	Emulsions	Foams	Gels	Spherification	Thickening
Agar			x	x	
Carrageenan Iota		x	x	x	x
Carrageenan Lambda		x			x
Carrageenan Kappa			x		
Gelatin		x	x		
Gellan	x	x	x		
Guar Gum	x				x
Gum Arabic	x	x			x
Konjac	x		x		x
Lecithin	x	x			
Locust Bean Gum			x		x
Maltodextrin					x
Methylcellulose	x	x	x		
Mono and Diglycerides	x	x			x
Pectin	x	x	x		
Pure Cote B790			x		
Sodium Alginate			x	x	
Ultra-sperse	x	x			x
Ultra-Tex	x	x			x
Versawhip		x			
Xanthan Gum	x	x			x

Ingredient Temperatures

When you are trying to determine which ingredient to use, the hydration, setting, and melting temperatures can be very important.

Ingredient	Dispersion	Hydration	Gel Sets	Gel Melts
Agar	Any	100°C / 212°F	40-45°C / 104-113°F	80°C / 175°F
Carrageenan Iota	Cool	Above 70°C / 158°F	40-70°C / 104-158°F	5-10°C / 9-18°F above setting
Carrageenan Kappa	Cool	Above 70°C / 158°F	35-60°C / 95-140°F	10-20°C / 18-36°F above setting
Gelatin	Above 50°C / 122°F	Cool	30°C / 86°F	30°C / 86°F - 40°C / 104°F
Lecithin	Any	Any	N/A	N/A
Maltodextrin	Room temperature	N/A	N/A	N/A
Methylcellulose				
Methocel F50	Any	Below 15°C / 59°F	Above 62-68°C / 143-154°F	Below 30°C / 86°F
Methocel A4C	Hot	Below 15°C / 59°F	Above 50-55°C / 122-131°F	Below 25°C / 77°F
Mono and Diglycerides	Above 60°C / 140°F	Any	N/A	N/A
Sodium Alginate	Any	Any	Any	Above 130°C / 266°F
Xanthan Gum	Any	Any	N/A	N/A

Sous Vide Time and Temperature

If you are looking for more sous vide information I have many articles covering the process and equipment used, as well as over 50 recipes.

http://www.modernistcookingmadeeasy.com/info/modernist-techniques/more/sousvide-cooking-technique

One of the most interesting aspects of sous vide cooking is how much the time and temperature used can change the texture of the food. Many people experiment with different cooking times and temperatures to tweak dishes various ways.

The numbers below are merely beginning recommendations and are a good place to start. Feel free to increase or lower the temperature several degrees or play around with the cooking time as you see fit as long as you stay in the safezone.

Doneness Range

One of the most common questions we get asked about our sous vide recipes is some variation of "the recipe says to cook it for 3 to 6 hours, but when is it actually done".

The short answer is that anytime within the given range the food is "done". As long as the food has been in the water bath for more than the minimum time and less than the maximum time, then it is done. There isn't a specific magical moment of true doneness that can be generalized. For more information, here's the explanation why.

The How and Why

To have this conversation we first need to determine what "done" actually means. For sous vide there are two main "doneness" concerns when cooking your food. The first is to the temperature you are cooking it at (or becomes pasteurized at for some foods). The second concern is making sure the food is tender enough to eat without being "over tender", mushy, or dry.

Once the food you are cooking is completely up to temperature and it is tenderized enough to eat (and not over tenderized), it is now "done". For some already tender cuts of meat like filets, loins, and chicken breasts you don't have to worry about tenderness since they start out that way. That means that these cuts are "done" once they get up to temperature. You can find out this time using our Sous Vide Thickness Rules.

However, despite them being "done" at the minimum time shown, they stay "done" for several hours past that time, depending on the starting tenderness of the meat. This is why we give a range. You can eat a 1" cut of filet mignon after 50 minutes but you can also eat the filet up to 3 hours after it has gone into the bath without any loss in quality, tenderness, or flavor.

This is how our ranges are determined. They specify that for an average cut of the given meat, they will become "great to eat" tender at the minimum time given. They will continue to get more tender the longer they are in the bath but will remain "great to eat" tender until the final time given, at which point they may begin to get mushy and overcooked. In essence, they will be "done", and very tasty, for that entire range between the minimum and maximum times.

Another Way to Look at It

Another way to think about how this works is to use the following analogy. Pretend you

> **Jason Says**
>
> I use the appendix a lot in my books. I always provide tables of time and temperature combinations for sous vide items, ratios for modernist ingredients, and other data-heavy information. I also provide essays on topics that don't work in the flow of the text, such as discussing time vs tenderness cooking in sous vide, addressing modernist misconceptions, and other more detailed topics.

BIBLIOGRAPHY

If you heavily rely on other people's work then a bibliography is key to giving them credit. It is a list of sources you used for your book, citing the author, title, publisher and date.

END NOTES

Some people prefer to remove some of the information for a topic and display it in end notes at the end of the book. (You can also display them on the same page as footnotes). The end note is commonly used to point to a citation of the source of some material, provide a website link to the topic, or provide a more detailed aside from the author.

OTHER BOOKS

The end of the book is a great place to highlight your other books. If the reader has gotten that far, they most likely enjoyed your work and would potentially be interested in other books you have written. If you don't have any other books, you can also use this space to highlight your blog.

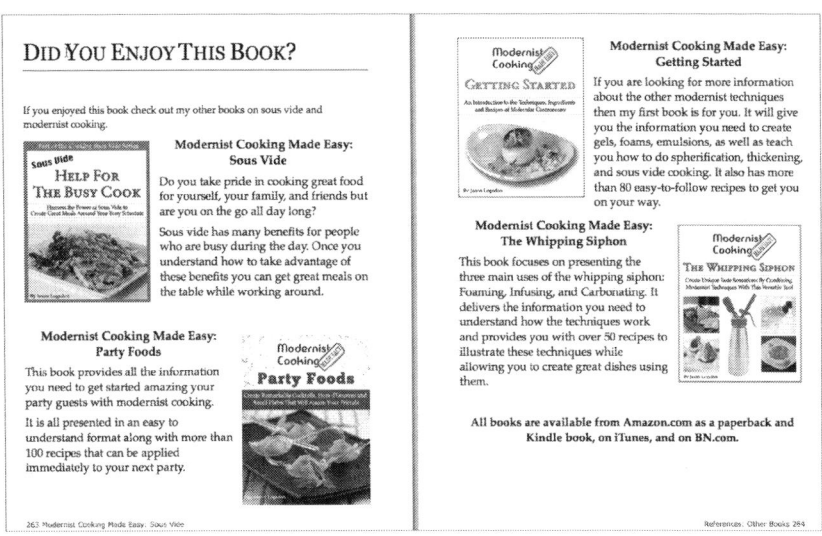

Jason Says

I try to market 2 or 4 of my other books on a nicely laid out page with covers of the books prominently displayed. This lets readers quickly see the books and better sells them on the content.

ACKNOWLEDGMENTS

Acknowledging the people who have helped you with the book can be done at the front or end of the book and is a great way to give thanks to the community of people who has helped you. This could be anyone who helped edit, outline, or otherwise assist with the creation of your book or other authors or cooks whose work you greatly leaned on. You can refer to the example in the previous "Front Matter" section.

GLOSSARY

The glossary is a place where you can provide definitions for terms you use elsewhere in the book. This can be very helpful if you assume your readers have a base of knowledge but worry that some people won't know every term you use. Instead of describing it within the text of the book you can add it to the glossary so your readers know they can turn there for any clarification they may need.

ABOUT THE AUTHOR

Providing more information about yourself is a great way to build trust with your readers. This section usually consists of 2 to 4 sentences about the author, followed by a listing of their most prominent books, articles, or websites. There is often a way to contact the author directly, either through email, Facebook, or Twitter.

ABOUT THE AUTHOR

Jason Logsdon is a passionate home cook, entrepreneur, and web developer. He helps cooks understand new modernist cooking techniques with easy-to-understand directions and recipes. He has a website and several books on sous vide and modernist cooking that are read by thousands of people every month including *Modernist Cooking Made Easy: Sous Vide*, *Modernist Cooking Made Easy: Party Foods*, *Sous Vide: Help for the Busy Cook*, *Modernist Cooking Made Easy: Getting Started*, *Sous Vide Grilling*, *Modernist Cooking Made Easy: The Whipping Siphon*, and *Beginning Sous Vide*. His website is www.ModernistCookingMadeEasy.com and Jason can be reached at jason@modernistcookingmadeeasy.com or through Twitter at @jasonlogsdon_sv.

In-Book Marketing

Your cookbook is a great place to market you, your blog, and your other books. Here are a few things you may want to market inside of your cookbook.

Opt-in to Your Newsletter

Giving your readers an indication of where they can sign up for your newsletter in order to get more great content is a wonderful use of space in your book. You are speaking directly to readers who thought enough of your book to purchase it and are currently reading it. This link can go anywhere in the book. I tend to put one in my introduction, in a chapter intro around the middle of the book, and at the end of the book.

You can also offer a freebie if they sign up, such as "If you liked my baking book sign up for my newsletter and I'll send you my foolproof recipe for pie dough".

Advertise Your Other Books

If you have other books be sure to advertise them in each book you put out. We highlight ours both on the "Other Books" page at the beginning, in the resources section, and on the final page of our books. If the readers are enjoying your book there's a good chance they will want to purchase more of your books.

Some people will go as far as having several pages from one of their other books in the back of a new book. It allows people to get immersed in it before prompting them where to purchase the entire book.

Link to Your Blog

If the readers are enjoying your book they will also probably enjoy your blog. Providing links to your blog is a great way to drive new readers. You can either provide a generic link to the front of your blog or create links to specific content on your site as a "for more information please see this article on my website at XXX".

Review Requests

Getting reviews for your books is always hard, especially if you never ask for them! Adding a short note to your book along the lines of:

> My cookbooks can't be successful without YOUR help. If you are enjoying this book could you spend 5 minutes and leave a review on Amazon here: XXX

It normally makes the most sense to leave these at the middle or end of the book. Placing them at the beginning means they will be read by people who haven't really read your book yet. If they are in the middle or end they are also more likely to only be seen by people who are enjoying your cookbook, leading to more 4 and 5 star reviews.

Use Live Links

For Kindle and ebooks, all of these items should be live links that the user can just click on. That will save them from having to type in urls or cut and paste them. Having a link they can click greatly increases the number of people who will follow the link.

Finding Outside Design Help

You don't always have to do everything yourself and often times outsourcing components of your book will result in a higher quality product. Design is one of the areas where a professional touch can go a long way.

General Book Design Help

If you know what you want done but just need someone to follow your instructions, with either Elance or Upwork you can find inexpensive contractors to hire for practically any individual aspect of the process. This includes book writing, designing and conversion between print and all e-formats.

Numerous self publishing companies also provide services in addition to their Print on Demand capability. For example, CreateSpace and Lulu have both general design and cover design services as well as proofreading and editing. However, we believe that often these services can be obtained elsewhere online with better quality and lower price.

HelpPublish.com offers cookbook editing, typesetting, book page layout design, illustration, book cover design, and many other services to help you publish your book. This group allows you to only pay for the services that you need as opposed to a package-type deal.

Jennifer Barry Design is a full service company that guides clients on all design issues, editorial matters, packaging and marketing. Depending on how much assistance you need, they offer their services both individually or in a package.

If you are looking to create a stunning, full-color cookbook, Life Rich Publishing (an imprint of The Reader's Digest Association) offers a choice of five publishing packages ranging from $1,000 to $10,000. These packages also include cover and interior book design and layout but do not assist with the writing portion of the cookbook.

Another high-end, full-service company is Dog Ear Publishing that offers a selection of five packages from $1,000 to $8,000. Unlike Life Rich Publishing, Dog Ear offers support with writing and proofreading the text in addition to designing the cover and general layout.

COVER DESIGN HELP

Generic job sites such as eLance or Upwork have designers for hire. There are also several design companies you can use such as 99 Designs or crowdSpring where you get dozens of custom cover designs for a flat rate starting around $300. Killer Covers also does custom ebook covers for $100 to $200.

Adazing, the "super awesome book marketing" website, specializes in designing cookbook covers for $450 to $650, non-illustrated and illustrated respectively.

Illuminating Graphics specialize in designing book covers and backs for both print and ebooks. They also have consultants who can help with inside layout issues.

There is also an in-depth 9-part DIY series on how to design your own book cover by Jason Gurley posted on his website (http://bit.ly/1qxUUwp).

eBook Design Help
eBook DesignWorks offers custom ebook design and conversion. They are geared to help authors develop professional-quality cookbooks and e-cookbooks. They also have a blog on their website that presents a lot of helpful information.

Lisa at ideastylist.com provides many ebook design services. Another ebook design and conversion company is Digital Dragon Designery who also offers assistance with the full line of print book and cover design.

Contractor Recommendation Help
In addition to personal contacts, it's nice to start with a contractor recommendation from someone who used them before. Here are two great places to get possible recommendations on who to hire to help you with needed tasks and who to avoid.

Absolute Write Water Cooler is a writers forum for self publishers (http://bit.ly/23oJKIE). This huge community of writers can offer conversation, discussion and enlightenment on many writing-related topics.

The Independent Book Publishers Association (https://www.ibpa-online.org/) is aimed at "helping each other achieve and succeed" and often has good recommendations.

eBook Specific Design

Many of the design considerations apply to both print and ebooks. However, there are a few specific things you need to know for ebooks. We offer our top tips for ebook design and then discuss creating an ePub file and testing your ebook.

How to Design an eBook

When you are creating an ebook for the Kindle, Nook, or iTunes, there are a few considerations to keep in mind.

Hard to Be Perfect

One thing to remember with ebooks is that with so many devices and user settings, it is hard to make your ebook look perfect on all devices. It's usually better to go with a simple design that works everywhere than a more complicated design that will look off on several devices.

Leave Fonts Free

It can be tempting to force the fonts into place but many readers like to change them to their own preferences. Leaving them unlocked allows the readers to pick the fonts that work best for them. You can read more about book fonts in the "What Fonts to Use in Your Cookbook" section.

Optimize Images

If you worked on a print version first, the images in your book will be much larger than you need for e-readers. Minimizing the file size will save you in delivery costs as well as make it faster for the reader to download.

Remove Page Numbers

Page numbers become arbitrary on many e-readers and it's best to leave them out. You can mention the section or recipe name you are referring to directly or better yet, include a clickable link.

More eBook Design Information

For a very detailed look at ebook design, we highly recommend The eBook Design and Development Guide (http://amzn.to/1SEzLqY).

HOW TO CREATE AN EPUB FILE

Once you've designed your ebook, you will need to create an ePub file so you can submit your book to publishers or distributors. "ePub" is the file format used by the majority of ebook publishers and is basically a miniature website, complete with meta information, that is compressed into a single file.

There are several ways to create an ePub file but the most common are to export it from a word processor, outsource the creation to a third party, or to create it yourself from scratch.

EXPORT AN EPUB FILE

The easiest way to create an ePub file is to simply export it from your word processor. Unfortunately, like most easy things, ePubs created this way are also the lowest quality. Depending on the word processor you are using, the quality of the resulting ebook will vary and you have very little control over the final ebook. Exporting does work for books with simpler layouts though, and Scrivener has a better ePub export than many other word processors.

OUTSOURCE THE CREATION

If you want more control over your ePub file but still don't want to do it yourself, you can find someone to do it for you. It usually costs $50 to $100 and you simply send them your Word or Pages document, a cover image, and any additional instructions and they will produce an ePub file for you.

Here is an example job we posted on eLance (we ended up using Ajmer as the contractor - http://bit.ly/23hPpDz).

> We have a cookbook we need converted for the Kindle. The book is about 170-200 pages long, needs a working table of contents, images optimized, and tables at the end of the book formatted. We can provide it in PDF, Pages, or Word format, whichever is easier for you to convert. We will also provide cover images if needed.
>
> We will want to make sure the book passes the Kindle specs and upload once they are completed.
>
> Thanks for your help.

CREATE IT FROM SCRATCH

If you want total control over your ePub file it is best just to do it yourself. As mentioned above, an ePub file is just a collection of HTML and CSS documents, images, and some meta information. If you have a decent understanding of HTML it's a surprisingly easy, if time consuming, process to create your own ePub file. If you go this route, we highly recommend purchasing The eBook Design and Development Guide (http://amzn.to/1SEzLqY). It's a fantastic resource that we used to created our first ePub files, complete with examples of all the documents in an ePub file and discussions of the nuances between publishers. It's only available as a Kindle book, but if you purchase it you can ask the author directly for a PDF copy as well.

> **Jason Says**
> When I got started publishing ebooks, I wanted a little more control so I outsourced the creation of the ePub file to Elance and for $50 I'd get back a customized file ready to submit to the ebook sites.
>
> Once I became more comfortable with the process I wanted to optimize my ebooks for the various e-readers so I looked into creating the ePub files myself. Since I'm very familiar with HTML I now just manually convert my book into HTML and put it into the ePub format. This allows me total control over the look and feel of the book.

PREVIEWING AND TESTING EBOOKS

Once you have created your ebook you will want to preview and test it.

Keep in mind that ebooks can look quite different depending on the device that's displaying them. That's one of the reasons we recommend keeping your ebook designs simple. We suggest viewing your ebook on numerous different platforms to be sure that it at least displays in an acceptable manner.

EBOOK PREVIEW AND TESTING TOOLS

There are numerous ways that this can be accomplished and we will cover a variety of them here. Some are more generic and others are specific to a device such as a Kindle or Nook.

ePub Validator

It always worth running your ePub file through the ePub Validator (http://validator.idpf.org/). This tool is provided by the International Digital Publishing Forum (IDPF) and will validate that your file conforms to the ePub specifications. It is important to be sure that your file passes this test.

Calibre
Calibre is a free and open source ebook library management application developed by users of ebooks for users of ebooks. It has a large number of features including ebook conversion, syncing to ebook reader devices, a comprehensive ebook viewer, and an ebook editor for the major ebook formats.

Kindle Direct Publishing (KDP)
During the setup process for publishing a Kindle book you can preview your book before actually submitting it for publishing. Once you upload your book file you can preview it using their online previewer or a downloadable previewer.

For most users the online previewer is the best and easiest way to preview your content. The previewer allows you to test many aspects of your ebook including the general layout, the table of contents, links, both landscape and profile views, different size fonts and your cover.

If you would like to see how your book displays on the Kindle Touch or Kindle DX you often need to use the downloadable previewer.

Nook Press
Once you have uploaded your manuscript to Nook Press you will be given the opportunity to preview it. The Nook online previewer will open a new tab in your browser with your book displayed and you can test the overall layout, the table of contents, links, various font sizes and types. Unlike the KDP previewer there is not a selection of different types of Nook devices to choose from. However, you can change the size of the browser window to get an idea how the book would display on various sizes of devices.

PRE-PUBLISHING STEPS

Once your cookbook is written and designed you are ready to actually start the process of publishing your book.

There are several factors you need to take into account before publishing. This includes determine the price for each format you are publishing the book in and writing a book description that will entice readers to buy it.

If you are publishing on Amazon or the Kindle you will also need to determine your Amazon categories and choose your Amazon Keywords.

How to Price Your Cookbook

Learning how to price your cookbook is as much an art as a science. It is a very important decision that can lead to a lot of stress. There's always the tradeoff between setting the price too high and losing sales, and setting it too low and leaving money on the table. There's no hard and fast rules to a successfully priced cookbook but there are several considerations you need to take into account.

> **Jason Says**
> Tracking the effects of book pricing on sales, especially on Amazon, is very hard and convoluted. There are people that try to figure out ideal pricing on Amazon for a living and I just don't have the time or inclination to compete with them. I'd rather spend my time cooking and writing books. If the information below feels overwhelming, don't worry, it's that way for everyone. I've found pricing my Monetizing books around the average price for a book in my genre works good enough for me.

Your Cookbook Goals

The pricing you pick will have a lot to do with the goals of your cookbook. Viral cookbooks will normally be priced lower than Monetizing or Marketing cookbooks to maximize their sales. Monetizing cookbooks will try to maximize the total revenue generated, or sales times royalties. Marketing cookbooks don't always fall one direction or another, it's highly dependent on the cost incurred in developing them.

Your Cookbook Format

There are very different pricing models for ebooks vs print books.

Print Books

The list price for print cookbooks typically runs anywhere from $15 to $30 for popular cookbooks and $25 to $50 for gourmet or restaurant cookbooks. Amazon usually discounts these by 30% to 50%. It is usually ideal for most Monetizing or Marketing books to fall somewhere in this range.

If you publish through CreateSpace Amazon may discount your books closer to a 10% to 20% rate. Remember, if Amazon discounts your book you still get paid a royalty on the list price, not the discounted price.

Kindle Books

Kindle books normally range from $0.99 to $14.99 and are usually not discounted. One quirk of Kindle royalties is that you only get a 70% royalty if the book is priced between $2.99 and $9.99. Otherwise your royalty is 35%.

So while you might be tempted to sell your Kindle book at $15.99 instead of $9.99, you would only make $5.60 per book sold at $15.99 instead of $7 per book selling at $9.99. So you would have to sell more books at the higher price to come out ahead.

The same is true at the bottom of the scale. Every book sold at $0.99 will earn you $0.35, but a book sold at $2.99 will earn you $2.10. It might be tempting to price your book at a dollar and try to sell more copies but you will have to sell 6 times as much to match the revenue at the higher price. For some books, especially Viral ones, this might be a trade off worth making.

Authors with Viral cookbooks in the Kindle format can also look at giving their books away for free. While it doesn't bring in any more money it arguably can lead to wider distribution for your book.

GENERAL PERCEPTION

It can be tempting to try and price your cookbook as low as you can while still making a decent profit. This is especially true for people who view their own work as less valuable than the work of "professionals", an unfortunately common occurrence. However, it is important to remember that lower-priced things tend to be viewed as less valuable and less well done.

If you were looking for somewhere to eat and a random restaurant had a full filet mignon dinner for only $5, would you eat there? Or would you be worried that there would have to be something wrong because otherwise they'd never charge that little for high quality steak? You want to avoid that situation with your book.

If all your competitors are priced at $40 and your book is only $10 then potential readers might start to worry that something is wrong with your book and that's why you are selling it so cheaply.

On the flip side, pricing your book higher, assuming it is a high quality book, will make people perceive it as being of higher quality than your competition. This can be especially important if you are publishing a Marketing book. Sales might not matter as much as the association of your name with high-quality books.

You can also price it in the middle, removing price as a factor in the reader's purchasing decision. For many Monetizing books this is a sound strategy.

> **Jason Says**
> Remember that a higher price doesn't always lead to less sales. Recently I raised the price of my Whipping Siphon book by four dollars, from $14.95 to $18.95 and sales actually increased.

BOOK PRINTING COSTS

Another large factor to consider when pricing your book is how much each book sold costs you. For print books sold through Amazon you are charged for the printing, handling, selling, and any wholesale discount if it's not through CreateSpace. A book sold on Amazon and printed through CreateSpace takes about 40% off the top, then about $1 per 100 pages in the book, plus an extra $1 on top.

For example, a 200 page book sold for $10 will earn you only $2.75. The same book sold for $20 earns you $8.75, over triple the royalty. With the lower price you have to sell over 3 times as many copies to come out ahead. You can find out more information about CreateSpace pricing here (http://bit.ly/22mc1gD) and their royalty calculator (http://bit.ly/1Ndj9Fb).

If you publish through CreateSpace there are also minimum amounts you need to charge based on the size of your book. If you are trying to produce a very inexpensive book this may affect you.

For non-CreateSpace books you have to pay a printing cost and a "wholesalers discount". This discount is usually 30% to 55%.

For Kindle books there are also delivery costs. These are about $0.15/MB of book size.

MORE SALES LEAD TO A HIGHER AMAZON SALES RANK

Another wrinkle in the pricing decision is the Amazon Sales Rank. Higher sales lead to a higher sales rank which leads to more promotion in different Amazon categories. This higher placement then potentially leads to more sales. This can be especially effective during your cookbook launch where the lower price can vault you up the ranks, keeping it relevant for a longer time. You can learn more about the Amazon Sales Rank in the Appendix.

HOW TO WRITE A SELLING BOOK DESCRIPTION

The description of your cookbook is the last chance you have to convince a potential reader that your book is exactly what they are looking for. A great cookbook cover will get their attention and a winning title will draw them in, but your book description is what will really sell new readers on your cookbook. Descriptions for cookbooks can vary but the successful ones have a few key similarities.

> **Jason Says**
> I highly recommend going to the Amazon Best Sellers for cooking (http://amzn.to/1WhETqz) and read through their descriptions to get a good idea of what is currently working in the industry. You can also view a list of my books to get a feel for the type of descriptions I use (http://amzn.to/1mXRzCr).

THE INITIAL HOOK

Much like a good blog post, you want the first line or two of your book description to intrigue the reader and make them want to read more. This hook often takes the form of an appeal to the reader or a question they want to get the answer to. Here's some examples from the top 20 cookbooks on Amazon.

"Lose weight and feel better one tablespoon of olive oil at a time."

"One pan + fresh ingredients = dinner for two!"

"Cooking a wide variety of Japanese meals doesn't have to require a lot of effort, multiple cookbooks, and guesswork."

The hook can also be in the form of a short summary of what you'll find in the book. Here's some more examples from the top 20 cookbooks on Amazon.

"A complete meat- and brisket-cooking education from the country's most celebrated pitmaster and owner of the wildly popular Austin restaurant Franklin Barbecue - winner of Texas Monthly's coveted Best Barbecue Joint in Texas award."

"Here from the celebrated California restaurant Big Sur Bakery is a stunningly photographed cookbook showcasing seasonal ingredients, local vintners, fishermen, and farmers--and the food that makes the Big Sur Bakery unique."

"Chris Chamberlain, author of the popular The Southern Foodie Cookbook, takes you back to the South for a tour of the restaurants that make the best pig dishes."

"Nearly 1,000 crowd-pleasing and award-winning recipes presented in an easy, step-by-step format to ensure success for anyone-even beginners."

"Filled with classic pie recipes such as apple and pecan, yet bolstered with modern pie innovations like pie pops, Thanksgiving Pie, and pies-in-a-jar, this is a collection of simple, straightforward recipes and stories of Amish life that will help bakers bring their families together around the table."

The key that all of them have in common is that they make you want to read more about the book.

DESCRIBE THE BOOK

Following the hook, the description usually will focus on what information the book will provide and what the user will get out of it. This often takes the form of a story and often speaks directly to the reader.

Sometimes the book description is very straightforward, like Japanese Cooking Made Simple (http://amzn.to/23hTWGf) and Me, Myself and Pie (http://amzn.to/1qxZ7jG). Other times they are stories to the reader like The Big Sur Bakery Cookbook (http://amzn.to/1V1UVWy) and Franklin Barbecue (http://amzn.to/25Pjc5r).

Regardless of the writing style you use for your description, there are several facts you want to convey.

- What the cookbook covers
- How the reader will benefit from your cookbook
- The type and number of recipes included
- A final "call to action" or sales pitch to the reader

FEATURES VS BENEFITS

When writing your description, it's helpful to keep in mind the differences between features and benefits. Features are the facts about your book such as the page count, number of recipes, the list of chapters and what they cover. Benefits show the reader what the features will help them accomplish.

For example, a feature would be "Step by step look at the bread baking process" and the benefit would be "bake tasty bread at home".

> **Jason Says**
> I like to think of the features as the "what", as in "what does the book contain", and the benefits as the "why", as in "why does the reader care about this". The reader doesn't care that the book has a "Step by step look at the bread baking process", they care that it will let them "bake tasty bread at home".

Most marketing is more effective when the benefits are focused on instead of the features. For book descriptions, a combination of features and benefits is usually very effective and a common practice is to state the feature then the benefit.

"[A step by step look at the bread baking process] will let you easily [bake tasty bread at home]."

"Containing [more than 100 cocktail recipes], this book will give you the knowledge to [wow your friends with your cocktail making skills]."

"With the [easy to follow weekly meal plans] you can [get dinner ready quickly and easily]."

For more on features vs benefits we recommend this article from Printwand (http://bit.ly/1PYvCfv).

USE YOUR KEYWORDS

It's important to use the keywords for your book in your book description. Both Amazon and Google will index your description and your book will be more likely to show up if you sprinkle the keywords throughout it. Try to use the keywords in a similar manner that you would when writing a blog post. You don't want to keyword stuff your description, but you should try to get them all in there at least once or twice.

For more help on finding and evaluating keywords, you can see the "Choosing Publishing Keywords" section later in this chapter.

TESTIMONIALS SHOW SOCIAL PROOF

A great way to show that your book has merit is by including testimonials in your description. These testimonials can come from Amazon reviews or comments of your testers or early reviewers. A one or two sentence blurb is a good length to use.

USE HTML WHEN AVAILABLE

On Amazon and Kindle descriptions you can use limited HTML. This allows you to call out headers or specific phrases you want to highlight. This is a great way to make your description look more professional and be more effective.

BE HONEST

It can be tempting to gloss over any issues with your cookbook but it is much better to be fully honest in your description. If you don't cover something, let people know. Only have black and white photos? Tell them.

Being honest might result in less sales in the short term, but if you mislead people about what your book covers you will start to get many negative reviews from people who feel misled. This will result in much lower overall sales, as well as hurting your credibility.

DETERMINING YOUR AMAZON CATEGORIES

When submitting your book to Amazon, one of the numerous selections you will need to make is which two categories to list your book. As it turns out, this selection of categories can have a significant impact on how many books you will sell so it's important to make this decision carefully.

Amazon loosely uses BISAC Subject Codes, an industry standard, to help determine where your book should show up for browsing and searching customers. You can read more about the BISAC Subject Code system and see the most up-to-date list of codes on their website (https://www.bisg.org/bisac-subject-codes).

How Categories Work

To understand the power of categories you need to think about how customers often look for books on Amazon. If they aren't looking for a specific book, they will often do a search to get them in the general area they want to browse. For example, searching for "baking cookbooks". At that point Amazon displays a list of categories on the left which the customer will use to select a subcategory they suspect will have the book they are after. Once they get to their desired subcategory they then will browse for the specific type of cookbook they need.

They will typically browse the first and perhaps the second page of the category before selecting their book. Consequently, it is critical that your book shows up on the first or second page of the category. As a new self published cookbook author it is unlikely that you will be able to sell enough books to get to the first page of the larger categories. For example, the category "Cookbooks, Food & Wine" (http://amzn.to/1WhETqz) has more than 60,000 books. As you can imagine you would have to be selling a ton of your books to make it to the first page of that category.

In order to rank in a category we need to move further down the category tree until we find a category we can rank in. To continue the example let's select the "Cooking Methods" category. It has over 9,000 entries and is thus still pretty competitive. Finally, we will take one step further to "Slow Cooking", which has about 1,500 entries.

My book Modernist Cooking Made Easy: Sous Vide is in the top 10 of that category and thus displayed on the first page. My book is also ranked at #25 in the category: Books> Cookbooks, Food & Wine > Kitchen Appliances which has approximately 3,500 books. As a reference my book is ranked #3,337 in Books.

Selecting Your Categories

The following is some advice on how to choose the best browse categories for your cookbook. You can also find more information about evaluating categories in the "Competitive Breakdown of an Amazon Sales Category" section of the "Determining Your Cookbook Subject" chapter.

Select the Most Specific Categories
As presented above it's better to choose more specific categories instead of more general categories. Customers looking for very specific topics will more easily find your book, and your book will be displayed in more general categories as well. For example, a book in the "Cookbooks, Food & Wine > Kitchen Appliances" category will also show up in searches for the "Cookbooks, Food & Wine" category. You should only select a "General" category if your book is actually a general book about a broad topic.

It is very beneficial to have your book in a category that will put you on the first page for customers browsing that category. If you aren't making much progress after a several weeks you can always try to change to another category. Keep at it until you find a category that works for you.

Pick the Most Accurate Categories
Make sure the categories you select correctly describe the subject matter of your book. Don't attempt to "play" the system by placing your book in some obscure category in order to be ranked. Amazon doesn't take kindly to this and will reassign your book to an appropriate category.

Ensure the Categories You Choose Are Not Redundant
Since your book will be displayed in a variety of searches by choosing even a single category, you shouldn't place it in both a category and any of that category's sub-categories (for example, selecting both "Fiction > Fantasy > Historical" and "Fiction> Fantasy").

A FEW GOTCHAS TO KEEP IN MIND REGARDING CATEGORIES

The more you get involved with studying and working with Amazon categories, the more you will find yourself occasionally shaking your head in disbelief. Here are some of the things that you may run across:

Multiple Sets of Categories
The categories for printed books and ebooks sold on Amazon are different. So it's highly likely that you will end up with different categories for the two formats of your Amazon books. Also the categories that you select as part of the uploading process for your

book normally turn out to be different than the ones that are shown on your book page.

Changing Categories
For reasons no one quite understands, Amazon often reorganizes their category listings.

Amazon Selects Categories for You
If Amazon believes that you will sell more books in a different category it may reassign your book to that category in an attempt to increase sales. Obviously, this is not a bad thing but it is a bit of a surprise if you're not expecting it.

Can't Easily Switch to Some Categories
You may study the categories online and determine which of those would be perfect for your book. You could then go on to the dashboard in an attempt to switch one of your books to that category. But to your surprise you see that the category that's online is not available to be selected from your dashboard.

In this case you need to write to Amazon explaining the situation and giving them the information required for them to assign the category that you desire. This can usually be done relatively quickly - it's just a bit of a hassle.

Although categories can be confusing, they can also have a tremendous impact on the number of books that you can sell.

CHOOSING PUBLISHING KEYWORDS

As a blogger you are aware of how important keywords are to having the search engines find your articles and present them in the search results for the subjects you cover in your blog. The keywords associated with your book play a similarly important role in increasing the popularity and sales of your book.

When you submit your book to most publishers they will request a list of keywords that will help readers to discover your book. Therefore, it's important for you to come up with 5 to 7 keywords (or short phrases) that accurately portray your book's content and use the words customers will use when they are searching.

Similar to Google, the Amazon search engine is very sophisticated and can be used to help you determine the best keywords for your book. We will list a few ideas that will assist you in coming up with the keywords that will help increase the visibility of your book.

BRAINSTORM A LIST OF POTENTIAL KEYWORDS

Try to create a list of 20 to 30 possible keywords that accurately describe the subject of your cookbook. Some of these may be broad such as "Grilling" and others might be narrow such as "Sourdough Bread". Remember to structure the keywords in the way that you think your readers would search for them.

EVALUATE YOUR LIST ON AMAZON

For this you will want to use the power of the Amazon search engine. In the drop down to the left of the search box select the word "Books" so that you will limit the Amazon search to their books. Then slowly begin to type in a keyword and study the types of suggestions that the search engine provides.

It would be ideal if your keywords show up as one of the "searched for" terms. Certainly the very broad terms will usually show up but keep in mind that there will be many search results for those broad topics, thus making it difficult to get to the first page of the search results. You may want to have a mixture of keywords addressing both broad and narrow topics.

EVALUATE YOUR LIST ON GOOGLE

Another valuable exercise is to input your list of potential keywords into the Google Keyword Planner. This tool will provide you with the number of times a particular keyword is searched for on Google, which will reflect its overall popularity. The more long tail keywords will definitely have lower search volumes, but that does not necessarily mean they are unattractive - especially if they are an accurate description of the content in your book.

PICK YOUR SEVEN KEYWORDS

Using what you've learned on Amazon and Google narrow down your list to the seven that you think would be the most effective. Remember to always be thinking like your readers - what would they ask a search engine in order to find your book. The keywords are not set in stone and you may want to do some experiments with different ones to see which seem to be most effective.

KEYWORD DON'TS

Single words or smaller phrases generally work better than longer phrases. Specific words usually work better than general words.

Don't use quotation marks in search terms. If you enter "savory desserts and snacks" only people who type all of those words will find your book.

Here is a list from Kindle Direct Publishing on what not to include in keywords:

- Information covered elsewhere in your book's metadata: title, contributor(s), category, etc.
- Subjective claims about quality (e.g. "best")
- Statements that are only temporarily true ("new," "on sale," "available now")
- Information common to most items in the category ("book")
- Variants of spacing, punctuation, capitalization, and pluralization (both "80GB" and "80 GB", "computer" and "computers", etc.).
- Anything misrepresentative, such as the name of an author that is not associated with your book. This type of information can create a confusing customer experience and Kindle Direct Publishing has a zero tolerance policy for metadata that is meant to advertise, promote, or mislead.

KEYWORD EXAMPLES

Here's some examples of the keywords we decided to use for several of our books. You can see how much overlap there is between the keywords in our books, this is largely because they are all in the same niche.

Modernist Cooking Made Easy: Sous Vide
Sous vide, under pressure, modernist cooking, modernist cuisine, slow cooker

Modernist Cooking Made Easy: The Whipping Siphon
Whipping siphon, modernist cooking, modernist cuisine, molecular gastronomy, whipped cream

Modernist Cooking Made Easy: Getting Started
Molecular gastronomy, modernist cuisine, foam, sous vide, gel

Modernist Cooking Made Easy: Party Foods
Modernist cooking, modernist cuisine, party, party food, molecular gastronomy

PUBLISHING YOUR COOKBOOK

Once the pre-publishing steps are complete, it's time you actually publish your book! This chapter is filled with several guides for how to publish on specific platforms, including CreateSpace, Kindle, Smashwords and several others. We also discuss creating and selling a PDF on your blog.

You can skim the following sections or just use them when you are ready to publish on a specific platform. We highly recommend reading the previous chapter, "Pre-Publishing Steps" before this one since it helps you come up with a lot of the information you need during the publishing process.

HOW TO PUBLISH ON AMAZON WITH CREATESPACE

CreateSpace is the easiest way to publish a book on Amazon. Here is a step by step look at the processes so you can easily get your book available for sale through the largest online retailer in the world.

CREATE YOUR CREATESPACE ACCOUNT

The first step to getting started with CreateSpace is by creating a free account with them (https://www.createspace.com/Signup.jsp). You need an email, password, and full name, along with your country and the type of material you expect to publish.

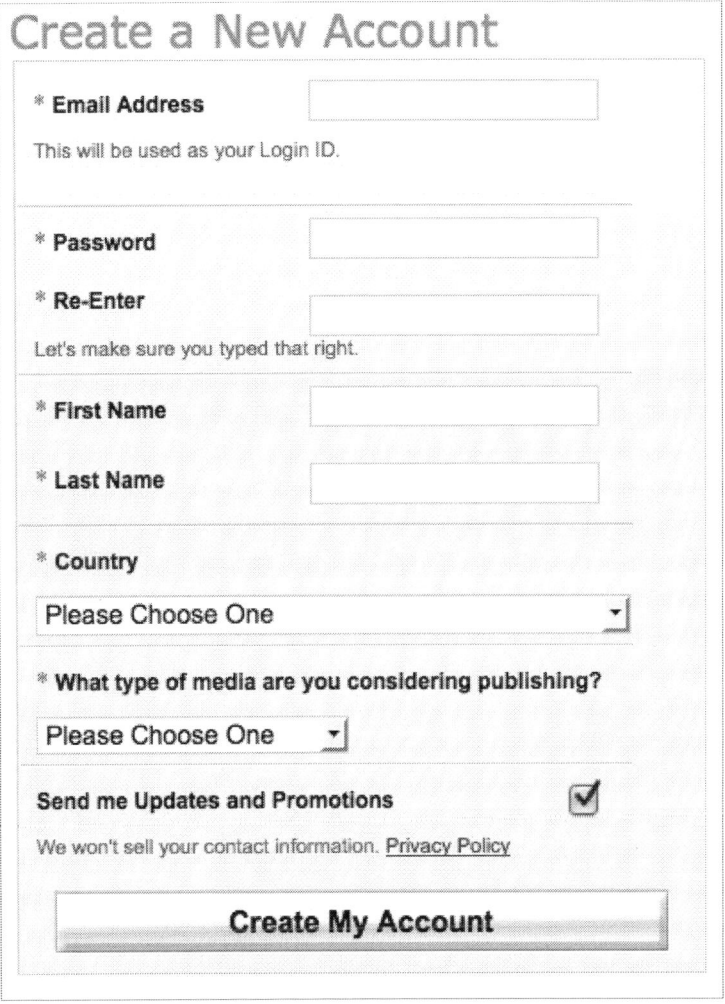

On the next screen you will need to accept their service agreement.

They will send you an email for you to confirm your identity. Click on the link there and then choose "Set Up Your Book Now" when prompted to choose between that and "Talk to a Consultant". This will take you directly into adding a new title.

ADD A NEW TITLE

To add a new title, click on the "Add New Title" link on the left. Then fill out the form presented. The "Name of Project" will be the title of your book. Choose "Paperback" as your project type. If this is your first time adding a book we recommended choosing the "Guided" setup process.

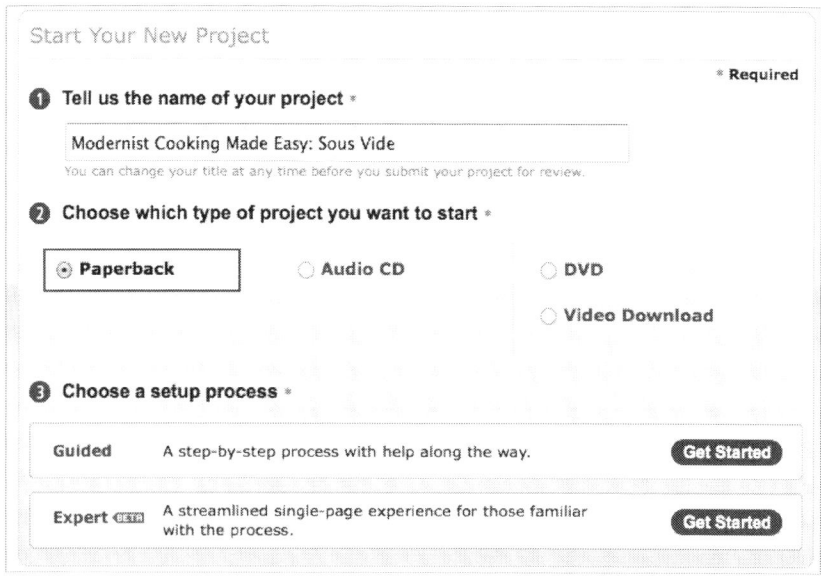

TITLE INFORMATION

This page has many different fields to fill out.

Title and Subtitle

Enter the name of your book and the subtitle. If you have a Kindle version, the name and the subtitle you enter should match your Kindle version exactly.

Primary Author

The primary author is most likely you, unless you are publishing someone else's book. Make sure you enter in the name as you want it to appear throughout Amazon.

> **Jason Says**
> When you enter your Primary Author name, be very careful to be consistent between books. For a while I had two author pages, one for "Jason Logsdon" and one for "Jason W Logsdon". This made it much harder for people to find and view all of my books and it also led to some confusion among readers.

Add Contributors

You can also add any contributors that were an integral part of the book creation process. Only add people here if you want them to get credit on your Amazon sales page, right next to your name.

Series, Series Title and Edition Number

If your book is part of a series then you should add the series title and edition number, otherwise leave it blank.

Language

If your book is in a language other than English, be sure to select it here.

Publication Date

This allows you to set a specific publication date for your book. It allows you to delay the launch of your book or release it right away. This helps to easily time the release with any launches you may have planned. Just leave it blank if you want it to be available immediately upon approval.

Save and Continue

Click "Save and Continue" to move onto the next step or just "Save" to save the content for later.

ISBN

The ISBN page allows you to choose the ISBN option you want to use. You can use a CreateSpace ISBN, create a custom one, or use one of your own. We highly recommend you provide an ISBN of your own, this keeps your distribution options open, allows you to be the publisher, and removes some stigma that publishing through CreateSpace can cause.

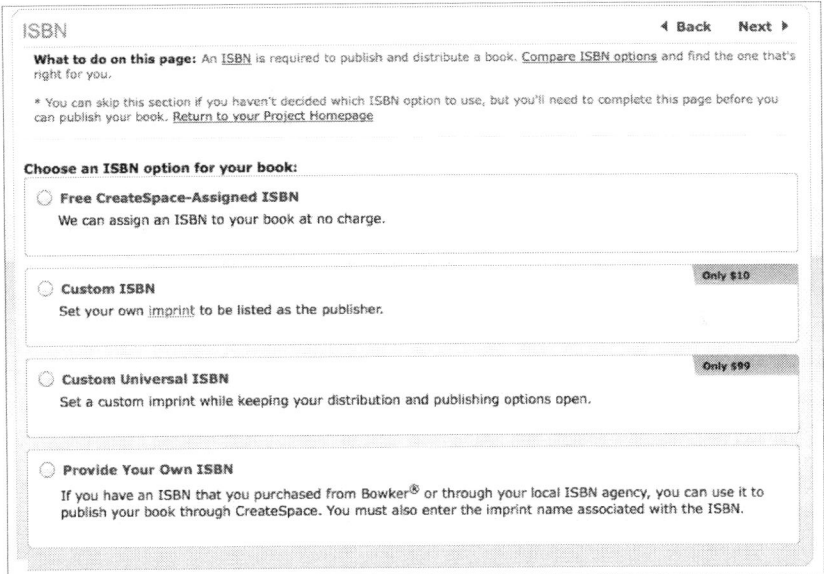

You can read a more detailed explanation of what is an ISBN and our recommendations for handling it in the "All About ISBN Numbers" section of the Appendix.

INTERIOR

The interior step walks you through uploading your interior PDF and setting your trim options.

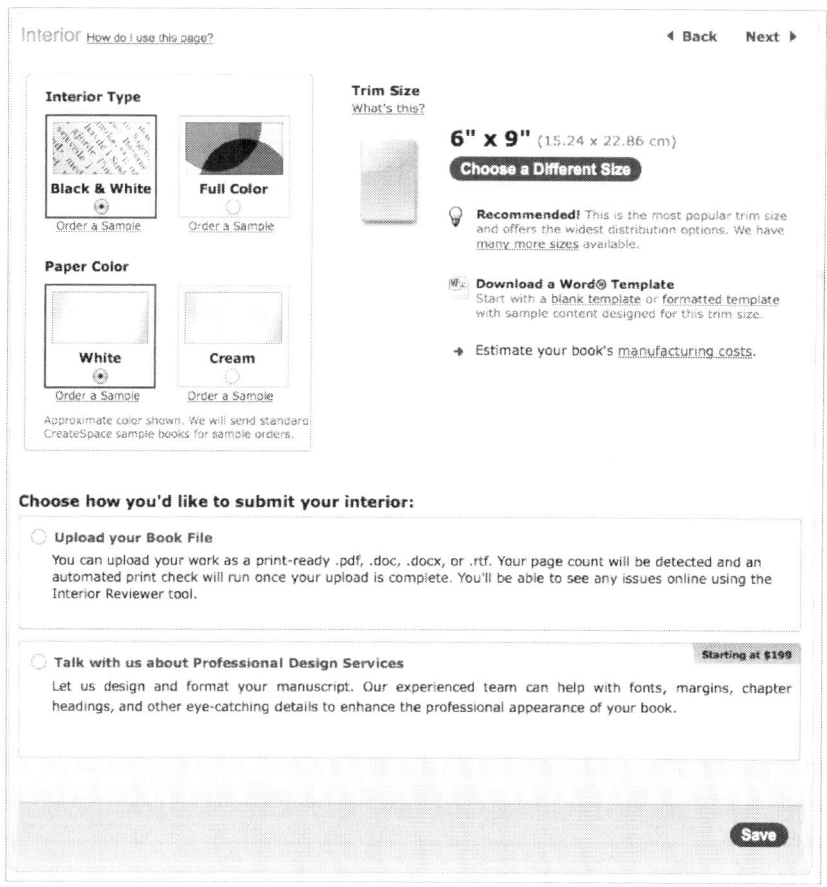

Interior Type and Paper Color

Choose "Black and White" or "Color", depending on how you want your book printed. This only affects the inside, the cover will always be in color. Also choose the paper color you prefer. We use "White" for all of our books but some people prefer "Cream" for books that aren't picture heavy.

Trim Size

The trim size is the dimensions of the book. Pick whatever trim size you designed your book around.

Upload Your Interior File

Upload your interior file that you created earlier using the "browse" button. Choose the bleed that you wanted to go with. We recommend leaving "Run automated print checks and view formatting issues online" checked because it never hurts to have your work double checked. Click save to upload your file and move on.

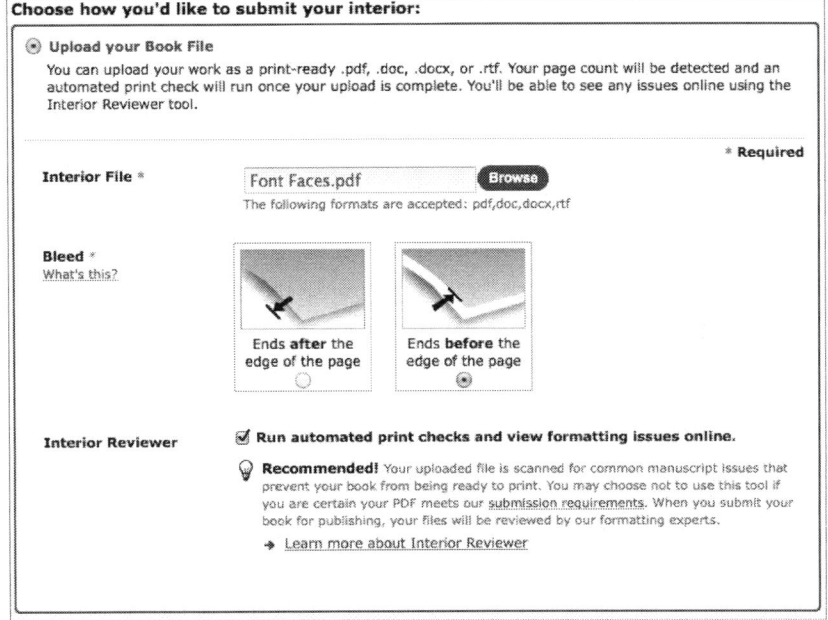

COVER

The next step is to upload the cover you created.

Glossy or Matte

The type of cover you want is completely up to you. Glossy covers are more shiny and bright while matte covers are flatter and a little more subdued.

Submit Your Cover

If you have already designed your cover, click on the "Upload a Print-Ready PDF Cover". Click "Browse" and choose the PDF cover file you exported. Click "Save" to upload the cover. Once it uploads successfully, click "Continue" to move on.

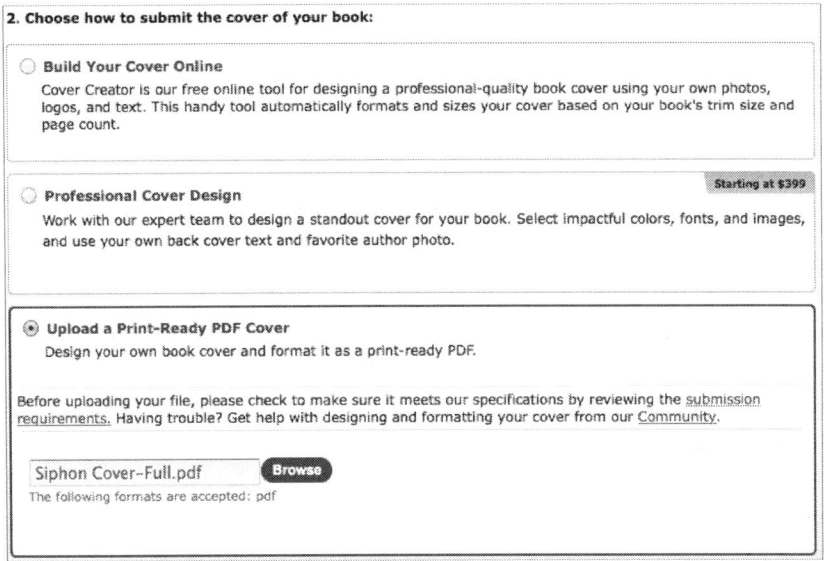

VIEW AND APPROVE A PROOF

Once your files have been approved by CreateSpace you will need to view and approve a proof. You have two options for this, view an online proof or have them ship you a proof to view.

If it is your first book, we recommend using both methods. Use their online proofing tool to make sure there is nothing major you see wrong. If it looks good, have them send you a proof to view.

> **Jason Says**
> Now that I've been through the process several times, I check and approve the online proof. Then as soon as it comes up on Amazon, typically in a day or two, I order a real copy of the book and pay for the overnight shipping. I have Prime so it only costs a few bucks. I get the print copy in the mail before it actually hits the search results and can un-post the book if there is something wrong.

CHANNELS

The channels you choose will determine where Amazon distributes your book. We recommend always using them for Amazon.com, Amazon Europe, and CreateSpace eStore. If you want ease of distribution then using the Amazon Expanded Distribution options work well but if you want to have the widest distribution, using IngramSpark instead of the CreateSpace Expanded Distribution is often the way to go.

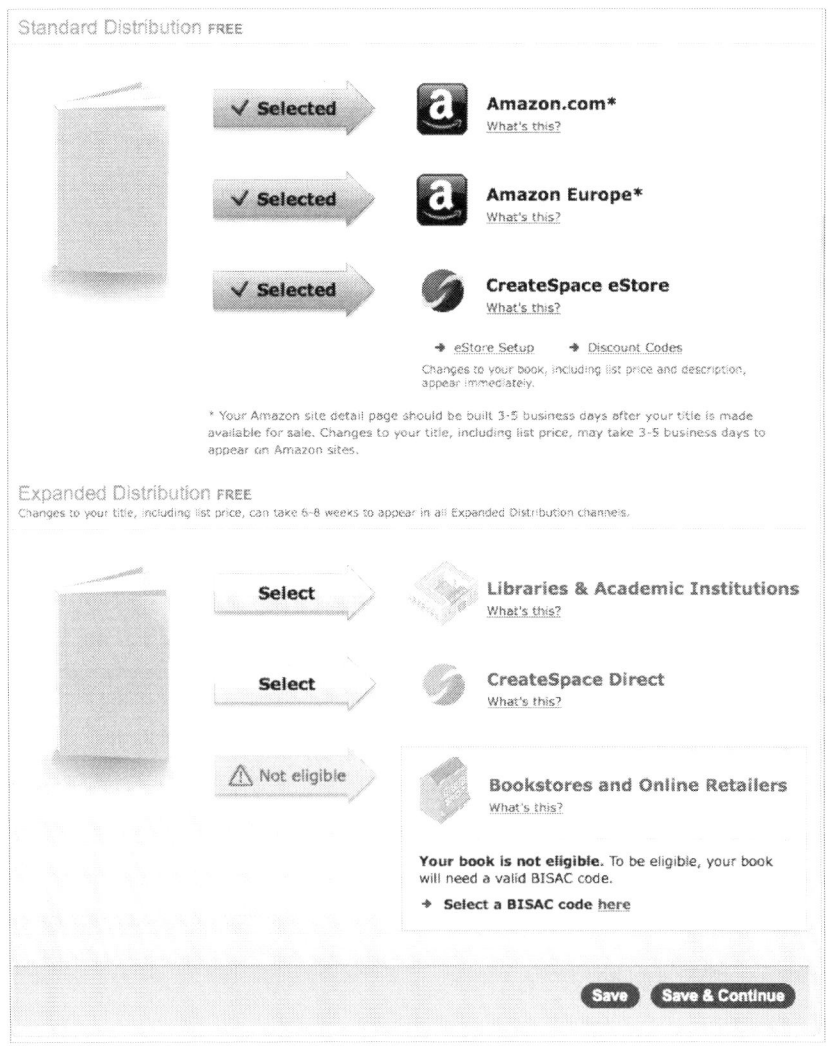

PRICING

Enter in the price of your cookbook then click "Calculate" to see what your royalty will be in various channels. To fill out your other prices you can enter a specific number or use the "Yes, suggest a price based on U.S. price" checkbox for an equivalent price.

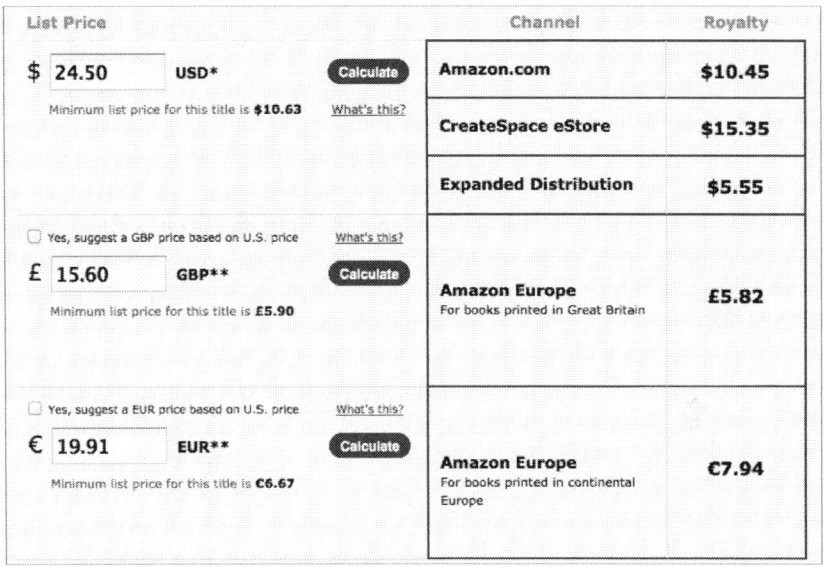

DESCRIPTION

The description page collects information that controls how and where your cookbook appears on Amazon.

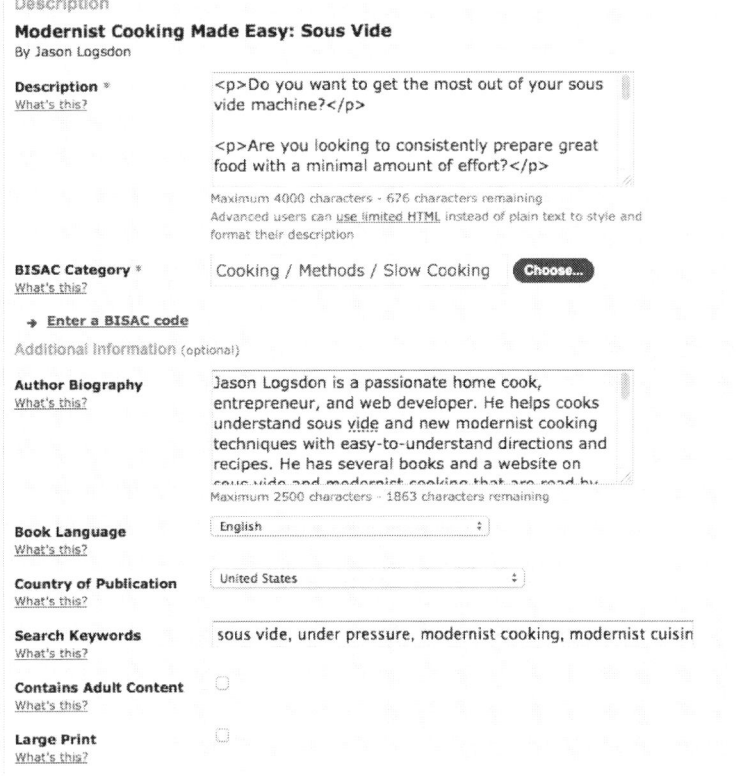

181 Self Publishing Made Easy: Cookbooks

Description

Paste in the cookbook description you created earlier. For CreateSpace you can use some HTML formatting including font size and faces, bold, italic, super and sub script, ordered lists and unordered lists.

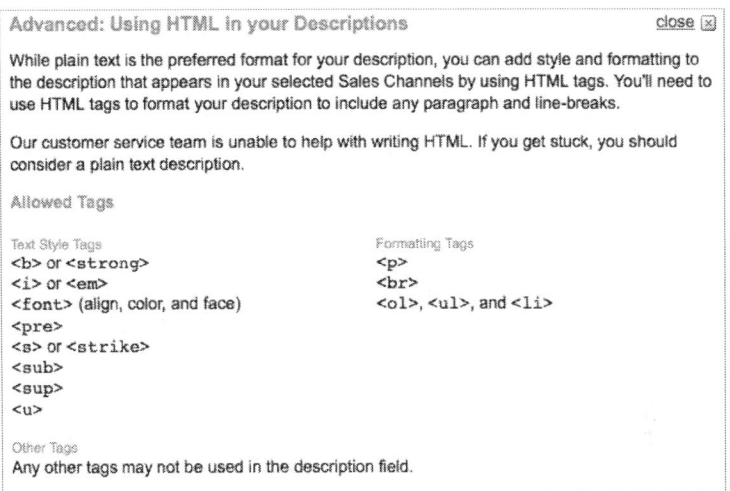

BISAC Category

The BISAC Category is the place that your cookbook will show up in the Amazon hierarchy. You can learn more about choosing Amazon categories in the "Determining Your Amazon Categories" section.

Author Biography

The biography is optional but it can be helpful to add a short one that informs potential readers about who you are and why you are qualified to write your book. Our standard biography is currently:

> Jason Logsdon is a passionate home cook, entrepreneur, and web developer. He helps cooks understand sous vide and new modernist cooking techniques with easy-to-understand directions and recipes. He has several books and a website on sous vide and modernist cooking that are read by thousands of people every month including Beginning Sous Vide, Modernist Cooking Made Easy: Getting Started, Sous Vide: Help for the Busy Cook, Modernist Cooking Made Easy: The Whipping Siphon, Sous Vide Grilling, and Modernist Cooking Made Easy:

Party Foods. He can be reached at jason@afmeasy.com or through Twitter at @jasonlogsdon.

Language
If your book is in a language other than English, be sure to select it here.

Country of Publication
Choose the country you are publishing from and that is listed with your ISBN number.

Search Keywords
You can add up to 5 keywords. For more help on finding and evaluating keywords, you can see the "Choosing Publishing Keywords" section of the "Pre-Publishing Steps" chapter.

Contains Adult Content
If your cookbook contains content not suitable for children then be sure to click this.

Large Print
If this version of your cookbook is a "large print" version, check the checkbox.

PUBLISH
Once you have all of the previous information entered, as well as a proof ordered and approved, you are ready to publish!

Just click the "Publish" button and your book will be made available on Amazon in a few days. You can get a sneak look at your book the instant it goes live from: http://www.amazon.com/gp/product/XXXXXX/ - where "XXXXX" is your ISBN-10 digit number. Your book will show up here before it shows up in any search results or other Amazon pages, usually in 1 to 2 days. You can also use this url when building any launch pages on your blog.

How to Publish On the Kindle

Once you have created an ePub file, which we covered in the "eBook Specific Design" chapter, publishing it through Kindle is relatively simple.

Create a KDP Account

If you don't already have a KDP account with Amazon, you will need to create one. You can do that directly from Amazon's KDP site (https://kdp.amazon.com/) and it will be associated with your general Amazon account.

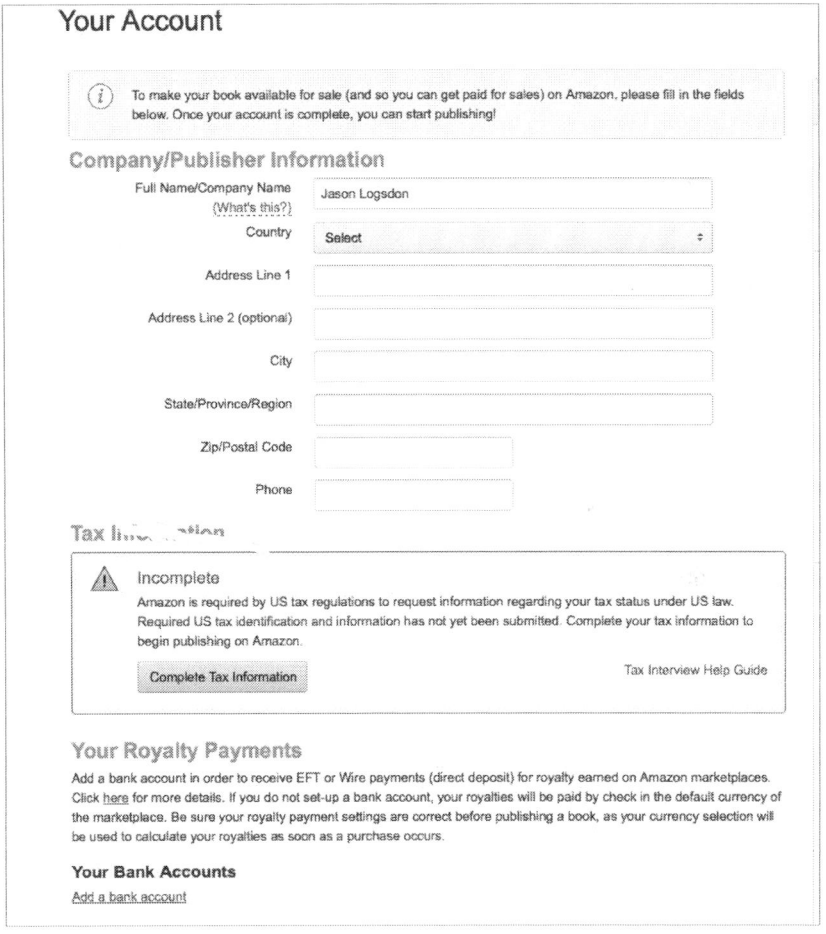

As part of this process you will have to enter several different pieces of information. This includes the name, address, and phone number of your company or publisher name. Your tax information and tax identification number. A bank account also needs to be added for direct deposits.

CREATE NEW TITLE

Once you have a KDP account you can start to add your book as a "title". To add a new title, you will first click on the "Create New Title" button from your Bookshelf page (https://kdp.amazon.com/dashboard). This will bring up step 1 of what we call the "Book Information" page.

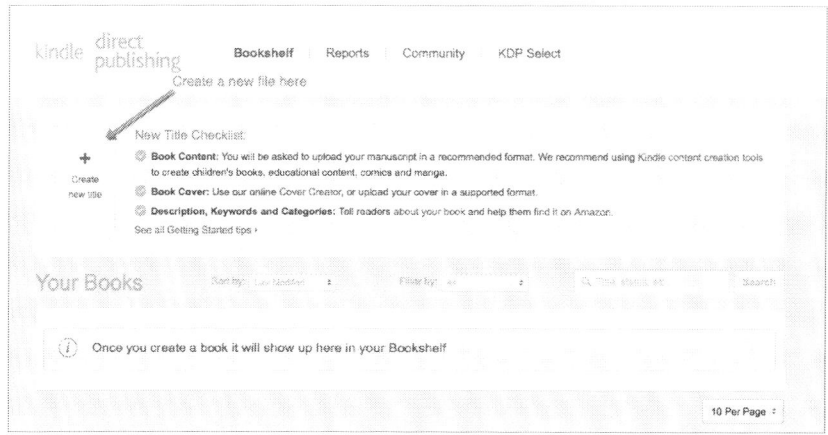

YOUR BOOK

Step 1 requires several different pieces of information.

KDP Select

KDP Select is the Kindle-specific plan. We offer much more information in our article called "KDP Select - What is it and is it Worth it?" in the Appendix.

Introducing KDP Select

Take advantage of KDP Select, an optional program that makes your book exclusive to Kindle and eligible for the following benefits:

- **Reach more readers** - With each 90-day enrollment period, your book will appear in Kindle Unlimited in the U.S., U.K., Italy, Spain, Germany, France, Brazil, Mexico and Canada and the Kindle Owners' Lending Library (KOLL) in the U.S, U.K., Germany, France, and Japan which can help readers discover your book.
- **Earn more money** - Every time your book is selected and read past 10% from Kindle Unlimited or borrowed from KOLL, you'll earn your share of the monthly KDP Select Global Fund. You can also earn a 70% royalty for sales to customers in Japan, Brazil, India and Mexico.
- **Maximize your sales potential** - Choose from two promotional tools including: Kindle Countdown Deals, time-bound promotional discounts for your book, available on Amazon.com and Amazon.co.uk, while earning royalties; or Free Book Promotion, where readers can get your book free for a limited time.

Learn more

☐ **Enroll this book in KDP Select**

By checking this box, you are enrolling in KDP Select for 90 days. Books enrolled in KDP Select must not be available in digital format on any other platform during their enrollment. If your book is found to be available elsewhere in digital format, it may not be eligible to remain in the program. See the KDP Select Terms and Conditions and KDP Select FAQs for more information.

Book Details

After deciding whether or not to do KDP Select you need to enter your book details.

Name and Subtitle
Enter the name of your book and the subtitle. If you have a print version, the name and the subtitle you enter should match your print version exactly.

Series and Edition Number
If your book is part of a series then you should add the series and edition number.

Publisher
The publisher is optional, but we recommend either using your name or the name of your blog.

Book Description
You will also need a compelling book description. On the Kindle you have very limited formatting options for your book description.

Book Contributors
You can also add any contributors that were an integral part of the book creation process. Only add people here if you want them to get credit on your Amazon Kindle sales page, right next to your name.

Language
If your book is in a language other than English, be sure to select it here.

ISBN
This ISBN number must be different than one you have used for the print version. The ISBN number for a Kindle book is completely optional and isn't really used by Amazon any more. We recommend saving your money and not using one for most Kindle books. You can learn more about ISBN numbers in the Appendix.

Publishing Rights

The publishing rights section just specifies whether this is a work of public domain or if you own the copyright to it. In most cases you will want to specify that it isn't part of the public domain, otherwise anyone can copy and use your work.

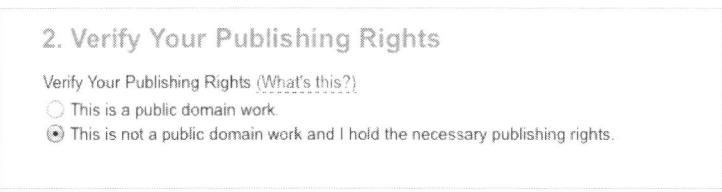

Target Your Book To Customers

In the Target Your Book to Customers section you can help let Amazon know what type of people your cookbook should be marketed to.

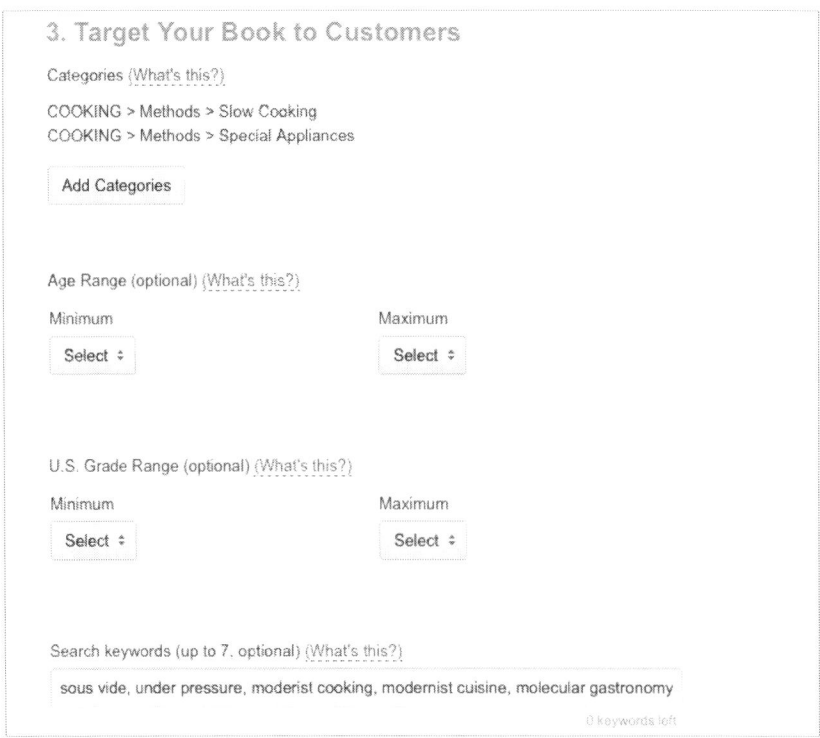

Categories
Picking your Kindle categories is an important part of the process. You want categories that are competitive but not too competitive. You can read more in the "Determining Your Amazon Categories" section.

Age Range
If your book is focused on a specific age range you can choose it here. You can only specify from a baby to 18 years old. It is usually left blank unless you are targeting your book at kids or teens.

US Grade Range
This specifies the suggested reading level for readers of your book. It only goes up to 12th grade and is usually left blank unless you are writing specifically for a younger audience.

Search Keywords
The search keywords is another important way to let users find you. They should be targeted to high traffic words that your potential readers would be using to try and reach your book.

For more help on finding and evaluating keywords, you can see the "Choosing Publishing Keywords" section of the "Pre-Publishing Steps" chapter.

Book Release Option
The book release allows you to delay the launch of your book or to release it right away. This allows you to easily time the release with any launches you may have planned.

> **4. Select Your Book Release Option**
>
> Please select if you are ready to release your book immediately or if you would like to make it available for pre-order (What's this?)
>
> ● I am ready to release my book now
> ○ Make my book available for pre-order

Upload or Create a Cover

This is where you upload your cover. We recommend creating your cover in another program, but it is possible to create a nice looking cover using their "cover creator".

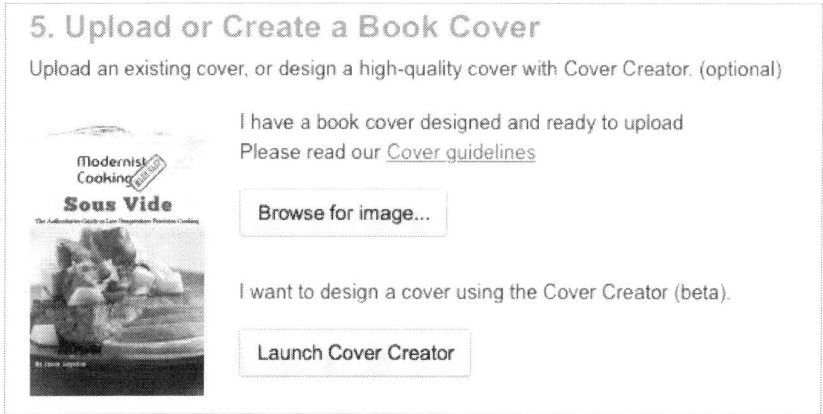

Upload Your Book File

Click on the "Browse" button and choose your Kindle-specific ePub file. Whether or not you "Enable Digital Rights Management" is up to you. We write more in-depth about what DRM means in the Appendix.

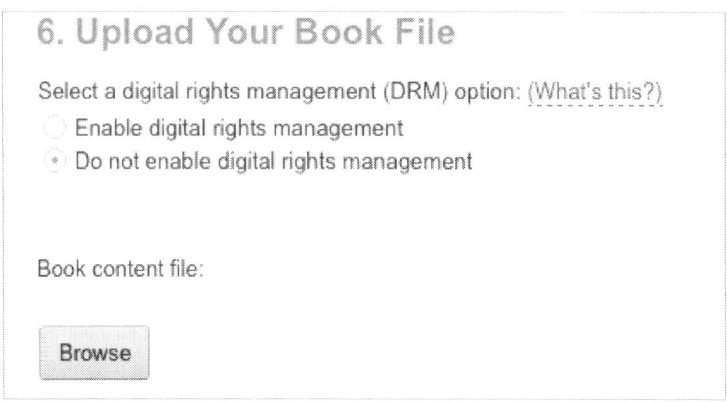

Preview Your Book

Once you've uploaded all the files for your book you can preview the book online or download any of the desktop Kindle preview programs. We highly recommend you do at least one final preview to make sure nothing got garbled during the upload process.

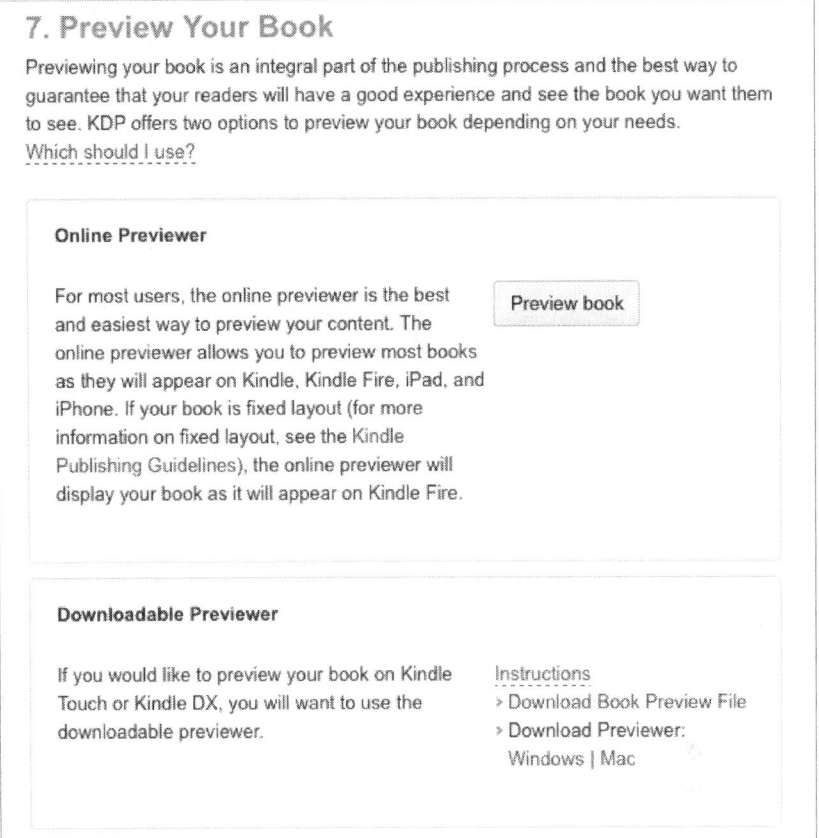

RIGHTS AND PRICING

The second page of the Kindle book creation process has to deal with the rights and pricing across various countries.

Select Your Territories

This option allows you to specify where you have rights to sell your book. You can either choose worldwide or select individual territories. If you are self publishing then you will want to choose worldwide.

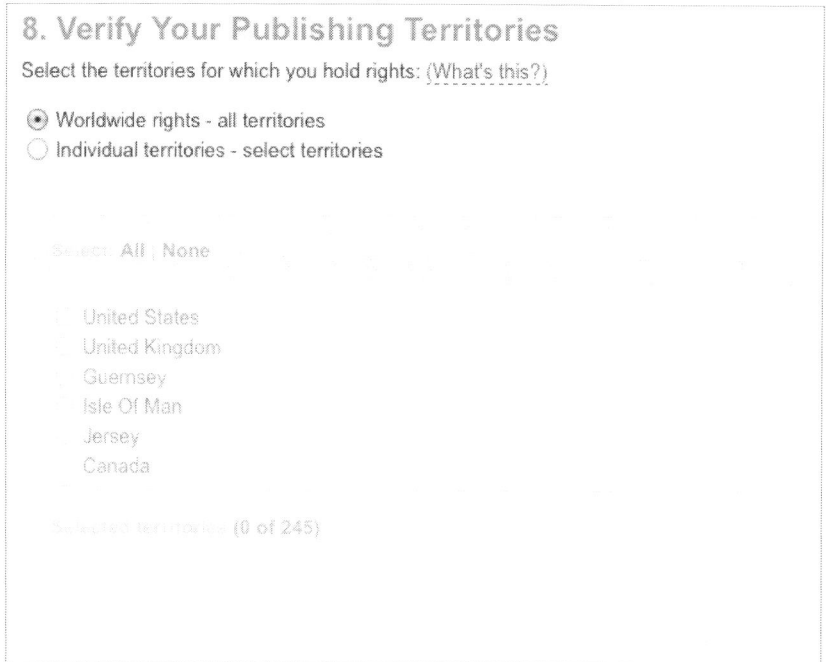

Set Your Pricing and Royalty

We talk more about pricing in our guide to how to price your cookbook. Once you've decided on your price, you need to select 35% or 70% royalty then fill in the US list price. The prices for the other territories will be automatically filled in, though you can overwrite it if needed.

9. Set Your Pricing and Royalty

KDP Pricing Support (Beta)

See the relationship between price and past sales and author earnings for KDP books like yours.

[View Service]

KDP Pricing and Royalty

 Effective January 1, 2015, list prices for EU marketplaces include VAT. Learn more about VAT

Please select a royalty option for your book. (What's this?)

○ 35% Royalty
● 70% Royalty

	List Price	Royalty Rate	Delivery Costs	Estimated Royalty
Amazon.com	$ 9.95 USD Price must be between $2.99 and $9.99.	35% (Why?) 70%	n/a $1.04	$3.48 $6.24
Amazon.co.uk	☑ Set UK price automatically based on US price £7.52 (£6.27 without UK VAT)	70%	£0.69	£3.91*
Amazon.de	☑ Set DE price automatically based on US price €9.51 (€7.99 without DE VAT)	70%	€0.83	€5.01*
Amazon.fr	☑ Set FR price automatically based on US price €8.43 (€7.99 without FR VAT)	70%	€0.83	€5.01*

Kindle Matchbook

The Kindle Matchbook program allows you to offer a discount to people that purchase the print version of your book. This program is something we have tried to take advantage of as a service to our readers. Some people enjoy having a digital copy in addition to the print copy so we allow them to get the e-version for only $2.99.

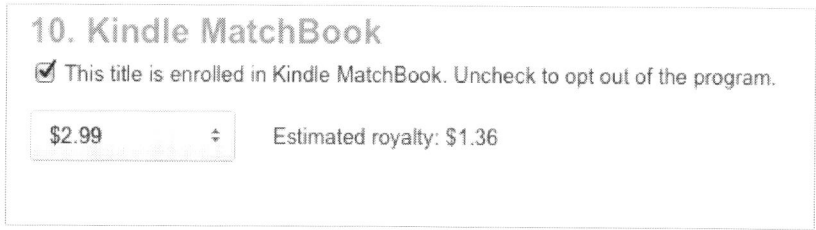

Kindle Lending

This allows your readers to lend your book to their friends and family after they have purchased it. We tend to allow this because we want to keep our readers happy, and hopefully the people they loan it to will want to purchase their own copy.

SAVE AND PUBLISH

Once you are happy with the information you have entered you are finally ready to publish your cookbook! Just hit the "Save and Publish" button and it will go live on Amazon in a few days. If you aren't ready to pull the trigger yet, you can "Save as Draft" and then publish it later at your convenience.

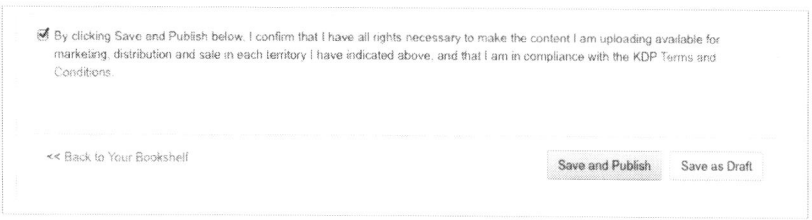

LINKING YOUR PRINT AND KINDLE VERSIONS

If you publish both a print and Kindle version of the same book you want to make sure they are linked up. This ensures that they share reviews and that potential customers are given the ability to switch formats. It will also allow you to enable the special Matchbook pricing.

If the title of your book was entered the same during both publishing processes the books should be linked together already. If they are not linked for some reason, you can contact Amazon by signing into your KDP account and clicking on help. At the bottom left there is a "Contact Us" button. Once clicked, you get a form that allows you to choose your reason for contacting them. The first option under "Amazon Product Page" is "Linking Print and Kindle Editions".

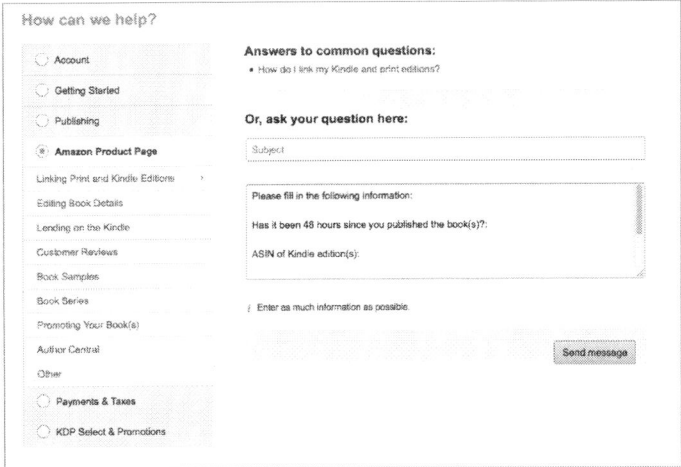

Fill out the information required and they usually take care of it in a few days.

How to Publish on the Nook

Once you have created an ePub file, which we covered in the "eBook Specific Design" chapter, publishing it through Nook is relatively simple.

First you will need to create an account with Nook Press (https://www.nookpress.com/). Once you create your account the new project process will start.

Manuscript

Just click on the "Upload Manuscript" file and you can pick the file you want to upload. We suggest you create an ePub file instead of having them convert your Word file. Creating your own normally results in a much higher quality ebook and gives you much more control over the process.

Cover Image

The next step is to upload the cover you created.

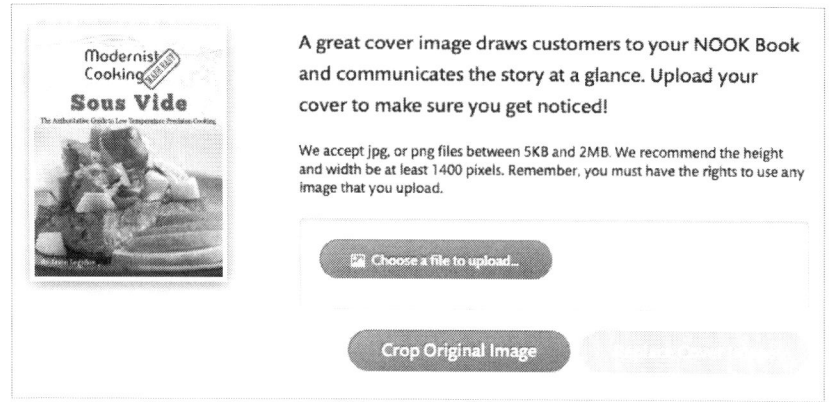

NOOK BOOK DETAILS

The information in this section determines what your book will look like on the Nook site and where it will appear. Click on any of the fields under a specific category to open the edit window for that section. You can hop around and enter the information in any order that works for you.

TITLE & DESCRIPTION

Title	Modernist Cooking Made Easy: Sous Vide - The Authoritive Guide to Low Temperature Precision Cooking
Publication Date	November 17, 2014
Publisher	Primolicious LLC
Description	Do you want to get the most out of your sous vide...
Contributors	1 Provided

1. Jason Logsdon: Author

CATEGORIES

Categories	5 Provided

1. Cooking » Methods » Slow Cooking*
2. Cooking Fundamentals & Reference
3. Cooking » General
4. Cooking » Reference
5. Cooking » Methods » Special Appliances

RIGHTS & PRICING

Prices	3 Provided

1. USD $9.95
2. GBP £6.25
3. EUR €7.98

OTHER INFORMATION

Num. Pages in Print	284

Title and Description

Title

Enter the title of your book you came up with earlier. Also include the subtitle if you want it to show up on the Nook sales page.

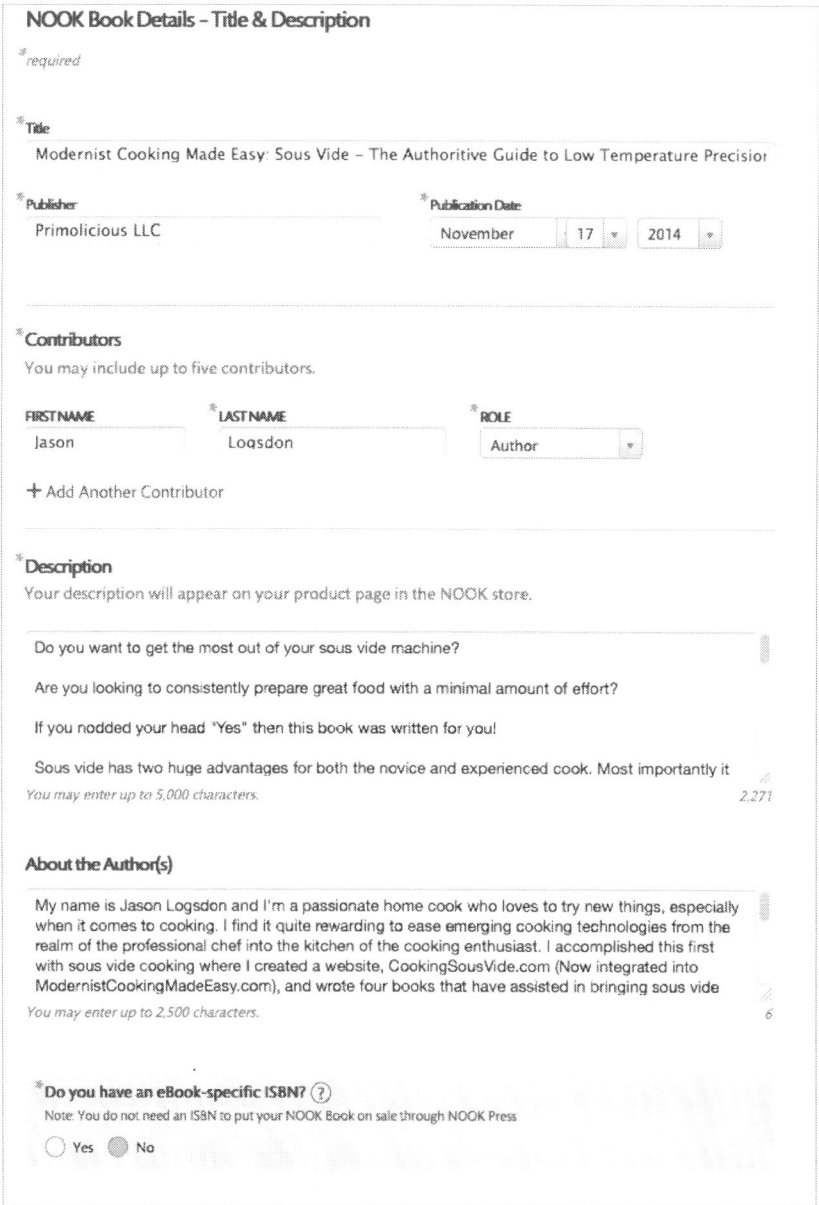

Publication Date

This allows you to set a publication date for when your book will go live. You can publish right away or choose to delay the launch of your book. This can help to easily time the release with any launches you may have planned.

Publisher
Enter in the publisher of your book, or your blog as the publisher.

Contributors
You can add any contributors that were an integral part of the book creation process. Any people you add will show up on your Nook page right next to your name so make sure you only add people here if you want them to have equal credit with you.

Description
Take the cookbook description you created earlier and enter it here. For the Nook you have very limited formatting you can add so it is best to use plain text here.

About the Author
The About the Author section is optional but it can be helpful to add a short one that informs potential readers about who you are and why you are qualified to write your book. Our standard biography is currently:

> Jason Logsdon is a passionate home cook, entrepreneur, and web developer. He helps cooks understand sous vide and new modernist cooking techniques with easy-to-understand directions and recipes. He has several books and a website on sous vide and modernist cooking that are read by thousands of people every month including Beginning Sous Vide, Modernist Cooking Made Easy: Getting Started, Sous Vide: Help for the Busy Cook, Modernist Cooking Made Easy: The Whipping Siphon, Sous Vide Grilling, and Modernist Cooking Made Easy: Party Foods. He can be reached at jason@modernistcookingmadeeasy.com or through Twitter at @jasonlogsdon.

Do you have an eBook-specific ISBN?
If you enter in an ISBN number it must be different than one you have used for the print version. The ISBN number for the Nook format is completely optional and isn't really used by the Nook for much. We recommend saving your money and not using one for most Nook books. You can learn more about ISBN numbers in the Appendix.

Categories
The categories determine where your cookbook will show up in the Nook hierarchy. You can add up to 5 categories. You can learn more about choosing categories in the "Determining Your Amazon Categories" section.

Keywords for Search Engines
You can add up to 100 characters of keywords. To save some space leave off the space after the commas. For instance: "keyword1,keyword2,keyword3" instead of "keyword1, keyword2, keyword3".

For more help on finding and evaluating keywords, you can see the "Choosing Publishing Keywords" section of the "Pre-Publishing Steps" chapter.

Your NOOK Book is most suited for...
Choose the category that best suits your cookbook.

Your NOOK Book is written in...
Select the language your cookbook is written in.

Rights and Pricing

This section determines where your book is sold and how much it is sold for.

NOOK Book Details – Rights & Pricing

Select where you have the rights to make your NOOK Book available for sale and then set the list price for each territory, or let us do the currency conversions for you!

*required

Sales Territory Rights

- ● Worldwide Sales Rights
- ○ United States Only

DRM

Do you want DRM encryption for your NOOK book?
○ Yes ● No

List Price

Convert currencies based on my USD list price ☑

CURRENCY	LIST PRICE		EST. ROYALTY	
USD $	9.95	USD	65%	$6.47
GBP £	6.25	GBP	65%	£4.06
EUR €	7.98	EUR	65%	€5.19

Sales Territory Rights

This option allows you to specify where you have rights to sell your Nook book. You can either choose worldwide or select individual territories. If you are self publishing then you will want to choose worldwide.

DRM

Enabling DRM protection is a personal decision that we cover more in-depth in the Appendix.

List Price

Put in the list price of your cookbook that you determined earlier. You can choose to let Nook convert the other currencies automatically or enter in your own.

Other Information

```
NOOK Book Details – Other Information
* required

* Is this NOOK Book public domain? (?)
   ○ Yes    ● No

* Is this NOOK Book a part of a series?
   ○ Yes    ● No

* Is this NOOK Book available in print?
   ○ Yes    ● No
```

Is This NOOK Book Public Domain
This option is only for works that do not have a copyright and currently exist in the public domain. If your cookbook was written by you it is doubtful you want it in the public domain.

Is this NOOK Book a part of a series?
If your cookbook is part of a series then choose this option. If you select it, it will also ask for the name of the series and the series number.

Is this NOOK Book available in print?
If you also have a print version of this book then select this option and enter in the number of pages it contains.

Editorial Reviews

You can add editorial reviews that people have written about your book. These reviews show up on the Nook sales page.

NOOK Book Details - Editorial Reviews

Editorial reviews aren't required, but they're a good thing to include if you have them. Make sure they're not written by you, and that you have permission to use them. You may include up to five editorial reviews.

*required

Current Editorial Reviews

New Review — hit save when done...

*FIRST NAME

*LAST NAME

*REVIEW SOURCE

*REVIEW EXCERPT

You may enter up to 500 characters   500

+ Add Editorial Review

HOW TO PUBLISH ON ITUNES

Once you have created an ePub file, which we covered in the "eBook Specific Design" chapter, publishing it through iBook and iTunes is a little more complicated than publishing on other e-readers. You can get a general overview of the process from the Apple Publishing FAQs (https://support.apple.com/en-us/HT201183). You also have to have a Mac computer to publish through iTunes. Though there are some workarounds (http://bit.ly/1MZ67QP), including publishing through Smashwords.

ACCOUNT CREATION AND SETUP
First, you need to create an iTunes Connect Account (http://apple.co/1PYCqK5). You may need to connect your iTunes Connect account with the book publishing arm by applying to be a book publisher (http://apple.co/1V26op3).

You will also need to download iTunes Producer, which is also linked up under your Resources and Help section of your iTunes Connect Account (https://itunesconnect.apple.com/WebObjects/iTunesConnect.woa/ra/ng/resources_page).

Once you are approved and have downloaded iTunes Producer you are ready to go.

CREATING A NEW BOOK
Open iTunes Producer and choose File -> New. Select "Book" and click "Choose".

DETAILS

The first step is to enter in some basic information.

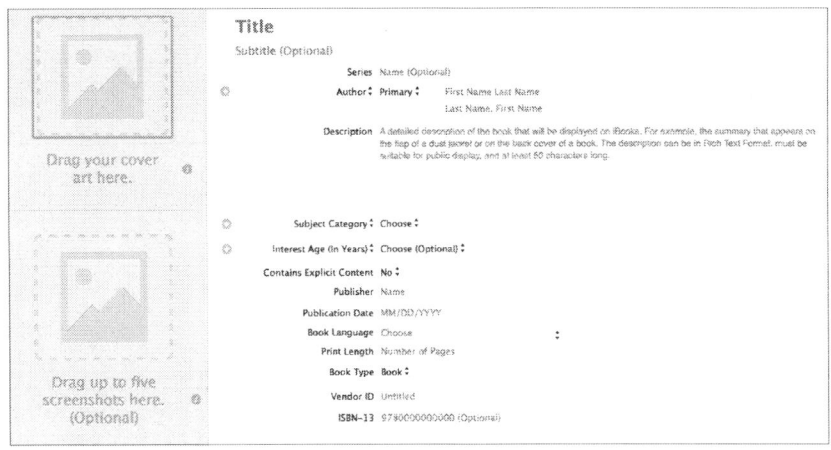

Name and Subtitle
Enter the name of your book and the subtitle. If you have a print version, the name and the subtitle you enter should match your print version exactly.

Series
If your book is part of a series then you should add the series title. You will then be prompted to enter the Number this edition is and the Display Text (Such as Volume 3, or Book III).

Author
Enter you or the main author as the Author -> Primary. You can also add any other contributors that were an integral part of the book creation process but be aware they get credit on your sales page, right next to your name.

Description
Paste in the cookbook description you created earlier. For iTunes you can use Rich Text Format (https://en.wikipedia.org/wiki/Rich_Text_Format) in your description, allowing you some control over the look and feel.

Category
You can enter up to three categories. They can be an iTunes subject, BISAC subject, BIC subject, or CLIL subject category. These categories are the place that your cookbook will show up in

the iTunes hierarchy. You can learn more about choosing categories in the "Determining Your Amazon Categories" section.

Interest Age
If your book is specifically targeted towards a younger audience you can enter the age range here.

Contains Explicit Content
If your cookbook contains content not suitable for children then be sure to select this.

Publisher
Enter in the publisher that is associated with this book, or your blog name.

Publication Date
Enter in when you would like this book to go live. It can allow you to delay the launch of your book or release it right away. This helps to easily time the release with any launches you may have planned.

Book Language
Choose the language this version of your cookbook is written in.

Print Length
If you also have a print version of this book enter in the length in pages here.

Book Type
This should be set to "Book" unless you are specifically publishing a textbook.

Vendor ID
This is a unique identifier created by iTunes Producer.

ISBN-13
If you want to use an ISBN number with the ebook version of your cookbook you can enter it here. You can read a more detailed explanation of what is an ISBN and our recommendations for handling it in the Appendix.

Cover Art
You can drag the cover you created earlier into the Cover Art box. It should be a JPG or PNG version and at least 1400 pixels wide and tall.

Screenshots

You can also include up to 5 screenshots and we highly recommend uploading them because they help provide potential readers with a feel for your book. We usually include a few intro pages as well as a few recipes. They need to be in a specific size, according to the iTunes Producer documentation the size needs to be:

> Screenshots must be full-sized iPad images in the PNG or JPEG format with a size of 1024 x 768, 768 x 1024, 2048 x 1536, or 1536 x 2048 pixels. For a cleaner look, you can also remove the status bar from your screenshots, making the size 1024 x 748, 768 x 1004, 2048 x 1496, or 1536 x 2008 pixels.

We tend to take the screenshots in our PDF view and then resize the canvas size in photoshop but you can also take them directly from your iPad.

PRICE

The Price view allows you to add the different territories your book will be sold.

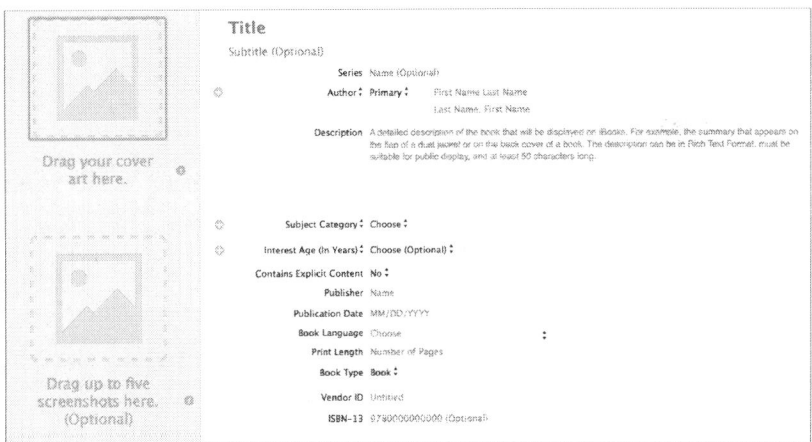

DRM-Free

This allows you to enable or disable DRM. We write more in-depth about what DRM means in the Appendix but the ultimate decision about whether DRM is right for your book is up to you.

Sales Start Date and Pre-Order Start Date

These determine when your book will go on sale or pre-sale in the selected territory. If you want them to go on sale right away just leave them blank.

Publication Type

If you have a specific type of publication, such as Digital Only or New Release you can choose it, otherwise select Other.

Currency

Choose the currency you would like to set the prices in.

Physical List Price

If you have a print book you can add in the list price for the printed version.

iBooks Store Price

The price you'd like to sell your book for in the iTunes store that you can determine from the price of your cookbook.

Choose Region

You can then choose the regions you want your book in. You can do it manually or click on the "Choose Region" drop down and select "All" or a specific region.

When you click "Save" it will auto-populate all the regions you selected with the information you provided.

FILES

On this screen you can upload your created ePub file here. The sample book is usually auto-created during the submission process.

SUBMIT

When all of your information is ready you can submit your book to iTunes. Just click the "Submit" button in the top right of the window. If there are any errors it will highlight them and let you fix them. Your book should show up shortly in your "My Books" section in iTunes Connect.

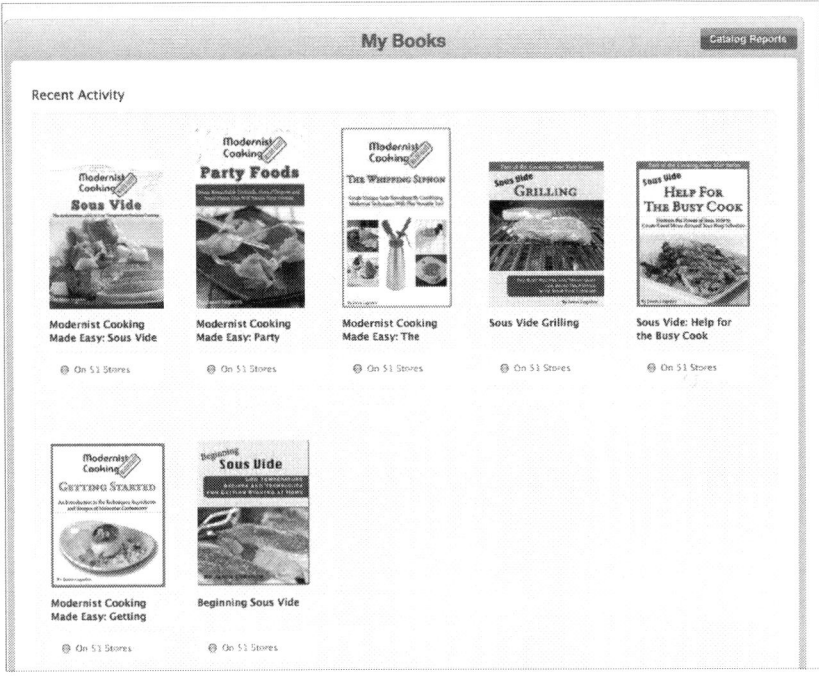

How to Publish Your Book Through Smashwords

If you read through the Smashwords website it would lead you to believe that publishing through them is essentially a no-brainer. Unfortunately, given our experience, as well as others we've read about, this is simply not the case in most situations. Perhaps you might get lucky and sail right through, but typically there are some bumps (sometimes walls) that need to be overcome in order to complete the exercise. We will try to present an accurate summary of what you might expect when publishing through Smashwords. We just want to be sure you go into this with your eyes wide open.

Your first step is to decide if you want to publish your ebook directly or through a distributor, which we cover in the "Should You Use an eBook Distributor?" section of the "Publishing Formats and Platforms" chapter.

If you do want to use Smashwords for some of the platforms, you need to sign up for a free account (http://www.smashwords.com/signup). Once you have signed up you will receive a confirmation email which will summarize your next steps.

ePub Creation

There are two options to publishing your book through Smashwords. The first is to let them convert a Microsoft Word document into an ePub file for you, and the other is to create the ePub yourself.

Smashwords ePub Creation

If you are letting Smashwords create your ePub file, the first step is to be sure that your book is prepared to the requirements of the Smashwords Style Guide (https://www.smashwords.com/books/view/52). To quote the Smashwords website, "Download The Smashwords Style Guide for simple instructions on how to format your manuscript as a Microsoft Word .doc file prior to upload. No technical expertise is necessary!"

Wow, that sounds simple. As it turns out this Style Guide is more than 100 pages long (27,000 words) and must be followed to the letter for your ebook to be accepted into the Smashwords Premium Catalog and distributed to all the major retailers.

In order to get your ebook accepted you need to understand the Style Guide and know enough about Word to make those necessary changes to satisfy the requirements in the guide. Once again quoting from the Smashwords website, "if you are relatively proficient with Microsoft Word, or you have the patience to learn by following our Style Guide, it's not difficult. We encourage authors and publishers to do their own formatting, if they're able. If you're not proficient with word processing, or you don't own Microsoft Word... an improperly formatted book will prevent or delay the distribution of your book."

If you are not "relatively proficient with Microsoft Word" then Smashwords suggests that you hire someone to create a professionally formatted Word document. Although this is expensive (usually $30-$60), Smashwords calls this "A good choice if you don't have the time, patience or ability to implement the Style Guide on your own."

From reading users' experiences online this first step to prepare a book to meet the Style Guide can be as simple as making a few minor changes to your existing Word file or involving preparing a large number of iterations. Unfortunately these "failures" can come without adequate explanations of why, leaving you in the dark. In these cases many authors give up and pay one of the formatters on "Mark's List" to create the file so it finally gets accepted (https://www.smashwords.com/list).

Smashwords Direct
Smashwords now has another option for preparing your book called "Smashwords Direct". This is definitely the way to go if you already have an ePub version of your book available. This is the method we used to prepare our books for Smashwords. Keep in mind that you still need to meet the Style Guide, which may require changes to the ePub file from what you might use in other places. For example, you must add the Smashwords branding to the first actual page of your book.

In addition to your book file, you will also need to have an ebook cover image that meets the detailed specifications provided on the Smashwords website. If you don't already have a cover you may need to create one yourself or pay a contractor to create it for you.

Smashwords also has a list of low-cost cover designers on "Mark's List" (https://www.smashwords.com/list).

CLICK PUBLISH AND UPLOAD THE BOOK
After you complete the Publish form and upload your ebook, ebook cover image and book information, Smashwords will display the conversion page where you can watch in real time as the Meatgrinder technology generates multiple ebook formats for your book. This takes anywhere from 1 to 3 minutes.

Once the conversion completes, the AutoVetter technology will instantly analyze the book and report back if it identifies any potential formatting errors. Whether you have errors or not, the next page you'll see is the conversion confirmation page to tell you the conversion is complete. With this step completed, Smashwords will provide you a link to your new ebook page where your book is available for immediate sampling and sale. If errors are found you will receive an email that will summarize the errors and provide instructions on how to fix them.

DASHBOARD
Once your ebook as been successfully converted you can manage it via the Smashwords Dashboard. From the dashboard you can upload a new version of your ebook or cover, change the price, change the title and categorization, track the sales of your book and a variety of other activities.

HOW TO CREATE AND SELL A PDF ON YOUR BLOG

There are three components to selling PDFs from your website. First, you need to create and design a PDF file of your cookbook. Second, you need to create a sales page for your book. Third, you need to collect money and send out the PDF file to buyers.

We do all of our cookbook PDF creation in Pages, but you can use most word processors to design it. It is covered in more detail in the "How to Design an eBook" section.

We have always used e-Junkie (http://www.e-junkie.com/?r=42616) for all of our files. They manage the whole selling process including the collection of money through PayPal and the delivering of the PDF file. You set up everything through an easy to use interface and tie into their program through a simple link. Plus they have plans starting at only $5 per month so it is very low cost to get started.

For more information about the entire processes of creating and selling ebooks we highly recommend this guide written by Pat from Smart Passive Income. It's a great free book about creating and selling ebooks that goes into much more detail (http://www.smartpassiveincome.com/ebooks-the-smart-way/).

Selling and Marketing Your Cookbook

PROMOTING YOUR COOKBOOK

No matter how good your cookbook is, no one will ever know about it unless you promote it. There are three facets of cookbook promotion: pre-launch promotion, launch promotion, and post-launch promotion. We try to give you ideas on how to maximize all three areas to achieve the widest possible promotion.

We also dive into more details about getting Amazon reviews, promoting through your newsletter, utilizing free content previews, and how to get others to write about your cookbook.

How to Launch Your Cookbook Successfully

Your initial book launch is the time when you first start to really promote your book. It usually includes several layers of promotions to maximize the amount of sales you can get right away.

The initial book launch is often the most important part of your marketing plan, especially if your cookbook is being sold on Amazon. A strong initial launch gets you out of the gate with a higher Amazon Sales Rank, placing you further up the search results and potentially getting you into the Amazon newsletter. It can also get your book into the "People Who Bought This Also Bought" section of many complimentary and competitive products. All of this snowballs into higher long term sales on Amazon, plus more promotion within Amazon itself.

Here is an overview of the various tasks you will want to focus on during your launch process. We also look at many of them in more depth in the sections following this one.

Pre-Promotion Tasks

Before you launch your cookbook, there are several tasks you need to accomplish. Many of these are best done as soon as you get started on your book. For instance, building up your newsletter is a key to a successful launch and priming your readers with content similar to that from your upcoming book also builds interest.

One of the keys to having a good launch and extended success on Amazon is through garnering good reviews. There are many ways to do this out of the gate, as early Amazon reviews will greatly help your launch maintain its momentum. Make sure you line up people to provide Amazon reviews for your book before your launch date.

Finding blogs to write about your book is also a task that needs to be done ahead of time. These articles help build up interest and expose new audiences to you and your work.

Cookbook Launch Techniques

There are an almost unlimited number of ways to launch your cookbook but here are some techniques that work across many launch strategies.

Time the Launch with the Release

If possible, your book launch should be timed to occur when your cookbook goes on sale on Amazon. This allows you to climb up the Amazon Cookbook Hot Releases (http://amzn.to/1RVkz9g) and get even more visibility. This initial push will have long lasting impact on the external promotion of your book.

You can tweak the time the book goes on sale when you add it to CreateSpace or another company by changing the "Publish Date" or "Publication Date" field to sometime in the future. This allows you to get your book up but not have it be released until later.

Use Giveaway Promotions

A great way to entice users to purchase your book early on is through promotions. We will often offer a discount on our other books, or a unique PDF file with special recipes in it for people that order the book in the first week it is on sale. We just have them email us the receipt from Amazon and then send them the file directly.

Offer a Discount

Offering a week-long discount is a great way to get people to make the decision to purchase your book. Even though you leave some money on the table in the short term, the boost to your Amazon Sales Rank will allow you to make more in the long run.

Free Content

Leading up to your book launch it can be a good idea to start posting a steady stream of free content from your cookbook on your blog. This will not only build anticipation but add to your newsletter list and provide great examples of what your book will be covering.

Articles on Other Blogs

Working with other blogs is a great way to drive traffic. You can offer the blogs things like free copies of your cookbook to give to their readers or guest posts based on your cookbook. Having these articles all come out at the same time allows you to maximize your exposure during your initial launch, leading to higher brand recognition and more potential buyers.

Newsletter Promotions
As your book launch nears, talking about it in newsletter promotions is a great way to drive interest. It can range from teasing it several weeks ahead of time to a full, advertising based newsletter on the day of the launch.

GETTING AMAZON REVIEWS

If your book sells on Amazon or another online retailer it is critical to get reader reviews up as soon as possible. The reviews provide social proof for your book and show that other people have purchased it and liked it. Many people will not purchase a book without reviews, fearful that they will be buying a bad book.

Think back to how often you have been ready to purchase a book or product on Amazon and realized there were no reviews for it. Did you still buy the item? If so, did the lack of reviews make you hesitate? Your goal during launch is to remove all hesitations from potential readers. Ensuring your book has a solid amount of (hopefully) positive reviews will convince many readers your book is worth buying.

How Many Reviews Do You Need?
It's critical to have some amount of reviews to minimize people's concern for buying your book. The number normally suggested is 5 to 10 reviews as the minimum you need for people to seriously consider your book. After that number, there seems to be no direct correlation between the number of reviews and the number of purchases that follow, especially for recently launched books. After books have been out for a while, the more books that have been sold, the more reviews it will have, mainly because there are more potential reviewers.

> **Jason Says**
> I always try to launch with a decent amount of reviews. However, I've occasionally had less reviews on higher selling books and lower selling books with more reviews. I've found that during the initial launch phase having 5 to 10 reviews is really enough to get people to take a chance on you, a handful more won't make a ton of difference.

How Do You Get Amazon Reviews

Once you acknowledge that reviews are critical to a successful launch, the big question becomes "how do you get reviews before people have read your book?" There are several ways, including reaching out to your business and personal connections, soliciting reviews online, approaching Amazon top reviewers, and many others.

One thing to remember when asking for reviews is that people are busy with work of their own. Many people, even friends and family, will not respond to your request at all. Several people who say they will write a review also will never get around to it. While a gentle follow up email is fine, after that it's usually best to just let it go. Don't be discouraged or let it affect your relationship with the person, it happens to everyone and it's not an indictment of you or your book.

> **Jason Says**
> One thing I can't stress enough is that when you solicit reviews you MUST ask for an honest review. I believe honest reviews, and honesty in general, are the keys to building up trust with your readers and will greatly pay off in the long run. Whenever I solicit a review, especially if I am giving them a free review copy, I always stress it should be an honest review so the reviewer is under no illusion they have to write a positive review.

For many early reviews, you can send out a PDF copy of your book, that way they can get started reading it before it is live. Once the book is available on Amazon you can have them go in and add their reviews right away, helping your launch.

PLACES TO GET REVIEWS

There are several different places you can turn to get Amazon reviews for your cookbook.

Friends and Network

The easiest way to get good Amazon reviews is by asking your friends and your blogging network. As long as the reviews are honestly written, Amazon is fine with them, even if you know the person. We often send review copies of our latest books to our more adventurous friends and connections and ask them for an honest review in return.

If you feel uncomfortable with the reviews coming from friends, it's easy to ask your friends to include the fact that they know you, or got a free copy of the book, in their review. This way you are still being upfront with any potential buyers.

Blog Readers

One of the best places to find potential reviewers for your book is from your readers. Unless your cookbook is on a vastly different subject than the one you blog about, many of your readers will be interested in it. It's especially valuable if you have relationships with some readers of your site. They are usually very excited to help out and happy you thought of them.

We often reach out to some of our more visible readers, or readers we have communicated with via email and ask them for an honest review in exchange for a copy of the book.

As a food blogger it is important to work on continually growing your email list. This is one of your most valuable assets since it includes individuals that are already familiar with, and ideally fans of, your content. It is also a great source of potential reviewers for your latest cookbook.

Other Bloggers

If there are other bloggers that are in a niche that fits with your cookbook they can be great places to turn for reviews. You can often provide them with several copies, one for them and a few to give away to their readers. These connections can lead both to Amazon reviews and reviews on the blogger's website that can result in more sales.

Social Media Contacts
If you have a decent presence on any of the social networks you can turn to your contacts there for reviews. Many people in your network will be more than happy to write a review in exchange for a free copy. They will also often discuss the book on the different social media platforms, leading to more sales.

Amazon Reviewers
It is also possible to contact other reviewers on Amazon that have reviewed similar books. There are two approaches that you can take to recruit Amazon reviewers. Unfortunately, both are very tedious and take a lot of patience to complete. However, it can be a way to increase the number of quality reviews your book has on Amazon.

The first approach is to solicit reviews from Amazon's top reviewers. You can find Amazon's Top Customer Reviewers listed here: http://amzn.to/1TGdwpB. You can click on the reviewer's name and it will take you to their personal page. The first thing to look for is to see whether they have provided their email address. If they have not, you should go on to the next reviewer. If they have provided their email address then read through the "About" portion of their page. This will typically give you enough information to know if they might be interested in reviewing a cookbook. If it sounds promising then add their email to your list of potential reviewers.

For example, we have gone through the top 10 Amazon reviewers and found they all provided their email address. Moreover, two of them #6 and #7 both indicated an interest in cooking and would probably be worth sending an email to. We have compiled all the emails we could find from the top 250 Amazon reviewers to create a list of the top Amazon cookbook reviewers (http://bit.ly/1GlLLbl).

> **Jason Says**
> Preparing for the launch of my Modernist Cooking Made Easy: The Whipping Siphon I sent emails to 20 top Amazon reviewer's. Of those, 6 asked for copies of the book, of which 3 entered high-quality 5-star reviews. It was quite a bit of work for three reviews but I have stayed in contact with those reviewers and have received reviews on some of my other books as a result.

The second approach to recruiting Amazon reviewers is similar. In this case you can search for cookbooks on Amazon which are addressing a subject similar to the one you are writing. For each of those cookbooks scan through their reviews sorted by "Most helpful". For each review you can click on the reviewer's name to determine if they have provided their email address. If they have you probably have located someone who is interested in your particular subject and is willing to write an Amazon review.

REVIEW REQUEST TIPS
Getting reviews can be difficult but there are a few tips you can follow to increase your odds of getting a review.

Always Ask for Honest Reviews
Make sure you make it clear you are asking for an honest review. Giving away a book in exchange for a positive review is against Amazon's terms, the book given away as a review copy must be in exchange for a review that can be positive or negative.

Of course, asking people who are more apt to like your work will result in much more positive reviews than asking people that don't know or like you.

Provide Talking Points
We almost always try to provide a few talking points about what we were hoping the book would accomplish. This will help focus the reviewer on specific items when they read and then review your book. This direction can help shape the reviews to discuss the things you would like them to discuss.

It's important not to tell the reviewer what to write, but just letting them know what you were trying to accomplish often results in them noticing those points when they are reading. These points are then more likely to show up in their review.

Don't Be Disheartened

The people you contact for reviews will be very busy with their own lives and might not get to a review for you quickly, or at all. We generally get reviews from about 10% of unsolicited requests, i.e. "Please review this book", and 33% of solicited requests, i.e. "I'd love to review your book".

We normally send one follow up email and then let the issue drop. The last thing you want to do is alienate someone that was interested in your book by badgering them about a review. It will be made apparent time and time again that no one cares about your book nearly as much as you do, so don't take it personally.

Provide Instant Access

Several people may want to check the book out right away, so providing access to an electronic version is a great way to let them hop right in. We usually have PDF files on DropBox or Amazon S3 that potential readers can download or share.

Provide the Review Link

Not everyone knows how to review something on Amazon. Providing them a direct link to the page where the review is entered helps increase follow through since they won't get frustrated looking for the link on Amazon.

Offer a Physical Copy

Unless your book is an electronic only book, offer a physical copy if they want one. For the low cost of providing it you will hopefully get a valuable review in return.

SAMPLE REQUEST EMAIL

To give you an idea of an effective email, here is a sample of the email we sent out for the Party Foods book.

> Hey NAME! I've got a big favor to ask of you. My latest book has come out and is available on Amazon. It's on modernist party foods and is focused on creating remarkable dishes.
>
> Anyway, one of the things that helps sales the most, especially in the first week, is reviews on Amazon. I was wondering if you would be willing to help me out and review the book?
>
> The things we were trying to accomplish with the book were:
> - Create easy to follow recipes that will delight your guests
> - Teach the basics of modernist cooking including the main techniques and ingredients
> - Give people ideas about unique foods they can serve at parties
>
> What it lacks:
> - Print version doesn't have color photos :-(
>
> So I'd love any help from you, especially if you can spare it over this weekend. I believe you can submit a review directly from here: https://www.amazon.com/review/create-review?ie=UTF8&asin=0991050169&ref_=dpx_acr_wr_link
>
> And feel free to pass this, and the link to the free book, along to any adventurous cooks you know.
>
> You can download a high resolution PDF (160meg) here: www.LINK-TO-PDF
>
> Or a lower resolution one (40 meg) here: www.LINK-TO-PDF
>
> If you would prefer the paperback version of the book please reply with your mailing address and I will be happy to ship it out to you.

Thanks again, I really appreciate your help making my new book a success!

Jason

With slight customizations for each person you send this to, the email becomes an effective way to gather reviews for your book, as well as help publicize your launch.

NEWSLETTER PROMOTIONS

Taking advantage of your newsletter is a wonderful way to kick off your book launch as well as to continue to promote it and drive long term sales. You can get many examples of the following emails from our cookbook newsletter promotion templates article (http://bit.ly/1QQ5lGY).

PRE-LAUNCH NEWSLETTER PREPARATION
While you are writing your book you should be focusing on driving signups to your newsletter. Both from general blog readers as well as from people specifically interested in your book. There are many ways to capture these email addresses.

General Newsletter Signup Forms
Placing signup forms throughout your site allows you to consistently add people to your newsletter. These links can either be inline or at the bottom of every post.

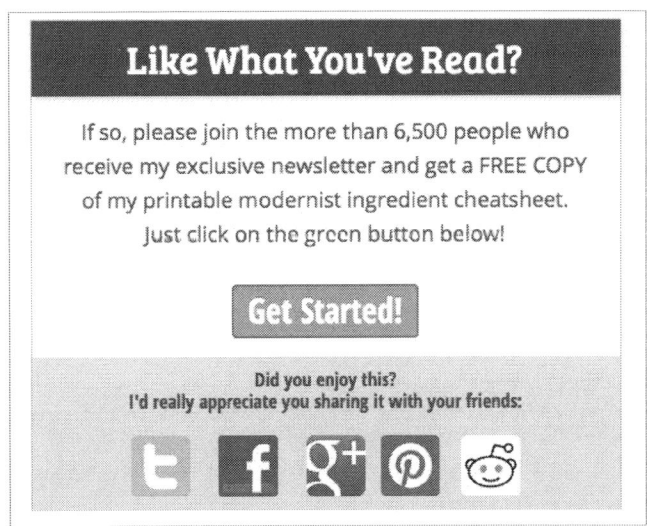

If you are just getting started writing a newsletter we highly recommend reading The Beginners Guide to Starting a Newsletter by Pat from Smart Passive Income (http://bit.ly/1SbUxE7).

Cookbook or Product Giveaways

You can create giveaways to draw in newsletter signups. This is an especially effective way to draw in subscribers who are interested in your new book. You can offer a prize to a randomly picked subscriber to your newsletter. Here was our giveaway page before we launched Modernist Cooking Made Easy: Party Foods (http://bit.ly/1WhYx5L).

You can offer just about anything as a prize. A free copy of your upcoming book is great. If you have multiple books you can offer a combo pack of them. You can also give away a piece of equipment or fancy ingredient that your readers would enjoy.

Cookbook Launch Newsletter Use

Leading up to and during your book launch there are many ways to take advantage of your newsletter list.

Tease Your Upcoming Cookbook

Several weeks, or even a few months, ahead of time you can tease that you have a new book coming out. From hinting at your upcoming book, to posting covers or sample recipes you can prime interest for you cookbook, leading to higher sales and better promotion when it comes out.

Get Amazon Reviews
When you are teasing your upcoming cookbook you can also solicit your readers for people interested in reviewing your book on Amazon in exchange for a free copy. This is a great way to get people that are biased in your favor to leave reviews on Amazon.

Launch Your Book
During the beginning of your book launch, your newsletter can be used to great effect to drive initial purchases. These purchases will kick up your Amazon Sales Rank, leading to much better promotion. The regular readers of your newsletter are also much more likely to purchase your book when there are only a few Amazon reviews available, which is often the case early on in your launch.

POST LAUNCH MARKETING
Not everyone will purchase your book during the initial launch. Many people will hold off until they learn more about it, read reviews on it, and develop more of an understanding about what it covers. This means that continuing to market your cookbook in your newsletter will result in additional sales.

Providing free content, either in the newsletter alone or on your blog, as well as testimonials, links to articles about your book, and other great content will push many of your readers over the edge and cause them to purchase your cookbook.

FREE CONTENT AND PREVIEWS ON YOUR BLOG

One of the best ways to market and promote books is by utilizing free content and previews on your blog. This content gives potential readers a preview of your writing style, photography, and the types of recipes your book has. There are many ways to implement free content and previews. You can also use any of these methods with other blogs to help spread your content throughout your blogging network.

RECIPE POSTS
Posting existing recipes on your blog is a great way to drive up interest in your book. Any recipes in your book that have nice

pictures and are creative, fun, or tasty are great candidates to share. These posts can be part of your normal blogging structure or added as special posts.

Highlighting the best recipes from your book on your blog has several benefits. Showcasing the best work from your cookbook drives interest for potential readers. Adding these posts to your blog helps increase the content and quality of the material on your blog.

To alert readers where the posts came from it is helpful to call out your book multiple times in the recipe post. Here's an example callout:

> If you like this recipe you can get it and more than 100 other recipes that will help you create remarkable cocktails, hors d'oeuvres and small plates that will amaze your friends. It's all in my book Modernist Cooking Made Easy: Party Foods - Get Your Copy Today!

Callouts like these will help drive people who are interested in similar content to the sales page for your book. From there you can give them more information and complete the sale.

> **Jason Says**
> I tend to make a recipe post out of any recipe in my books that has a nice photograph. You can see a few examples of my recipe posts here with my Sous Vide Fennel (http://bit.ly/1RmDIjh) and Chicken Piccata with Lemon Caper Air (http://bit.ly/1U84we1). Sometimes it's hard to give away content from your book, but it definitely seems to pay off in the long run.

SAMPLE RECIPE PDF DOWNLOADS

You can also provide PDFs of recipes for people to download. This has the benefit of being able to show the formatting of your book. Here are two examples, a recipe for Monkfish in Dashi with Spring Vegetables (http://bit.ly/25PwOxF) and one for Flank Steak with Argentinian Chimichurri (http://bit.ly/25PwPBC). You can also require users to provide an email address to download the PDFs, increasing your newsletter mailing list at the same time you market your book. I generally provide these free PDFs as a bonus to people on my mailing list.

INFORMATIONAL POSTS

Similar to the recipe posts, informational posts are a great way to highlight the best content from your cookbook. Picking parts of your book that will really resonate with readers and/or hits good Google keywords is ideal for successful informational posts. Including callouts for your book in the posts will lead interested users to the sales page for your book.

CHAPTER PREVIEWS

Chapter previews are similar to the sample recipe PDF downloads. They are PDF snapshots of certain chapters in your book. Often the first few chapters are good to use because they provide an overview of what the book is about without giving away too much information. You can see an example of a sample chapter from my sous vide book (http://bit.ly/1RJ0Lt0).

Placing ads and alerts for your books in the sample PDF is another great way to let people who like the sample buy your actual book. You can also require users to provide an email address to download the PDFs, increasing your newsletter mailing list at the same time.

PHOTO GALLERIES

Another way to showcase the content in your books and drive potential readers is by posting photo galleries of all the images in your book. This is especially helpful if you publish in black and white, as it allows you to provide full-color images to people that have already purchased a copy.

If you provide a description of each image you can also harness some Google traffic based on the descriptions. You can see some examples of photo galleries for my Sous Vide (http://afmeasy.com/SVGallery) and Infusions (http://afmeasy.com/InfusionsGallery) books.

How to Get Blogs to Write About Your Cookbook

There are many ways to get other blogs to write about your upcoming cookbook. It's important to start developing relationships with other bloggers before you will be asking them to promote your content. The longer you've been working together, and the more you've done to support them, the more receptive they will be.

Here are several options for successfully working with other bloggers to garner promotion for your book. Feel free to combine methods for maximum impact.

Author Interviews
If you have a good relationship with another blogger, you can offer to do an interview for their blog. You can discuss your book and talk about tips and tricks that might help their readers. This helps spread awareness of your book while providing good content for the other blogger. Make sure when you present your pitch you discuss what the readers of the other blog will get out of your interview so it isn't just straight marketing.

Book Giveaways
A great way to get cheap promotion is by providing free copies of your book to other blogs for giveaways. These blogs can then pass these books on to their readers, spreading the word about your books and leading to lots of additional promotion.

Guest Posts
Providing recipes from your book, or articles discussing techniques and equipment used in your book is a great way to get the name of your cookbook in front of new readers. Pitching these posts to other bloggers offers a clear benefit for them in the form of free content. Make sure you tailor each guest post so it matches up with what their audience is looking for.

Affiliate Network
If you have created a PDF for sale you can pass along the affiliate network information to other bloggers. This allows them to get paid for promoting your cookbook.

WHOLESALING YOUR COOKBOOK

Wholesaling is a great way for a self publisher to expand their distribution and bring in additional revenue. Once you have a published print book, setting up wholesaling isn't a hard process, assuming you can find companies that want to work with you.

The first step to wholesaling is understanding the different wholesaling methods. Next you should develop a wholesale line sheet and figure out places that would be interested in carrying your cookbook.

Once you find a company willing to work with you, they will place an order for a certain number of books. You will have those books printed and shipped to them, at which point they will pay you per the terms of your agreement.

Methods of Cookbook Wholesaling

There are generally two ways to sell books wholesale. The first is on a "consignment" basis where you only get paid when your books sell. The other is on a "resale" basis where the company will purchase your books up front and then sell them to their own customers.

Sometimes there is also a hybrid method where the retailer will purchase your books upfront but reserve the right to return them to you if they don't sell. This is the way most major bookstore chains work and many smaller bookstores follow that model.

All three methods have their advantages and disadvantages.

With a resale model, you are guaranteed payment for your books, even if the retailer never resells them. However, you will normally make less money per book with this method. Most resale books are purchased at 50% of list price, leaving the retailer ample room to mark up the books to help cover the costs of any unsold ones.

Consignment books generally bring in the most money, typically 70% to 80% of the list price. But if the retailer can't sell them you will never be paid for them. The retailer also has less incentive to sell your book since they have taken no risk with it.

The hybrid method generally results in the lowest prices, about 50% to 60% of the list price with the highest risk since if they don't sell they will be returned to you. This risk of book returns with the hybrid method is something to keep in mind if you try to get in a larger chain. While it might be nice to get a $100,000 order for 10,000 books, if they don't sell you will have to return the money and try to figure out what to do with all of those books. On top of that, the printing costs will usually have to come out of your own pocket, resulting in a lot of risk up front.

Where to Wholesale Your Cookbook

Selling your cookbooks wholesale through retailers, manufacturers, and other partners is a great way to widen your distribution network. There are several different areas you can look for potential wholesalers, depending on the content of your cookbook.

When possible, try to focus on places that your book meshes well with. This will provide more value for the companies you are wholesaling through and make them more likely to listen to your pitch.

GENERAL RETAILERS

General retailers, both online and offline, are companies that sell a wide variety of goods, usually including ingredients, equipment, products, and books. They are a great place to try to wholesale your books. Some examples of larger general retailers are For The Gourmet, Dean & Deluca, Williams Sonoma, and Sur La Table.

Many local cafes, delis, and general stores also carry books. These local retailers are often open to supporting local authors and usually easier to get into. Explore your local area and see what types of stores you can find whose products would complement your cookbook.

NICHE-SPECIFIC RETAILERS

There are also many smaller retailers around, either online or offline, especially in individual niches. These retailers can be a great place to start your wholesaling. Our books are sold through several modernist-centric sites such as Cedarlane Culinary, Modernist Pantry, and Creamright. Look around your niche and see if you can find any specialized retailers where your book might be a great fit.

EQUIPMENT MANUFACTURERS AND RESELLERS

Similar to the general and niche-specific retailers, equipment manufacturers are often great places to wholesale your books. Many people buying equipment are also looking for detailed directions on how to use it. If your book has recipes or directions focused around their equipment, you can offer it as a great add-on to their equipment.

We have bundled our sous vide books with sous vide manufacturers, our whipping siphon book with whipping siphon resellers, and our modernist introduction book to a company reselling modernist ingredients. These are all great ways to bundle your cookbook and provide value both to the manufacturer and their customers.

LOCAL AND REGIONAL BOOK STORES

It can be very hard to get into large bookstores but there are many local and regional stores that might be interested in carrying your book. Finding these types of stores in your area and approaching their owners can open up many opportunities. Some restaurants or delis also have a decent book selection. These more local stores are often very open to working with local authors.

FARMERS MARKET STANDS

Stands at local farmers markets often carry books from local authors to supplement their income. If your cookbook complements the offerings of a stand, they might be willing to sell your book alongside the rest of their products.

If your book is really focused around artisanal or farm food you can look into selling them at your own booth but it is usually more efficient to work with an existing partner.

TOP BLOGGERS

Many bloggers are looking to add streams of revenue to their blogs and selling your books can be a great source of income for them. Make sure your book complements the writing of the blog before approaching them. Many bloggers do prefer to work through affiliate relationships instead of wholesaling. This makes it so they don't have to manage any book inventory.

PRODUCE OR INGREDIENT COMPANIES

If your cookbook is focused around a specific type of ingredient like a certain type of produce or meat, you can often team up with a seller of that ingredient. For example, if your book makes a lot of use of onions, you can look into working with the National Onion Association to sell your books. Both of you will benefit from the association and it will help educate consumers on how to get the most out of their products.

DEVELOPING A WHOLESALING LINE SHEET

To appear as professional as possible when looking for companies to wholesale through it is a good idea to create a wholesale "line sheet". A line sheet is basically a marketing flyer with information about your book, the purchasing and payment process, and any other terms and conditions. You pass this line sheet along to any companies interested in carrying your books.

COMPONENTS OF A LINE SHEET

There are many variations on line sheets but there are similar types of information on many of them.

Your Brand or Logo

Your brand or logo should be front and center. This helps remind them who they are working with as well as build brand recognition towards your website in the future.

Contact Information

You should include your contact information in a prominent location so the companies can easily find out how to contact you. The minimum information should be your email address and physical address. Often times a phone number and fax number will also be included.

Book Information

Make sure you provide enough information about your book so they can make a buying decision. At a minimum you should include the cover, title, list price, and a wholesale price. We also recommend including a description and potentially a link to a sales page for the book, either on your website or on Amazon.

Billing Information

While you often have to work with the billing system a company prefers, it doesn't hurt to have your preferred billing method on your line sheet. Some billing information includes the forms of payment accepted (credit card, check, bank transfer), the payment terms (net 30, net 60, consignment, etc), any bulk discounts offered (10% off for purchases of more than X books), any minimum order amounts, and whether or not shipping is included in the price.

MORE LINE SHEET RESOURCES

Line sheets can be very diverse and we have just scratched the surface. If you would like to dive deeper into line sheets, there are several places we recommend for more information.

Indie Retail Academy has two great articles about line sheets: So what the hell is a linesheet, anyway? (http://bit.ly/1qca1ey) and How to Make a Line Sheet that Makes Selling Easy (http://bit.ly/1XlthkK). Oh My Handmade (http://bit.ly/1Ne4kSA) also has a good article covering them. We highly recommend reading through those articles for the full scoop on line sheets, including many samples. For more examples of line sheets, you can simply do an image search on Google for "line sheet".

How to Get A Cookbook in Bookstores

It's the goal of many authors to be on the shelves of big chain booksellers. However, it is a very hard and risky enterprise for a self published author.

Many large chains work directly with established publishers, leaving you out of the loop. They also take a large chunk of the profit for themselves, usually 45% to 55%.

Even if you can get into a large chain, they typically require the right to return any unsold books. So while an order for several thousand books can look great, if they don't sell you'll be footing the bill for the printing and stuck with several thousand copies.

The majority of books are now sold online, so with the higher royalties, lowered risk, and ease of publishing online it's a great place to start.

Local bookstores, on the other hand, can be a great place to get distribution, you just need to go out and talk to them.

Appendix

Deeper Looks

Some topics require a deeper look and/or influence multiple areas of the publishing process. We've broken many of them out into their own sections for easy reference.

All About ISBN Numbers

The ISBN is the International Standard Book Number and is typically required to publish a printed book. It's 13 digit number, or 10 digits if it was assigned before 2007, uniquely identifies your cookbook.

How to Get an ISBN Number

There are several ways to obtain an ISBN number for your book.

Some print-on-demand publishers will provide you an ISBN number free of charge. CreateSpace is one of these. Be aware though that using this free ISBN number may have some negative impacts as detailed below.

You can purchase your own ISBN number from an ISBN company. There are several that you can use, depending on your location. The US company is My Identifiers, run by Bowker (https://www.myidentifiers.com/get-your-isbn-now). You can get 1 ISBN number for $125 or if you are planning on doing multiple books, 10 for $295.

If your ebook has an ISBN it needs to be different from the print version. The same is true for hardback and paperback versions, they would each need their own.

When Do You Need an ISBN?

You need an ISBN number if you are going to sell a printed book through almost any bookstore or retailer, either online or offline. If you are only going to be selling the book yourself then you usually don't need one.

Some ebook retailers also require them but not Kindle, iTunes, or Nook. Kobo recommends using an ISBN number. If the book is an electronic book you can usually get away without using one.

WE RECOMMEND PURCHASING YOUR OWN ISBN NUMBERS

If your aspirations as a publisher are to obtain a wide distribution of your cookbook, we suggest you make the investment in purchasing your own ISBN numbers for multiple reasons.

YOU ARE LISTED AS THE PUBLISHER

This is perhaps the most important reason for owning your cookbook's ISBN number. If you take advantage of a low-cost or free ISBN number provided by your print-on-demand publishing company, they would be listed as the publisher. In most cases this would cause your book to be disregarded by many bookstores and reviewers as being a self published book. This may not be fair, but it is unfortunately a fact of life in the book business. Moreover, if the publisher is listed as "CreateSpace" it gets even worse since Amazon is viewed as the enemy by many of the companies you are trying to sell your book to.

ALL ORDERS FOR YOUR BOOK WILL GO TO YOU

Since you are the publisher, you are assured that any special orders for your books will have to go through you rather than being handled by another party. If your book takes off this could amount to a significant difference in your financial outcome.

YOU CONTROL THE METADATA

As the owner of the ISBN, you control the metadata which is put into the Books in Print database. This metadata includes your book's description, cover image, and PDF file which librarians, reviewers, search engines, booksellers and the publishing industry at large use to find your book.

FREEDOM TO CHOOSE ANY PRINTER

As a publisher, you can take your book to any printer you choose. If your book takes off you have the freedom to go to a short run or offset printer to reduce your costs and make more money from your book. With a free ISBN you are stuck with the original printer of your book.

We feel that making an investment in your own ISBN numbers is the correct strategy for most self published authors.

WHERE DOES THE ISBN NUMBER GO?

The ISBN number is used in a few places. When you enter the information for your book for printing you will need to enter it into their form. You will also need it displayed on the back cover of your book, along with a bar code. Many printers do this automatically for you. The final place you need to put the ISBN number is on the Copyright page of your book.

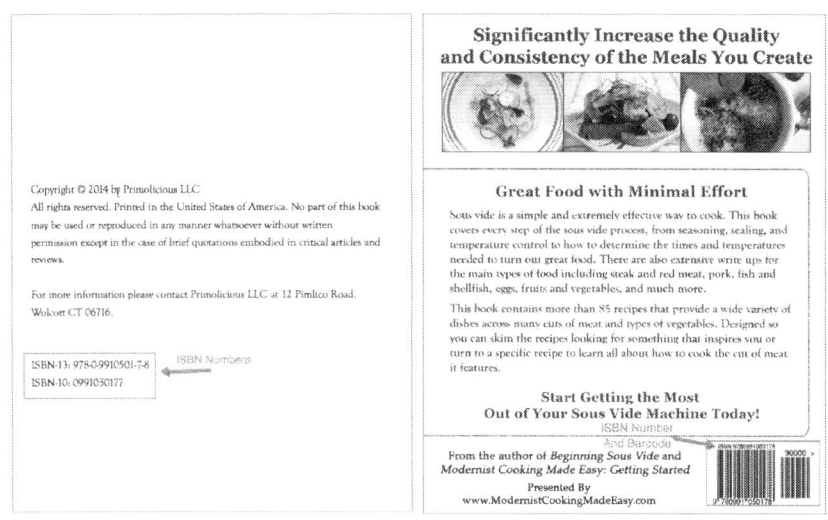

How Do Cookbook Royalties Work?

Royalties are one of the main concerns for many authors. They are simply the amount of money the author gets paid every time a book is sold. Royalties work differently for a traditionally published book and for self published books but there are a few similarities.

With either royalty type, the price of the book greatly affects the amount earned per book. The higher the price, the more money you will get. With traditional publishing you don't have control over the book price but with self publishing you want to maximize your profit if you are publishing a Monetizing cookbook.

The price of the book can also change greatly depending on the channel you are selling through. Selling a single book on Amazon will generally result in a higher cost-per-book and higher-royalty amount than selling 500 copies to a wholesaler.

Royalties in Traditional Publishing

Royalties in traditional publishing are negotiated up front. They are usually paid in one of two ways. Either price-based, as a percent of the retail price the book is sold for; or profit-based, dependent on the profit of the book. For example, if you have a 5% royalty on a book that sells on Amazon for $25 you could earn $1.25 with a price based royalty. If you are on a profit-based royalty, the profit of the book may just be $10 after expenses, so you would earn $0.50.

> **Jason Says**
> Recently I was in negotiations with a traditional publisher to write a cookbook they could publish. Their initial offer to me, someone they were trying to convince to work with them, was a 6% royalty. That came to about $0.50 - $1.00 per book sold compared to the current $8-$10 I make through self publishing. So to bring in comparable royalties the book would have to sell about 10 to 20 times as many copies.

SELF PUBLISHING ROYALTIES

Self publishing royalties are easy to calculate. Just take the total price you sold a book for, minus out the cost to print it and any fees or shipping costs and the remainder is your royalty per book. Also, as a reminder, on Amazon even though the price will fluctuate, you still get paid for the full-list price. Here are a few examples of royalties.

You have a book that costs you $10.00 to print and ship from the print-on-demand company you are using. The list price on Amazon is for $35. Amazon typically takes 40% to 60%, or say $17 per copy. So every copy that you sell on Amazon would get you $35 - $10 - $17 = $8 in profit. Since royalties are traditionally expressed in percents, you would be earning about a 20% price-based royalty.

When selling the same book direct to a wholesaler, they may pay you 50% of the list price per book. So they put in an order for 100 copies of your book and will pay you $17.50 per book. Since the book still costs $10 to print and ship you would get $17.50 - $10 = $7.50 per book sold.

Kindle, Nook, and other ebook royalties are usually paid at either 30% or 70% of the retail price. So if you sell a book for $9.99 on the Kindle, you will get $9.99 - $3 = $6.99 royalty per book sold.

If you are working through CreateSpace, you can easily see what your royalty will be based on their royalty calculator (https://

www.createspace.com/Products/Book/#content6). You can also buy books directly from them for wholesaling at much lower prices.

Royalty Calculator*
Use the royalty calculator to figure out how much you'll make every time your book is manufactured.

Print Options

Interior Type	Black and White	Number of Pages	200
Trim Size	7.5" x 9.25"		

List Price

	Channel	Royalty
	Amazon.com	$11.75
USD $ 25 [Calculate]	eStore	$16.75
	Expanded Distribution	$6.75
☑ Yes, suggest GBP price based on the U.S. price GBP £ 16.46 [Calculate]	Amazon Europe For books printed in Great Britain	£7.17
☑ Yes, suggest EUR price based on the U.S. price EUR € 22.73 [Calculate]	Amazon Europe For books printed in continental Europe	€10.63

> **Jason Says**
> Most of my print books earn $8-$10 per book sold through Amazon and $6-$8 per book sold wholesale. My books are published through CreateSpace, are black and white, about 150-250 pages long, and retail for $20 to $25.

In additional to the higher royalties for self published books, you also have control over the royalty amount because you can adjust the list price. This allows you to increase royalties for Monetizing cookbooks to increase your profit or decrease the royalty for Marketing or Viral cookbooks in order to increase sales.

Appendix: Deeper Looks 248

What is the Amazon Sales Rank?

If you publish on Amazon, the Amazon Best Sellers Rank, or just "sales rank", is something you will start to pay a whole lot of attention to. It is updated approximately hourly and in general is an indicator of how well your book is currently selling in relation to other books. The book ranked #1 at any point has sold more copies than any other book on Amazon. Some people live or die by their sales rank, however, I think total book sales are a much more valuable tool when determining if a book of yours is successful.

Many people say that another way to think of the sales rank is the amount of time that has passed since the book has sold, in relation to other books. For example, when you sell a copy your sales rank improves. Then as other people sell copies of their books, your sales rank starts dropping until you sell another copy.

It's important to remember that this is a snapshot of where your sales currently are, not an aggregate, so the sales rank can fluctuate greatly during the week, or even during a single day.

Here is a screen shot of the sales rank for one of my books over a 2 week period. It ranged from 36,000 to 415,000, a large variation.

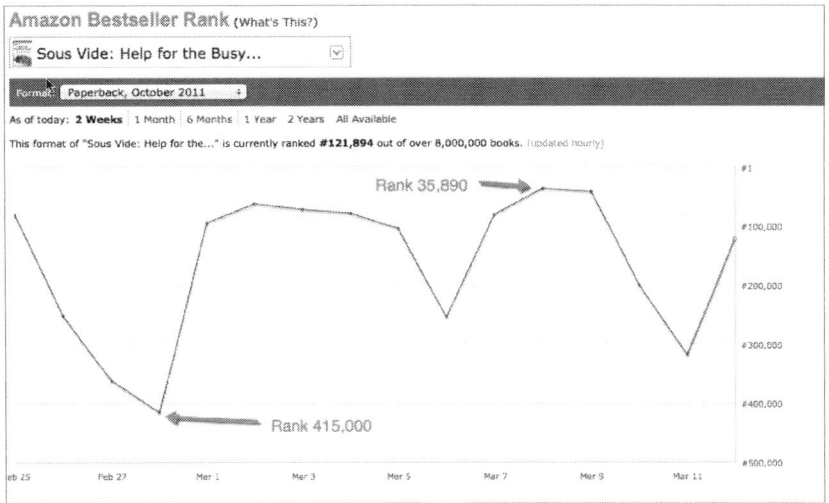

There are many factors that affect the sales rank. The largest and most obvious is the amount of books you sell. More books sold equals a better sales rank. Though technically, it is more books sold in relation to other books. If you sell 10 copies more than normal but other books sell 11 extra copies, your sales rank will get worse, despite the fact that your sales have increased. This is one more reason I focus on sales instead of the Amazon Sales Rank, I generally don't care if my rank gets worse as long as I'm selling more books.

Another factor that complicates the sales rank is the historical stability of your book sales. If your book usually sells several copies a day, its sales rank won't be hurt as much by going a day or two without sales as a book that doesn't sell well. Amazon gives better selling books the "benefit of the doubt" for a longer period of time than it does to worse selling books.

Jason Says

I think many people get hung up on their sales rank by trying to monitor it closely, track it to sales, and trying to manipulate the number. This can be so frustrating because of the huge fluctuations in sales rank. I personally find it better to focus on book sales and just have a general idea of what your rank is. I've been caught up tracking the sales rank, especially during launches or when it's getting high (as you can see from my tweet below), but maintaining a focus on sales will save you time and pay off in the long run.

Jason Logsdon
@jasonlogsdon_sv

Very excited, finally broke a sales rank of 1,000! Sous Vide is sitting at 890 best selling book on all of Amazon! amzn.to/1H2ezI0

SALE RANK RANGES

The amount of sales associated with a specific Amazon Best Sellers Rank varies throughout the year. In summer you usually need to sell less books to get a higher rank than you do during the holidays. As a general guideline, I tend to break the sales rank down into broad categories.

5,000 OR BETTER

A sales rank in the top 5,000 is very high and can be hard to beat, especially once your book sales plateau. The number of books sold to get into this range varies greatly, but a top 1,000 book may be selling 50 to 100 copies a day while a top 5,000 book might be selling 20 books a day.

5,000 to 30,000

A sales rank of 5,000 to 30,000 is what I would consider a very successful book. They are usually selling anywhere from 10 to 20 books a day.

30,000 to 100,000

Books in this range are successful without being too popular. They are normally selling around 10 books a day, down to a book or two a day. While this range is huge, the difference between the 30,001 book and the 99,999 book might be an extra 15 to 30 copies sold during a whole month.

100,000 or Worse

Anything out of the top 100,000 I don't consider a real successful book for myself. They still may be selling several copies a week but if you are aiming for a Viral or Monetizing book, they aren't resonating with your audience or need to be marketed differently.

> **Jason Says**
> Here is the general breakdown of my 8 books over the last year. I have had one consistent top 5,000 book, plus most books during their launch week hit that mark. At any given time, 2 to 3 books are in the 5,000 to 30,000 range and 2 to 3 books are in the 30,000 to 100,000 range. Another 2 to 3 regularly drop out of the top 100,000. Those books that don't sell well still contribute a few hundred dollars a month, but it's a lot more fun to have a top selling book!

Category Sales Rank

In addition to the overall sales rank described above Amazon also tracks the sales rank for each of its individual categories. You can see two of these listed under the overall sales rank in the image at the top of this article. These are only displayed if the book is in the top 100 books in a category.

WHAT IS DRM?

Depending on where you publish your ebook you will need to determine whether or not you want to protect it with DRM. DRM stands for Digital Rights Management and it is a form of copy protection that attempts to prevent the unauthorized use and copying of ebooks.

The only advantage of DRM is that it makes it harder for people to download unauthorized copies of your cookbook. However, this comes at the cost of some customer trust, and also makes it harder for legitimate purchasers of your cookbook to share it among their own devices. In general, copy protection only stops legitimate readers from using your book as they want to, most pirates and other copyright infringers can easily get around DRM and other copy protection.

> **Jason Says**
> I do not use DRM on any of the latest cookbooks that I have published. I'd rather lose a few book sales by someone sharing a book than prevent a paying customer from using my book how they want to. I also believe that people who read an illegal copy of my book may become fans, follow my website, and maybe purchase a different book of mine in

You can read much more about DRM from its Wikipedia page (http://en.wikipedia.org/wiki/Digital_rights_management).

KDP Select - What Is It and Is It Worth It?

KDP Select is Amazon's side program for ebooks that can offer different services to authors and publishers. However, these come at a price.

What is KDP Select?

When you use Kindle Direct Publishing to make your ebook available for the Kindle on Amazon you are given the option to join the "KDP Select" program. Amazon contends that KDP Select will "allow you to reach even more readers and gives you the opportunity to earn more money". If you choose this option you are required to make your book exclusive to the Kindle store during the 90 day period that you are enrolled in the program. You cannot even sell a PDFs version from your own website.

Why Enroll in KDP Select?

There are several reasons to consider enrolling in KDP select

Earn Higher Royalties In Some Parts of the World

You can earn 70% royalties rather than 30% for sales to customers in Japan, India, Brazil, and Mexico. If you believe you will be selling a lot of copies in those markets it might be worth it for that reason alone.

Earn Payments from Kindle Unlimited (KU)

Kindle Unlimited is a subscription service that lets customers read as many books as they like, and keep them as long as they want. Any customer can choose whether to subscribe to Kindle Unlimited. They don't have to be Amazon Prime members, but they do need to pay a subscription fee. KU may help readers discover your books by making them available through Kindle Unlimited in the US, UK, Germany, Italy, Spain, France, Brazil, Mexico and Canada.

As a result of a recent change authors will now be paid based on the number of pages read by members of KU that have borrowed their book. There is a pot of money specified by Amazon that will be divided based on the number of pages read. Since this is a recent change it's difficult to assess what type of income an author might receive from this. However, we feel that in general cookbooks are probably not borrowed and read like novels or non-fiction books. So for cookbook authors we don't know that this is a real benefit. For additional information on KU we suggest you read this article by John Scalzi (http://bit.ly/1qAs6nt).

EARN PAYMENTS FROM THE KINDLE OWNER'S LENDING LIBRARY

With an Amazon Prime membership, Kindle owners can choose from thousands of books to read for free once a month, with no due dates. This is similar to the KU program above where as an author you can be paid for the books people borrow from the Lending Library. The Kindle Owners' Lending Library (KOLL) is in the US, UK, Germany, France, and Japan. Once again the amounts for cookbooks we suspect would be relatively negligible.

MAXIMIZE YOUR BOOK'S SALES POTENTIAL

Choose between two different promotional tools. You can only choose one of these two tools during any 90 day period:

Kindle Countdown Deals

Kindle Countdown Deals is a KDP Select benefit that allows publishers to run limited-time promotions on their books, which can help earn more royalties and reach more readers. Customers can see the regular price and the promotional price on the book's detail page, as well as a countdown clock telling them how much time is left at the promotional price. The idea of this deal is to leverage the scarcity psychology of sales. People see a good deal and that it's going to end soon and therefore are forced into a decision, hopefully to purchase.

Amazon has a "Kindle Countdown Deals" page that also may highlight your book on it during the deal (http://www.amazon.com/b?node=7078878011). You can have the deal last up to seven days and all books sold under the Kindle Countdown will count on the paid list helping to increase your ranking.

Free Book Promotion
If you are in KDP Select you can make your Kindle book available for free for up to five days during the 90 day period. You may wonder, "Why would I want to give my book away for free?" The greatest claimed benefit is that it can help you broaden your audience by allowing readers to try your book for free.

There may be some validity to this but we are not sure how large a factor it really is. There are a lot of folks out there who simply watch the free lists and download everything they can - rarely ever accessing them. Conversely, if you announce your free giveaway to your email list and fans they will probably download and use your book. Unfortunately, as one of your fans they would've probably been fine with purchasing it.

Early on the free promotion was a great way to increase the ranking of your book since at that time the books given away free counted. However, now there is both a free list and a paid list, so the books given away free will normally not affect your book's ranking at all.

Sometimes in discussion of the free promotion you may hear the term "free-promotion bounce back". This describes a phenomenon that once the free promotion stops that the volume of sales will continue at a high rate for a while longer. With the new way in which the free books are accounted for this phenomenon is not what it used to be and typically has a minor impact on sales long-term.

Perhaps the authors who benefit most from the free promotion are ones that are writing a series of books. They could use the strategy of making the first in the series free in hopes of selling later volumes once they have hooked their readers. Or give the third volume away in hopes of selling volumes 1 and 2.

This strategy may also work for cookbook authors who have multiple books in a similar subject. We did a three day free promotion when we launched the Modernist Cooking Made Easy: The Whipping Siphon book. We had several other books on Amazon at that point in time and felt that individuals that received the book for free would consider purchasing other books with complementary content.

We would suggest authors with only one book not use the Free Promotion capability if it is a Monetizing book. Once someone receives the book and reads it, even if they like it there's not much they can do that will benefit you financially in the long term. For viral or marketing books, the Free Promotion capability can help drive traffic and readers to your blog.

WHAT ABOUT EXCLUSIVITY?

As we mentioned in the first paragraph in order to enroll in the KDP Select program you need to agree to exclusively sell your ebook through Amazon. This can be a hard pill to swallow if you have some meaningful sales on iTunes, Nook, Smashwords, Kobo, BookBaby and your own website. On the other hand if you have few readers then building an audience on Amazon before branching out to other venues might be an excellent choice.

There are a few interesting downsides to exclusivity. Although Amazon may be the biggest player in the US and UK, there are large numbers of potential readers scattered elsewhere on the planet. By giving exclusivity to Amazon you may not be able to address the rapidly growing emerging markets.

Having lived through the recent economic chaos we believe that any company, at any time, can be vulnerable to a downturn. The way to handle that in the stock market is through diversification. We believe it may make sense to use the same strategy as we pick publishers for our ebooks. Amazon could make one "simple" change in their process which could have a very negative impact on our income. For that reason we are selling our books through as many formats and channels as we can. Right now the volume on those channels is very small but we're confident that over time it's possible to build a reader base in those channels as well.

CONCLUSION

I hope you have gathered from this article that there is no "correct" choice of whether to go with KDP Select and take advantage of the free book promotion. It really depends on your particular circumstances as well as your book and the goals of your book. One solution may be ideal for one of your books while an alternative solution may fit another just perfect. We encourage you spend some time online studying your options so that you can make this important decision wisely.

CASE STUDY: SALES CHANNEL BREAKDOWN

For a more detailed look at the breakdown of revenue from the various sales channels we decided to dive more deeply into where my book money comes from. We had 8 active books in 2014 that brought in over 6 figures across more than 11 sales channels.

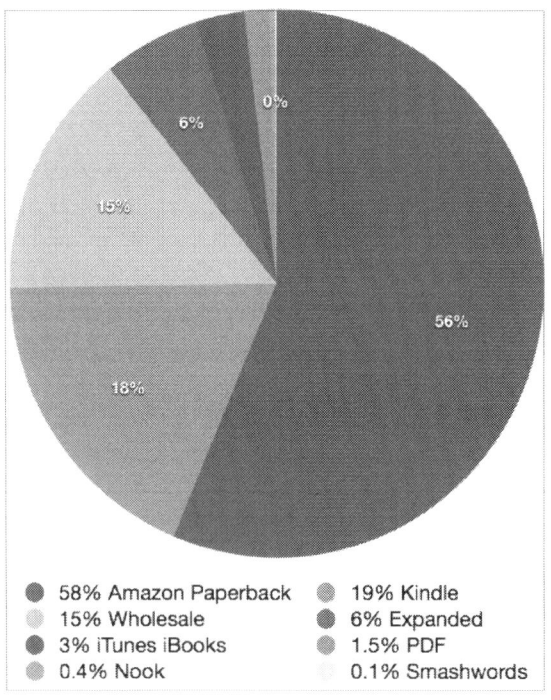

In 2014 our revenue breakdown was as follows:

- 58% Amazon Paperback
- 19% Kindle
- 15% Wholesale Purchases
- 6% Expanded Distribution
- 3% iTunes iBooks
- 1.5% PDF
- 0.4% Nook
- 0.1% Smashwords and Affiliates

Of the total sales revenue for 2014, Amazon accounted for about 77% of them. Wholesaling and direct sales were about 15% and other platforms including iTunes, Nook, and Smashwords were 4%.

There is always some fluctuation between paperback and Kindle on Amazon, but in general our books made about 25% to 35% as much from Kindle books as paperbacks.

Wholesale purchases have generally been increasing year to year as we add more books and expand our wholesale network.

The drop off between the two Amazon platforms and the iTunes and Nook is pretty shocking. Once you have a Kindle version it is very easy to release it on iTunes and the Nook, otherwise we might skip those formats all together.

PDF versions of the book are low for us but we try to focus on driving people to the Amazon sales pages instead of selling PDFs from our site. This has the added benefit of making affiliate commissions off of the sale of the book and anything else they purchase while on Amazon.

Note regarding the small amount of Smashwords sales: Since it is much more profitable for us to work directly with Amazon, iTunes, and Nook we have opted out of those for our Smashwords distribution. If you were to allow Smashwords to distribute to these three channels you could expect a significant increase in the amount sold through that channel, though at a lower overall royalty.

Cookbook Writing and Marketing Templates

We have put together many self publishing templates you can use in book creation, recipe writing, recipe testing, and marketing your book. They can all be downloaded from our website at http://bit.ly/1G4zlEA.

Financing Your Self Published Cookbook

When people think of self publishing they often start to wonder how they can afford to pay for it all. The truth is, these days self publishing doesn't take much up front money at all.

If you already have a successful food blog, you are probably able to self-finance your own cookbook. With your knowledge of recipe writing and food photography you already have the majority of the skills needed to write a cookbook covered.

Print on demand publishing companies eliminate the majority of the upfront costs including purchasing inventory. Most cookbooks can be published for under a few thousand dollars depending on how much external expertise you need for editing and design help.

> **Jason Says**
> Now that I've done several cookbooks, the entire cost of producing a new one is very small because I handle all aspects myself. I only need to purchase an ISBN for about $25 and a proof copy for $25.

If you do need more money for any reason, there are several ways to finance your self published cookbook including taking on friends and family as investors, taking pre-orders from your readers, or going through KickStarter.

SELF PUBLISHING RESOURCES

Self publishing can be a very complex process and there is much more to learn about it in addition to what has been covered in this book. Here are some resources to help you continue to learn more.

WRITING AND PUBLISHING RESOURCES

The Sense of Style: The Thinking Person's Guide to Writing in the 21st Century

The Sense of Style (http://amzn.to/1VUFCgS) is an engaging, to the point book on the modern art of writing well by New York Times bestselling author Steven Pinker. He applies insights from the sciences of language and mind to the challenge of crafting clear, coherent, and stylish prose. Pinker shows how writing depends on imagination, coherence, grammatical competence, and empathy. He replaces usage dogma with reason which allows writers and editors to accomplish the intent of the guidelines in other ways, rather than blindly follow a rule for a rule's sake.

On Writing Well, 30th Anniversary Edition: The Classic Guide to Writing Nonfiction

On Writing Well: The Classic Guide to Writing Nonfiction by William Zinsser (http://amzn.to/1VUFHBl) offers you fundamental principles as well as the insights of a distinguished writer, editor and teacher. This book is well known for its sound advice, its clarity and its style. It is a book that is applicable for a wide variety of disciplines, for anybody who wants to learn how to write or who needs to do some writing to get through the day. With more than a million copies sold, this volume has stood the test of time and remains a valuable resource for writers and would-be writers.

The Book on Writing: The Ultimate Guide to Writing Well

Paula LaRocque's The Book on Writing: The Ultimate Guide to Writing Well (http://amzn.to/25ZJl1q) contains 25 chapters divided into three sections beginning with easy-to-apply guidelines to good writing, from the importance of clarity to the value of a conversational tone. Section 2 addresses how to tell a story, from building suspense, to effective description, to the uses of metaphor and literary devices. The final section deals with common problems in grammar, usage, punctuation, and style. Paula LaRocque is a celebrated writing and a master writer herself with a long and distinguished career in both teaching and practicing the art of writing.

Style: Lessons in Clarity and Grace (11th Edition)
Style: Lessons in Clarity and Grace by Joseph M. Williams & Joseph Bizup (http://amzn.to/1VUFRst) is a self-teaching book that is widely used in university composition classes throughout the United States. This classic expose explains the reasons of what drives writing excellence and offers practical advice in cultivating a quality style. These ten chapters of Style focus on clarity, emphasis, organization, conciseness, elegance, and usage. The tips are practical and the descriptive passages come from a broad range of contemporary disciplines.

The Elements of Style
The Elements of Style by William Strunk (http://amzn.to/1Q6FJPE) is a dogmatic writing style guide covering rules of usage, principles of composition, form", and lists of commonly misused and misspelled words. The biggest drawback often noted about The Elements of Style is its lack of more in-depth explanations of style elements. Although a little staid, this book is one of the most influential books written on formal style over the years.

Will Write for Food
The book Will Write for Food by Dianne Jacob (http://amzn.to/25ZHIkv) provides a great overview, tips and how-tos for food writing of all kinds including blogging, cookbooks, recipes, food critics, and even food-related fiction novels. The book is teeming with references to books, websites, and groups that cover general writing, recipe writing, and other food writing topics. For all types of writing, Jacobs strongly recommends starting with a "clear notion of your audience, your medium, and your medium's picture of their audience". As a successful journalist, editor-in-chief, freelance writer, teacher, and blogger, Dianne Jacob brings a wealth of practical hands-on information with a style that radiates genuine enthusiasm.

Recipe Writer's Handbook

The Recipe Writer's Handbook by experienced food editors Barbara Gibbs Ostmann and Jane L. Baker (http://amzn.to/25ZIiyw) is a great resource on all aspects of recipe writing, including testing, formatting, nutrition and other general guidelines. These authors stress that measurements must add up, vocabulary must be clear, and the whole process must be broken down into simple steps with straightforward instructions and error-free presentation. However, you will also discover how to write concise and complete recipes without sacrificing your creativity or personality. You may find the final section interesting; it presents the philosophical views of food professionals as to what makes a good recipe good. The Handbook shows you how to "think" your way through a recipe in order to make important decisions and troubleshoot potential problems before they occur.

FOOD INFORMATION, CONNECTIONS AND DESCRIPTIONS

The Flavor Bible

The Flavor Bible (http://amzn.to/1VUE5aB) provides pairings of various foods. It's an invaluable resource for recipe creation and creativity by making connections between foods that you wouldn't have made on your own. Discover how to work more intuitively and effectively with ingredients; understand the relationship between temperature and texture; excite the senses with herbs, spices, and other seasonings. This book contains no recipes. However it does provide valuable alphabetical index of flavors and ingredients, and the means to search for complimentary combinations of them. The Flavor Bible by Karen Page and Andrew Dornenburg is Amazon's #1 seller in the "Herb, Spice & Condiment Cooking" category.

Deluxe Food Lover's Companion

The Deluxe Food Lover's Companion written by Ron and Sharon Herbst (http://amzn.to/1VUEb2d) contains more than 7,000 entries on types of food, cuisine, dishes, food-related culture and other gastronomic items. It's a good culinary dictionary for foodies; it gives you the quick answer for most questions in the kitchen. With Ron's background in hotel & restaurant management and Sharon's in journalism with awards as a cooking & dining author, they bring experienced information to the table.

Technical and Scientific Resources

On Food and Cooking: The Science and Lore of the Kitchen
On Food and Cooking by Harold McGee (http://amzn.to/23u6p9T) delves deeply into the science behind many of the food techniques, reactions, and reasons behind cooking. He pioneered the transformation of technical food science into cook-friendly kitchen science. In addition, he helped bring about the inventive culinary movement of molecular gastronomy. McGee has the authority to write with clarity and thoroughness as he blends the chemistry of food and cooking into the science of everyday life. Not only does this book provide useful information for anyone who has ambitions to develop their own recipes, but the book is simply interesting to amateur foodies and culinary professionals alike.

Keys to Good Cooking
Harold McGee's follow up book Keys to Good Cooking: A Guide to Making the Best of Foods and Recipes (http://amzn.to/1Q6EO1q) is a less scientific, but still a strong look into many aspects of cooking. From his standpoint, every great dish relies on proven science, and this compilation of well-researched data is a textbook for proper food preparation. It offers indispensable information on how to make the most of any recipe, a user's manual that enables home cooks to achieve maximum results.

Ratio
The book Ratio: The Simple Codes Behind the Craft of Everyday Cooking by Michael Ruhlman (http://amzn.to/25ZIvSi) is an effort to break down many of the more complicated cooking techniques into simple ratios that can easily be applied to create a wide range of foods. He explains what essential properties make the ratios work and the subtle variations that differentiate, for example, bread dough from biscuit dough.

The Science of Good Cooking
The team at Cooks Illustrated has spent the past 20 years investigating every facet and every detail associated with home cooking through tens of thousands of kitchen tests. In The Science of Good Cooking (http://amzn.to/25ZIyxt), they condense the past two decades of test kitchen work into 50 basic cooking concepts, scientifically-minded approaches that every home cook should know.

How Baking Works
How Baking Works: Exploring the Fundamentals of Baking Science (http://amzn.to/1MtUNfu) was written by Paula I. Figoni, a food scientist and associate professor at the International Baking and Pastry Institute in the College of Culinary Arts at Johnson & Wales University in Providence, Rhode Island. Figoni believes that the heart of baking is chemistry, and anyone who wants to master this skill must understand the principles and science that make baking work. This book explains the whys and hows of every chemical reaction, essential ingredient, and technique used in baking.

Cooking For Geeks
In his book Cooking for Geeks: Real Science, Great Hacks, and Good Food (http://amzn.to/1VUEXMD) Jeff Potter, a self-proclaimed science and food geek, provides the tools for you to express your creativity instead of just following recipes. He aims to help you discover what makes a recipe work so you can improvise and craft your own unique dishes. This book is an excellent, humorous and informative resource for anyone who wants to experiment with cooking.

Modernist Cuisine
Modernist Cuisine: The Art and Science of Cooking by Nathan Myhrvold, Chris Young, and Maxime Bilet (http://amzn.to/1MtUPnF). This five-volume, 2,400-page set reveals science-inspired techniques for preparing food. It is a landmark contribution to the art of cooking and our understanding of its underlying principles. Besides the large quantity of clear, concise information, the stunning photography of the equipment and ingredients, graphic design and even printing gives the book a "coffee table" type quality.

DID YOU ENJOY THIS BOOK?

If you enjoyed this book check out my other books on sous vide and modernist cooking.

Modernist Cooking Made Easy: Sous Vide

Do you want to get the most out of your sous vide machine and consistently prepare great food with a minimal amount of effort?

This book is the authoritative guide to low temperature precision cooking and it will help make sous vide a part of your everyday cooking arsenal.

Modernist Cooking Made Easy: Party Foods

This book provides all the information you need to get started amazing your party guests with modernist cooking.

It is all presented in an easy to understand format along with more than 100 recipes that can be applied immediately to your next party.

Modernist Cooking Made Easy: Getting Started

If you are looking for more information about the other modernist techniques then my first book is for you.

It will give you the information you need to create gels, foams, emulsions, as well as teach you how to do spherification, thickening, and sous vide cooking. It also has more than 80 easy-to-follow recipes to get you on your way.

Modernist Cooking Made Easy: The Whipping Siphon

This book focuses on presenting the three main uses of the whipping siphon: Foaming, Infusing, and Carbonating. It delivers the information you need to understand how the techniques work and provides you with over 50 recipes to illustrate these techniques while allowing you to create great dishes using them.

All books are available from Amazon.com as a paperback and Kindle book, on iTunes, and on BN.com.

ABOUT THE AUTHOR

Jason Logsdon is a passionate home cook who loves to try new things, exploring everything from sous vide and whipping siphons to blow torches, foams, spheres and infusions. He has self published 9 cookbooks which have sold over 60,000 copies in paperback and electronic formats.

His books include Modernist Cooking Made Easy: Sous Vide which made the Amazon top 20 cookbook list and hit the #1 spot on Amazon for both Slow Cooking and Gourmet Cooking. His other books include Modernist Cooking Made Easy: Party Foods, Sous Vide: Help for the Busy Cook, Modernist Cooking Made Easy: Getting Started, Sous Vide Grilling, Modernist Cooking Made Easy: The Whipping Siphon, and Beginning Sous Vide.

His websites are www.AmazingFoodMadeEasy.com and www.SelfPublishACookbook.com. Jason can be reached at jason@afmeasy.com or through Twitter at @jasonlogsdon.

Made in the USA
San Bernardino, CA
20 December 2019